THE ULTIMATE YOUNGER WOMAN MANUAL

How To Bring Younger Women Into Your Life and Keep Them There

BY BLACKDRAGON

Published in 2018 by DCS International
Copyright © 2018 DCS International LLC and Caleb Jones
19363 Willamette Dr. #119
West Linn, OR 97068
USA

This publication is designed to provide accurate and authoritative information in regard to the subject matter covered. It is sold with the understanding that the publisher is not engaged in rendering professional services.

ISBN: 978-0-9995133-1-6

Printed in the United States of America

First Printing June 2018

TABLE OF CONTENTS

Chapter 1

AN OVERVIEW OF DATING YOUNGER WOMEN

With changes in our culture and economics, relationships comprising much older men with much younger women are becoming more the norm. This has already been the case for many years in regions of Asia and Europe. Now, these changes are coming to places like the USA, Canada, England, Australia, and New Zealand as well.

This is due to several factors.

These days, the term "younger men" is encapsulating more and more men. It used to be that a typical "younger man," who spent his time playing video games, watching porn, and getting drunk while either working at a shitty job or not working at all, was a guy around age 23 or under. Today, that classification accurately describes many men throughout their twenties and well into their early to mid-thirties. Many younger women in their late teens and twenties are getting very tired of this.

Economics also play a factor. It's much harder these days for younger adults to make their own way in the world, with devalued currencies, lower wages, higher (real) rates of inflation, higher unemployment, and higher amounts of debt. This often gently entices many younger women into the arms of men older than usual.

On the other side of the equation, the utter failure of modern marriage has created a huge population of men in their thirties, forties, and fifties who are either divorced or have never been married, creating a large pool of available older men for younger women to draw upon.

This good news is that these kinds of younger women / older men relationships are bringing a lot of happiness to a lot of people. Older men enjoy the happier, carefree, less jaded company of younger women, as well as the younger and tighter bodies. Younger women are enjoying the reduced drama, chaos, and financial problems that so often accompany young men their age.

The bad news is that most older men have no idea how to actually attract and date women much younger than them. Attracting and dating women within your own age group is one thing, but what if she's 15, 20, 25+ years younger than you?

Dating women this much younger than you requires a unique set of dating, seduction, and relationship management techniques. Without them, you'll be stuck either dating women your own age or paying for prostitutes. With them, you'll be ready to date women of any age; your own or much younger, opening up your options for a lot of excitement, happiness, and fulfillment in your dating life.

As of this writing, I'm in my mid-forties. I've spent the last ten years of my life dating women of all ages; not only women my own age, but women as young as 18, early twenties, late twenties, and beyond. As a matter of fact, around 50% of all the women I've had sex with (not a small list) were under the age of 24. I have also had many very long-term relationships, mostly casual but some at least partially serious, with women within this age range. In this book, you will learn exactly how to attract and date women this young, or women who are older but are still much younger than you (since, if you're well over the age of 55 or so, even women in their thirties, for example, are "younger women" to you).

Do I think younger women are better than older women? Not necessarily; it depends on which aspects you're talking about. Younger women are indeed better looking than older women (though there are obviously many exceptions to the rule on both sides), have less sexual resistance than older women (allowing you to have sex with them much faster once you overcome the age difference issue), tend to be happier and less jaded about life than older women, and tend to be more flexible. On the down side, younger women are far more flakey and disorganized than older women, tend to have more drama (they whine and complain more), are usually not as intelligent (though yes, there are exceptions) and often lack emotional and intellectual depth. We will examine all of these positive and negative aspects in this book, and how to make the best use of them.

Since I only do nonmonogamous relationships and thus date multiple women at a time, my personal preference has been to date mostly younger women, but always have at least one woman in my own age group. This way I experience the good aspects of both younger and older women. If I wasn't proficient at dating much younger women, I wouldn't be able to do this, which would result in a much more limiting experience in my woman life.

How to Use This Book

This book is specially written for men over the age of 30-35, all the way to their sixties and beyond, who wish to date much younger women. (I'll clearly define what "much younger women" means in a minute.) It is a guide to both the seduction/dating process, when you meet a new woman and want to get to sex with her as quickly as possible, as well as the relationship management process, which is once you've had sex with a new woman at least twice and are now seeing her sexually on a regular basis, either casually or seriously.

This book builds on the material I've already presented in my other Blackdragon dating manuals. I'm not saying that reading my other books is required to make the material in this book work for you; they are not. However, the other dating books I've written that specifically cover the areas that you're interested in are **strongly** recommended for you if you're serious about making the concepts in this book work, namely:

The Ultimate Online Dating Manual[1], if you're interested in meeting younger women via online dating.

Get To Sex Fast[2], which is about getting women to sex as quickly and cheaply as possible from a real-life first date.

The Ultimate Open Relationships Manual[3], if you're interested in ongoing relationships with younger women in a nonmonogamous fashion, where you are dating multiple women at once.

This book will *touch* on all three of those topics above, as well as many others, but if you want the full details of the how-to systems those books describe, I strongly recommend you read the ones applicable to your situation, and then calibrate that information with the methods you are about to learn in this book.

For example, there is a chapter on online dating with younger women in this book (Chapter 11), but it won't include all the how-to detail of the *Ultimate Online Dating Manual*[4]; it will just include those aspects of online dating necessary for online dating as it directly applies to younger women.

Often I will include reference points in this book to the above three books as sources of more information. I will try not to do this too often, but some of this is unavoidable. Consider those three books above as the "core" Blackdragon books, and this book as something that "stacks" onto those for calibration for older men.

---

[1] http://www.onlinedatingsuccessnow.com/
[2] http://www.gettosexfast.com/
[3] http://www.haveopenrelationships.com/
[4] http://www.onlinedatingsuccessnow.com/

My History with Younger Women

Many years ago, when I was still a traditionally married beta male and well into my thirties, I had occasional thoughts, like all men do, of what it would be like to date or have sex with a woman who was much younger than me, a woman who was 19 years old, for example. It wasn't an overwhelming desire, like that experienced by Kevin Spacey's character in the movie *American Beauty*. Rather, it was simply a passing, pleasurable curiosity. "I wonder what that would be like?"

At age 35, I happily found myself divorced and single once again. For the first time in ten years, I started dating. A lot. I dated and had sex with many women in a relatively short period of time, as I've talked about in detail in my dating book, *Get To Sex Fast*[1], as well as my dating and relationships blog for men[2].

Most of these women were within my age range, within about eight or nine years plus or minus my age. I enjoyed these women, but after a while my thoughts started returning to that curiosity about younger women. For the first time I seriously considered attempting to date not only women in their early twenties, but 18 and 19-year-olds as well. I thought, "Why not?"

I did my best to approach much younger women, both in real life and online. After a few weeks of trial and error, to my surprise, I was soon on a date with an extremely attractive 20-year-old. The youngest woman I had ever dated up until that point was 26, and I thought *that* was pretty amazing. Yet here I was, on a date with a 20-year-old girl, myself 15 years older than her. There were some good and bad things about this experience.

The bad was that she acted like a teenager. She swore like a sailor. Though I could tell she was intelligent, her speech patterns were that of a moron. At one point she spent 20 minutes talking about her hair. I'm not kidding. Her hair.

---

[1] http://www.gettosexfast.com/
[2] http://www.blackdragonblog.com/

The good news was that she was so beautiful, so full of energy and life, and so fun to just be with, I was able to overlook a lot of this immaturity. I was extremely turned on. Moreover, there was a certain effortlessness to the sexual attraction that seemed less forced somehow than with women in their thirties or forties. There weren't as many "shields" up in front of her sexually like there were with women over 30.

The first date was very brief, like most of my first dates. When I got back to my home, I was overcome with a wave of horniness, a powerful, sexual euphoria that I had never experienced before. It was really something. I was so randy that I was tempted to have sex with my couch. The interesting thing was that I wasn't really *that* attracted to her. Sure, she was attractive, but a lot of women are attractive. This was… different.

There is, without a doubt, a powerful biological mechanism within men of all ages that generates powerful sexual attraction to women of prime childbearing age, i.e. women in their late teens and early twenties. I have experienced it many times, and you probably have too, even if you're an old man. I don't think this biology diminishes much just because you turn 30, 40, or even 50+, even if your preferences in women evolve over that time.

That first date with the 20-year-old never went anywhere, primarily because I was new at this younger woman stuff and I did a lot wrong. Yet, despite being a little turned off by her silliness and immaturity, I remembered the powerful attraction I had for her. I thought to myself "Okay, I got *one* out on a first date. **If I did it once, I can do it again**. If I can do it a few times, I should be able to actually have sex with a woman that young."

It made sense. What did I have to lose?

So while still dating women within my own age range, I also attempted to date women who were much younger, primarily the 18 to 23 crowd. After several months of mostly trial and error, it finally happened. I had sex with a very pretty 18-year-old. I was 36 at the time. A few months later I had sex with another 18-year-old, and actually had an open relationship with her that lasted several months, during which I had sex with two of her friends, both of them 18 years old as well.

That was all many years ago. As of this writing I am now 46. Over the last ten years I have had sex with, and long relationships with, a huge number of women ages 18 to 23. Some of them were quick flings. Most of them I've had ongoing relationships with, including casual ones (FBs) and more serious ones (MLTRs; we'll get to these terms later). Many of these relationships lasted many, many years. Some are still going strong even to this very day.

I've dated older women during that time frame as well, since women over 30 have their advantages too, at least in my opinion. But they simply cannot beat the ease, fun, excitement, and happiness of younger, less angry, less jaded, and often better-bodied younger women.

Since I don't do monogamy, I fully intend on continuing to date women this young for many decades, at least as casual FB relationships or sugar daddy relationships, well into my fifties and sixties. I have personally worked with, known, and coached men in their forties, fifties, and sixties who are dating women from age 18 to 35 with minimal problems. When you're done with this book, you will be able to do this too.

Two Types of Interest

Usually, I'll refer to the women we're talking about as "VYW," which stands for Very Young Women, defined as women from the age of consent in your city (usually 16 or 18) to age 23. For much of the Western world, 18 is the highest age of consent, so for the rest of the book I'm going to assume 18 as our lowest target age, but feel free to mentally reduce that age if the age of consent is lower where you live.

If you're reading this book, you likely fall into one of two categories:

1. You're a guy who's over age 30 who is interested in dating VYW.
2. You're an older guy who is well over age 45 or 50 who is interested in dating women who are much younger than you, but older than 23 (i.e. women in their twenties or thirties).

The majority of the techniques I'm going to describe in this book will apply equally to both types of men. When necessary, however, I will differentiate the two types of men when discussing certain topics, since often dating a younger woman who is 37 is quite different than dating one who is 22, even if you're 57.

What Is Too Old?

One of the more common questions I'm asked is, "I'm a really old guy. I'm X years old. Is it reasonable for me to expect to date / have sex with an 18-year-old or 22 year-old? Or should I just forget about learning game or relationship techniques and just pay for sex?"

It's a valid question. After teaching thousands of men these techniques over the last ten years, the age categories of men break down into something like this:

Men in their teens or twenties are not "older men" so they don't require any special changes in their approach with younger women.

Men age 30-34 are also not what I consider "older men," and these days, by and large, most younger women don't either. As I mentioned earlier, most men age 30-34 look and act like younger guys. Therefore, they usually don't need to do anything radically different for VYW, though some adjustments might be required depending on the circumstance.

Men age 35-39 are indeed "older men." Once you cross over age 35, younger women are definitely going to place you into that "older" category. Everything in this book applies to you, and you don't need to do anything special beyond what this book teaches unless you really want to. The good news about men this age is that while they are considered "older," they are often still youthful in appearance. I personally consider age 37 as the age where a man peaks in physical attractiveness, and some of my own informal polling in my real life and on the internet seems to indicate many men and women agree with this.

Men in their forties are still able to date younger women of any age, but the difficultly level is increased a little, and personal appearance becomes much more of a factor. The upcoming chapters regarding physical appearance are going to be much more important for you to follow. It's also important to do literally everything right when in your forties when dating much younger women, since the margin for error is razor-thin.

Sugar daddy game, a game style where men find women on sugar daddy dating sites and either pay women for sex or imply they will pay, is an option for men in their forties, but it's not required.

I'm in my mid-forties and I date VYW women with zero problems. I know many other men in their forties who do the same.

Men in their fifties break down into two subcategories. The first category, by far the smaller of the two, are men over 50 who are still reasonably physically fit (not like Schwarzenegger in his prime, but reasonably fit for a guy in his fifties), have decent skin, have a (reasonably) full head of hair (or a completely shaved head) and know how to dress well. If that's you, then in terms of women, you're essentially a man in his forties, so what I said above regarding men in their forties more or less applies to you.

The other type of guy in his fifties, a much more common type, is the typical fifties beta male who has let his physical health and appearance go after decades of monogamy or neglect. He's either chubby, with a nice pot belly, or way too skinny with no muscle to speak of. He's also balding, has poor skin and/or teeth, slovenly grooming, dresses like a dork, and has an overall beta male demeanor. He looks like the typical "dad."

If that sounds like you, you must focus very hard on the chapters in this book regarding physical appearance, and set a goal to maximize your appearance as much as humanly possible, even if it costs money and time to do so, which it probably will. We'll discuss fitness, fashion, and grooming in this book as it applies to older men in great detail in upcoming chapters.

While you're improving your appearance, I *don't* recommend you focus completely on VYW, since dating them at this point will be a challenge. Instead, you can temporarily focus on dating women within your own age range, or focus on dating women much younger than you but not quite as young as VYW (women in their thirties, for example), or focus instead on sugar daddy game where some money is involved. I generally advise men over 50 who are still in appearance optimization mode to avoid normal (non-sugar daddy) game with VYW until they get their appearance under control.

I personally know several men in their fifties who are dating women in their early to mid-twenties, without paying for it, with no problems, but these are men who take the time (and money) to take extra care of their appearance.

Men in their sixties or beyond should either focus on sugar daddy game if they want VYW (which should not be a problem financially for you, since by the time you're in your sixties you should have plenty of disposable income) or, if they optimize their appearance, focus on younger women in their thirties or forties. Non-sugar daddy game with VYW for men over age 60 isn't really an option unless the scenario is unusual.

If you have questions about any of this stuff, don't worry. I will get into very specific detail on what you need to do based on your age in upcoming chapters.

The Process

When I say "online dating," I'm talking about the entire process from when you sign up on a dating site all the way to when you walk into a first real-life date with a woman you met via a dating site or dating app. As soon as you sit down with that woman in real life, online dating is over with, and now you've transitioned into real life dating, or just "dating." Like I said, you need both skills to make this work: online dating and real-life dating.

Therefore, this book covers the entire process of online dating all the way to that first date. It does not cover what to do on a first date or afterwards. I have several other books (in both paper and digital form) that cover real-life dating skills, available at blackdragonsystem.

com and blackdragonblog.com. I highly recommend my best book of all, *The Unchained Man*[1], which covers dating in detail. It's located at alphamalebook.com.

Alright, enough of that. Let's get you started with the system.

Serious Relationships or Just Having Fun?

The next aspect you'll have to determine is specifically how you'd like to fit younger women into your life. Do you just want to get laid and have fun? One night stands? Casual relationships? Serial relationships? Long-term serious relationships? We'll address all of these options in future chapters, as well as my recommendations for these things based on how old or young these women are.

The key point is that you must know, very clearly, what you want from younger women. If you don't, if you just want to "get laid and see what happens," you will fall into the trap of oneitis so many other men fall into, where they fall head over heels "in love" with a hot younger woman who seems to be smarter than the rest, only to get piles of drama and chaos down the road.

Before you actually attempt anything in this book, I strongly recommend you sit down for a few minutes and clearly define how you want younger women in your life. My book on relationships, *The Ultimate Open Relationships Manual*[2], will act as a good guide, if you have it; since that book thoroughly describes the different types of serious and casual relationships. If you don't want relationships per se and just want to get laid, that's fine too, just make sure you define exactly what you want before you start implementing these techniques in your life. Otherwise, I promise you will encounter serious problems.

---

[1] http://www.alphamalebook.com/
[2] http://www.haveopenrelationships.com/

Legal Ramifications

Speaking of problems, having sex with younger women, unfortunately, brings up the topic of legalities and governmental entanglements. If you are an older man who has no desire to sleep with VYW, then this doesn't apply to you. However, if you are planning on sleeping with women under the age of about 24, it does, perhaps strongly.

If you've already read my lifestyle design book for men, *The Unchained Man**, you know that I do *not* recommend you do anything illegal, regardless of how silly or arbitrary you find your local laws to be. I do not recommend, promote, or endorse getting sexual with women under the legal age of consent in your city. Do *not* get sexual, in any way, with women under the age of consent in your area. In most areas of the West this is age 16 to 18.

Regarding women who *are* legal, sadly, we live in an era were some countries, particularly the United States, Canada, Australia, and a few others are overly hypersensitive regarding the concept of women age 18-23 having consensual sex with much older men. That means it's incumbent upon you to be aware of this, be very careful, and take a number of precautions that you would normally not need to take with women your own age.

Over the course of my life, I have both heard of and seen a myriad of horror stories about this. The 23-year-old guy who was on house arrest, had to wear an ankle bracelet for four years, and was legally branded a sex offender for the rest of his life, all because he had fully consensual sex with his girlfriend, a 17-year-old girl three months before her 18th birthday. The 18-year-old boy who was arrested right after his 18th birthday because his long-term girlfriend was still 17, and who was then raped in jail by another man his second night there. The 32-year-old man who met a 20-year-old woman on a dating site, had sex with her three times, found out she was actually 15, instantly stopped seeing her, then to

---

* http://www.alphamalebook.com/

be a good guy, told her parents what she was doing on the internet. Her parents immediately called the cops on him and he was sent to prison, a sex offender for the rest of his life.

I could go on and on. You do not want to be one of these horror stories. In this overly politically correct, hypersensitive, overly litigious, quasi police state we find ourselves in today, you *must* take the time to ensure that every woman you have sex with is 100% legal before you touch her. Here's how you do it.

1. Determine the *precise* legal age of consent in your city. Remember that all countries, states, and provinces are different about this, and the exact age can vary to a shocking degree. Some regions have very clear-cut ages of consent, yet others don't, and instead have a number of conditional aspects that are often confusing. You can't be confused about this; use the internet as a starting point, and if you are at all unclear, spend $50 if necessary to have a quick phone discussion with a family law attorney in your city to get clarity.

   The legal system in your Western country will not care if you didn't know the specifics of the age of consent laws in your area, so you need to know them cold. Moreover, getting sexual with someone under the age of consent is considered a "strict liability" crime. This means *the law does not have to prove you did it in order to punish you.* Yep, you read that right. Messing around with underage women is serious business.

   What if you live in a country outside of the West? It's true that many countries in South America, Asia, and even some in Europe don't really consider age of consent a big deal. That's fine, but don't assume anything. You still should be aware of the laws of your local city and stick with them.

2. Check her ID before you touch her. Have her show you her state ID, driver's license, passport, or some other form of photo ID with her birth date on it. Young girls can and do lie about their age to make them appear older. The recent upswing in sugar

13

daddy game has exacerbated this problem; I have encountered far more underage women lying about their ages in the last few years than I did the many years before that, combined.

If she lies about her age and you get sexual with her in any way (you don't even have to have full intercourse to get in trouble), you're in the realm of "strict liability" and you will go to jail regardless of anything else.

Do not be afraid to ask women for this. Many men seem to feel like this will scare women away. It doesn't if you do everything else correctly, but even if it did, tough shit. If you were polite with her only to wind up in jail, you weren't being polite; you were being stupid.

I have a strict policy of never even touching a much younger woman until I've seen her driver's license or similar ID. If she can't show me one because she "forgot it" or "lost it" or whatever, it's hands-off until she can procure it and present it to me, no matter how hot she is or how badly she wants me. I always remember that the law will not be on my side if there is a problem.

3. If a suitable photo ID is unavailable, verify her age through other means. As we'll discuss later, younger women tend to be somewhat irresponsible, especially when it comes to paperwork issues. Often, they really don't have an ID yet are still telling the truth regarding their age.

    If you still want to pursue this with her, get her full name (and if you don't know her well, verify it really is her name) her social security number (or equivalent if you live outside the US) and the name of the city she was born in. Call a local private investigator and have him verify her date of birth. It will cost you less than $40 to do this in most cases. There are also web sites that provide services like this, but they seem to go out of business all the time. Google around and locate some if you wish. Some regions have sites that actually show you a scan of her birth certificate for a small fee.

Usually, you will not need to go this far, but I have done this more than once with several younger women I've had sex with, and just the assurance that they were indeed legal helped a lot with my confidence (an extremely important thing you're going to need; more on this later) and peace of mind.

4. Do not get sexual with any underage women who pressure you for sex, even gently, no matter how hot you think they are.

    When you get to the point where you are very good at dating much younger women, the odds are near 100% that "word will get around" within the social circles of the younger women you're dating, and women will approach *you* for money, sex, a relationship, or all three. Some of these women may be underage, and you'll know it. You've got to say no to these women. Be nice and be polite, but say no, and get the hell out of there. Going to jail and being branded as a sex offender for the rest of your life isn't worth it.

    Over the years, I have had multiple experiences where women I knew were under the legal age of consent pressured me for sex or sexual activity. Every time, I refused. It's not that hard, and frankly, I'm surprised at the number of older men who just go for it anyway. You're playing with fire.

    If you really think she's hot, feel free to get her phone number and/or friend/follow her on social media. There's nothing illegal about that. Then *stay away from her* until she has her 18th birthday (or whatever age she becomes legal in your area), *then* hit her up if you still want to.

    Lastly, don't worry about "missing out" on any scenarios like this. There are plenty of 18-year-olds (and slightly older) who are readily available for you. Focus on them instead.

Chapter 2

TERMS AND DEFINITIONS

If you are already familiar with my other books[1] and/or my blogs[2], you can safely skip this chapter, or perhaps quickly scan through it. If you are not familiar with my other writings, you need to be aware of several terms and acronyms I use to describe different types of women, relationships, and conditions. I will use these terms for the rest of book; feel free to return to this chapter if you ever forget a term's definition.

ASD

ASD is a term coined by the pickup artist community many years ago. It stands for Anti-Slut Defense. I define ASD at the Blackdragon Blog[3] glossary thusly:

---

[1] http://www.blackdragonsystem.com/productsservices.html
[2] http://www.blackdragonblog.com/
[3] http://www.blackdragonblog.com/

A condition created by Societal Programming experienced by women wherein they attempt to avoid sex, even if they want it, so as to not look or feel like a "slut" or "inappropriate" or not like "a lady." ASD is a cause for major confusion, frustration, and psychological dysfunction in women since they strongly desire sex but are repeatedly told there is something wrong with it. ASD often drives women, even very intelligent ones, to extremely irrational behavior and rationalizing.

ASD is created in women's minds by many societal factors (that I describe in detail in *The Unchained Man**), including a puritanical cultural past, other female competitors, and right-wing men. These sources repeatedly tell women that sex is bad and that if she has sex, or too much sex, or sex under certain conditions, that she's a bad person who needs to be ashamed of herself, i.e. a "slut." Even though women love sex, they grow up with an extreme barrage of Societal Programming that tells them sex is bad or wrong.

If you think this sucks, you're right. All this anti-sex messaging makes it that much more difficult for you and I to get to sex with women quickly, with minimum money and effort, *even if the women are attracted to us and want to have sex with us.* Maddening. Other than your own appearance and dating skill, ASD is, and will always be, your greatest enemy in terms of getting to sex fast with women, as well as experiencing enjoyable sex with a woman once she's in a relationship with you.

The following factors increase ASD:

- **Age.** Since ASD is a direct result of exposure to false Societal Programming, a woman's ASD slowly rises for every year she ages, and dramatically spikes upward when she hits age 33 (which we'll discuss in the next chapter). Perhaps the greatest advantage of VYW is that their ASD is *extremely* low.

---

* http://www.alphamalebook.com/

- **Religion.** Regardless of the actual religion, the more devoutly religious a woman is, the more ASD she will likely possess. I'm talking here about *devout belief* in a religion, not simply *membership* in a religion. A woman from a strong Christian family may have very low ASD even though she self-identifies as a Christian. This is because she doesn't believe all the Christian dogma; she just goes along with it because that's what her family expects her to do, whereas a hardcore born again Christian, who really buys into her faith, will have higher ASD.
- **Conservative cultures.** Women from traditional cultures, such as places like India or Taiwan (as just two examples) are, generally speaking, going to have much higher ASD than women from more sexually liberal cultures, such as in South America. Culture makes a big difference.
- **Provider Hunter status.** Regardless of her age, if a woman is a Provider Hunter, i.e. actively seeking a husband or very serious, long-term boyfriend and nothing else, her ASD instantly jacks up several levels, regardless of how casual or relaxed she was about sex in her past. Again, the good news here is that provider hunter status is *extremely* rare with VYW. They're out to have fun, not find a husband.

EFA

I cover EFA, or Early Frame Announcement, in great detail in my dating book, *Get To Sex Fast**. It's critically important during the pick-up and dating phases when you're trying to have sex with a woman the first time, though it's also important during the early phases of relationship management as well.

---

* http://www.gettosexfast.com/

To briefly summarize, your EFA is your overall vibe that you convey to women, mostly nonverbally. It is the strongly conveyed, but mostly unspoken message you send to a woman conveying these three things:

1. Who you are.
2. Who you are not, which in many ways is even more important than who you are.
3. Who she is to you.

Your EFA consists of your behaviors with her. These tell her who you are, who you aren't, and what she is to you, regardless of what you verbally tell her.

For example, if you are calling her every day, seeing her several times a week, always telling her how pretty she is, always taking her out on romantic dates, and giving her largely vanilla sex, this is the EFA of a monogamous boyfriend. Even if that's not what you want her to be, that's what you're "telling" her via your EFA.

On the other hand, if you only see her once a week or less, almost never contact her, virtually never compliment her, and bang the shit out of her while giving her multiple, amazing orgasms every time you have sex, that's the EFA of a very attractive Alpha Male who is probably seeing other women. It also indicates that the relationship is more casual rather than that of a girlfriend.

Obviously, EFA is very important.

Oneitis

Oneitis is a common, though hugely dangerous and destructive emotional condition. It is a set of actions and behaviors where a man does things in order to get one particular girl or keep one particular Girl At the expense of pursuing other girls and/or at the expense of his own freedom and happiness. A man struck with oneitis will start to ignore all other women in his life and overly focus on one. His stress and neediness skyrocket. He loses his outcome independent frame and starts acting like a pussy. If he's a beta male, he starts getting sad, whiny, frustrated, and worried. If he's an Alpha Male, he becomes jealous, territorial, overly domineering, stressed, and angry.

Men experiencing oneitis stop focusing on all other women in the world and start focusing on the one he wants. He completely ignores the fact there are thousands of other attractive, high quality women in his city, and has brainwashed himself into thinking that he won't be happy until he has sex (and/or a relationship) with this one individual woman. He's either been on a date or two with this woman, or he's in true friend zone, where he's platonic friends with her but she's not interested in him sexually.

He goes on blogs and forums and lays out the situation, hoping to find some kind of magic bullet that will make this one, individual woman have sex with him. When others tell him to forget about this woman and go focus on others, he gets upset.

He becomes obsessed with this woman and starts stalking her on social media, often masturbating to her photos. He can't get her out of his mind and experiences a form of hyper-needy psychosis.

Another form of oneitis, called relationship oneitis, is the most common form of oneitis by far. This is when a man is dating or married to a particular woman, and he's so needy with her that he's terrified she'll leave him if he does anything she might not like. She gives him drama, and he puts up with it. (If he's a more confident guy, he may fight back, but he'll still put up with it; he won't leave her.) She makes demands of him, and he complies. If they have arguments, he always goes back to her. If she leaves, or threatens to leave him, he cowers, says he's sorry, and makes whatever promises he can to keep her.

His life is full of major compromises that he would never normally make, just to keep her. These compromises, in addition to the drama, make him unhappy. Yet, because he has oneitis, he doesn't care. He just continues to suffer like a pussy-whipped wimp (in the case of a beta male) or a high-drama, argumentative asshole (in the case of an Alpha Male).

Relationship oneitis is the default setting for monogamous relationships, and the societal default for most men (Alpha Males included) when they get into serious, traditional relationships with women. It his horribly destructive to all aspects of a man's life, happiness, and masculinity.

Betaization

Betaization is a hugely critical process that has major ramifications for your long-term happiness as a man. It permeates just about every medium or long-term relationship or marriage, yet the vast majority of human beings have no idea it exists. Once you understand betaization, how it works, and how to avoid it, your life will be changed forever, for the better. Just understanding betaization will shed light on many of your past relationship problems, and prevent you from experiencing them again in the future.

As I talk about in detail in *The Unchained Man**, we have bodies that were not designed for the modern, high-tech 21st Century. Instead, we have bodies and brains designed for the caveman era of 100,000 years ago. Because of this, we are full of Obsolete Biological Wiring (OBW) that tells us to do things that made perfect sense when we were cavemen, living in a harsh world, dressed in furs and living in a cave, but that makes absolutely no sense in the modern, free, abundant, high-tech era we live in today.

Women have OBW too. As a matter of fact, because women are the ones who get pregnant and have babies, women have even more OBW than men (which is really saying something, since men have a lot!). One of these forms of OBW is how women attract and keep men.

Back when she was a cavewoman, she wanted to bear children, or at least was subconsciously compelled to do so by her biology. The world of 100,000 years ago was full of lethal dangers. Harsh weather, scarce food, saber-toothed tigers, ice ages, disease, volcanoes, and enemy tribes all threatened her life and the lives of her tribe on a regular basis. Therefore,

---

* http://www.alphamalebook.com/

her powerful biology instructed her to make babies with very strong men. The stronger the man, the more likely he would successfully protect the baby, and the more likely the baby would be strong and thus survive the harsh environment.

"Strong" in this case meant not only physically strong, but mentally and emotionally strong as well. She was attracted to more confident, capable, badass leader types. In other words, Alpha Males. She would then have sex with an Alpha Male or two (or perhaps many more than two) and get pregnant.

When the baby came, she was more or less incapacitated. She didn't have the physical ability to go out and get food, provide warmth, and protect the baby all while raising the baby who was unable to live on his own. Therefore, she had to convince the Alpha Male father to stop running around the fields, hunting tigers, playing with his buddies, and banging other women so he could stand watch at the cave to protect and help feed her and the baby. Back then, masculine gallivanting around was dangerous behavior, and if he died, she would likely have no protection at all.

So, through various feminine means, she had to convince, negotiate, trick, and/or coerce the Alpha to calm down, stay with her, and follow her instructions. She didn't want a strong, confident Alpha Male anymore. She now wanted a compliant, submissive beta male. In other words, she had to transform the Alpha Male into a beta male to ensure the survival of both herself and her baby. She had to "betaize" the Alpha.

Women today have the exact same outdated biological urges as their cavewoman ancestors. When she's single or dating around, what attracts her are Alpha Male traits; confidence, strength (physical and otherwise), adventure, drive, motivation, masculinity, cockiness, sarcasm, roguishness, rebellion. However, once she gets this attractive Alpha Male into a relationship, and they start spending lots of time together, having sex on a regular basis, and start getting close, the process of betaization kicks in. She now needs to betaize the Alpha and turn him into a beta. Now she wants beta traits like compliance, obedience, calmness, intelligence, organization, peace, nurturing, reliability, and conformity.

At this point, the very Alpha Male traits that turned her on so much now actually annoy or even offend or anger her. A man acting like a confident, no-nonsense, charismatic rogue really turned her on during the first month they dated, but that same man who's been dating her for a year and/or is now living with her who is exhibiting the same traits is going to enrage her. He's the same guy, but her perception of how he should behave has radically changed.

Therefore, betaization is the process by which a woman slowly and gently starts to transform a man she's dating from an Alpha to a beta. There is no malice or ill intent behind this desire; it's simply her stupid, outdated biology kicking in. When she first had sex with you, she wanted a badass. Now that she's regularly dating you, she wants a complaint, good little boy, a "gentleman."

Betaization has been confusing the hell out of men for decades. It's caused all kinds of problems and conflict between dating and married couples. Worse, even women don't know anything about betaization and usually have no idea that they're doing it, or why.

If your goal in life is to be a beta male who is forever submissive to women's demands, betaization is fine. However, if you want to be a long-term happy Alpha Male, your goal is to constantly avoid betaization with every woman you date, no matter how serious you two get. Certain actions stimulate a woman's betaization desires, and you must never do these things with the women in your relationship life.

Disney

Disney is a trait that most women have in some capacity. Some women have a lot of Disney, some have a little, and a very small percentage have none. I define Disney at the Blackdragon Blog glossary* thusly:

> *Any thought derived from societal programming that monogamy, child rearing, or traditional marriage is pleasant and/or*

---

* http://www.blackdragonblog.com/glossary/

permanent in the modern era. Disney is usually suffered by women, but a certain variation can be suffered by men as well.

Disney is not nearly as bad as betaization or ASD, since Disney doesn't usually prevent women from having sex with you or getting into a long-term relationship with you. Instead, Disney tends to come up later in a relationship, once a woman decides she really likes you. If she has a decent amount of Disney, she'll start fantasizing about a beautiful, fairytale wedding, the two of you living together in heavenly bliss in a perfect white house, and, if she's young enough, two or three cute children running around. At this point, she's going to gently push for these kinds of things, whether you want them or not.

The key word there is "gently." Unlike with betaization, Disney means she won't demand things and get upset if you say no. She'll just gently, carefully, and patiently push, prod, and imply. If betaization is a hammer, Disney is a feather. You could almost consider Disney as "betaization light."

Disney is usually more prevalent with these kinds of women:

- Women with more feminine personalities
- More traditional women
- Religious women
- Foreign (non-Western) women

Unfortunately, unlike with betaization and ASD, there's not much you can do about Disney if a woman has a decent amount of it. If Disney is not something you want or like, you can simply refrain from making any woman with Disney anything more than a casual relationship.

The problem is, you might actually be attracted to women who have more Disney traits. A recurring problem I've had for a long time is that since I'm a very masculine man, I tend to be attracted to extremely feminine women (opposites attract!). Thus, I sometimes get "stuck" with women who have a decent amount of Disney despite the fact that I think it's all bullshit.

In these cases, you simply need to stay strong, and draw a line over which you will never cross. If you want kids but never want to get married, fine. If you never want kids or marriage, fine. If you never want to get legally married but don't mind having a wedding ceremony at some point in the future, fine. Whatever it is, define it internally with yourself and stick with it. Then don't ever compromise on the aspects of Disney you don't want, with any woman, no matter what. If she hates that, she can leave (and she'll probably come back later if you managed the relationship correctly).

In other words, Disney is only a danger if you puss out and agree to things you don't want because you don't want to lose her... which is, of course, oneitis. Therefore, Disney will never be a problem for you if you never get oneitis.

VYW

As I mentioned in the last chapter, VYW stands for very young women, meaning women from the age of consent, usually 16 or 18, to age 22. There are several types of VYW that I'll describe in the following chapter.

FB

An FB, which stands for friends with benefits or fuck buddy, is a woman you don't have romantic feelings for at all, but whom you enjoy having sex with. Beyond the sex, you're just friends (or less). There is no romance or dating. You just meet up and have sex. Maybe you both chat a little or watch a little TV afterwards or something like that, but that's about it. No dates, no cuddling after sex, no spending the night, none of that. There is no expectation of commitment or exclusivity by either of you. A person can even have several FBs at once (I often do).

That doesn't mean you treat your FBs like trash. The "F" in "FB" stands for *friend*. She's your friend, perhaps even your close friend. That means you treat her with kindness and respect, just like you would one of your guy buddies. Just because you're not romantically serious with her doesn't mean you don't treat her nicely. Plus, treating your FBs like crap invites drama, which will damage your happiness. We don't want that!

It's important to understand that you don't *date* an FB. An FB is someone you're having sex with, not someone you're "hanging out" with or dating. If you're in a sexual relationship with a woman where you're going to dinners, movies, or hiking together, that's an MLTR or OLTR (described below), not an FB. The FB relationship revolves around sex, and sex is your primary activity.

The beauty of FBs is that because you're not serious, these women largely don't care what you're doing with your life or if you're having sex with other women. They have virtually zero drama, require very little time and very little work. They're fantastic.

The downside of FBs is that they don't offer an emotional connection (assuming you want one, and maybe you don't). FBs also tend to not last nearly as long as MLTRs or OLTRs, since most women in FB relationships (though not all) will vanish out of your life as soon as they get a boyfriend, get engaged, or encounter a new man in their life they get excited about.

The vast majority of VYW you will date will likely be FBs.

MLTR

AN MLTR, or "multiple long-term relationship," is a woman you're in a relationship and with whom you actually have feelings for. Unlike the FB, an MLTR is a woman you're actually *dating*. Not only are you having sex with her, but you also have at least some romantic feelings for her as well. You go out on dates and events with her. She spends the night with you and even, perhaps, spends the weekends with you. You cuddle after sex and have no problem discussing your feelings with her. You can even be in love with an MLTR.

Like with the more common acronym LTR, the word "long" in the term multiple long-term relationship is not necessarily accurate. Some MLTRs last a few months, others can last many years.

The "M" in "MLTR" means multiple. This means you are not monogamous to, or emotionally exclusive with, an MLTR. You can date and have feelings for her, and you can also date, and have sex with, and have feelings for other women too. Thus, you can have several MLTRs at the same time if you wish.

Unlike with an FB, which is a binary "yes she is" or "no she isn't" status, an MLTR is actually a 1-to-10 scale. The higher the number, the more serious the relationship is. AN MLTR can exist anywhere on this scale.

For example, you can have one MLTR who you somewhat like, but not that much. She's a 2 on the MLTR scale; just barely higher than an FB. You may also be seeing another MLTR who you really like. She's a 9 on the MLTR scale. This is what you would call a "high end" MLTR. (Consider zero on this scale an FB, and an eleven on this scale as an OLTR.) This is normal when you have multiple MLTRs; you will always like some more than others, which is perfectly fine.

The great thing about MLTRs is that you can have a real emotional connection with them. You can go out and do fun things with them. You can be romantic with them. You can have many "girlfriendish" experiences and feelings with them.

The downside to MLTRs is that while they don't take nearly as much time and effort as a normal relationship, they definitely take more time and effort than an FB. If a woman is an MLTR, she likes you, so you'll have to manage her expectations, frame, and drama similar to (though not nearly as much as) you would a real girlfriend.

OLTR

The OLTR, or open long-term relationship, is the highest level of nonmonogamous relationship hierarchy (FB, then MLTR, then OLTR). This is the deepest and most serious type of nonmonogamous relationship. This is the nonmonogamous equivalent of a serious girlfriend. An OLTR is a woman who you truly love, and you love no other. Unlike with an FB or MLTR, with an OLTR you've actually made some real commitments.

You are emotionally exclusive to her and her alone. However, you are still allowed to have sex with other women provided those women are *just* FBs or one night stands. MLTRs on the side are not allowed.

Because of the committed nature of the OLTR, there are some ground rules you will both have to follow regarding sex outside the relationship. These rules are completely up to you and her, and every OLTR is different.

Also unlike an FB or MLTR, a woman must prove her qualifications for an OLTR over a long period of time; at least six months. You don't just have sex with a woman a few times and make her your OLTR. Rather, she's an MLTR for a few months, and if after six months she's still happy and low-drama, then you can upgrade her from MLTR to OLTR if you wish. Awarding "girlfriend" status too quickly to any woman, even a high quality one, often results in drama and other problems down the road.

You cannot have multiple OLTRs. You can only have one. If you have one OLTR, you cannot have any MLTRs, just one OLTR and multiple FBs.

If you would like more detail on how to create and manage FBs, MLTRs, and/or OLTRs refer to my relationship management book, *The Ultimate Open Relationships Manual**.

As I will explain in upcoming chapters, I do *not* recommend having an OLTR with VYW. Keep women under the age of 23 to mostly FBs and perhaps the occasional MLTR, and save the OLTR stuff (if indeed you want that at all) for women over the age of about 25. More on this later.

---

* http://www.haveopenrelationships.com/

Chapter 3

THE DIFFERENT TYPES OF YOUNGER WOMEN

Not all younger women are the same. There are several different age ranges, each one with their own priorities, outlook, and sexual tendencies. Within each type of age range are several different subcategories.

It's critical that you fully understand the different types of women within the subcategories that you're targeting. Men all over the world make the mistake of attempting to game or date women of different age groups the exact same way, only to get problems and chaos as a result. Many years ago, I was one of these men. I would attempt to date women in their late teens, twenties, thirties, and forties all the same way, and I got no where fast. Once you fully understand the different types of younger women and adjust your approach accordingly, your results will instantly increase.

Female Age Ranges

Listed below are the different age ranges of younger women and how they differ. As always, the term "younger women" can be subjective. Most guys consider women in their early twenties as "younger," but if you're 60 you may consider women in their thirties and forties as "younger" as well. Given this, I will cover women age 18 to forties.

It's important to note that everything I'm about to say are *generalizations*. There will always be exceptions to the categories I'm about to describe, sometimes extreme ones. Yet, over the large population of millions of women in your city, these generalizations will tend to be accurate.

VYW – Very Young Women, Age 18 to 22

Women this age are essentially "adult teenagers." Even though some have the numeral 2 in the first digit of their age, they are still teenagers in terms of their behavioral patterns. Women in this age range are wild, free, happy, fun, dramatic, irresponsible, chaotic, and fickle. Unsurprisingly, at this age women make the most irresponsible decisions of their entire lives. Having a baby with the wrong guy, marrying the wrong guy, moving in with the wrong guy, doing hard drugs, getting too drunk, getting into serious financial trouble, having car accidents, having regular and huge drama with their friends and family, all of that is more common at this age.

VYW are fickle as hell. They are constantly leaping in and out of relationships all the time, changing their Facebook relationship statuses constantly, and not seeing anything wrong with it. They will dump you on a whim and find a new serious boyfriend within a week… then dump him a few weeks later and monkey-branch to the next guy.

ASD is at an all-time low at this age. This means that, once you overcome the age difference resistance (if indeed you get any, and sometimes you won't), you can get to sex with these women extremely fast, so fast that it may surprise you if you're accustomed to only dating women over the age of 30. Unlike older women, VYW have no problem whatsoever having sex very quickly with new men. This is to your advantage if you want to sleep with these women, and to your disadvantage if you get exclusive or monogamous with one of them. VYW are almost incapable of sexual monogamy and will cheat on their "boyfriends" constantly. Indeed, many of VYW I've had in casual relationships had "serious" boyfriends at the time. (I talk about how to manage this in Chapter 26.)

Because of this unusually low ASD, VYW tend to be more promiscuous. It's not uncommon to see some of those women have sex with five, ten, or even more guys within a six-month period. Not all VYW do this, but many do.

Despite all this sexuality, a woman's Disney fantasies are at extreme levels at this age, and many of these women are consumed with falling in romantic love, getting married (or the equivalent) with her Prince Charming, and having babies. This often causes them to, as I mentioned above, get serious with, move in with, marry, and/or have babies with the wrong men. And again, these relationships (or marriages!) are almost always brief until she moves on to the next guy.

Women this age tend to have elevated levels of drama and tend to be more whiny. However, very unlike older women, in the face of a strong, confident man, VYW will happily divert their drama to other targets besides him. (This diversion is usually impossible with older women, who feel they have a "right" to throw drama at their man if they're in a bad mood.)

At this age, a woman is all about *fun*. The goal of *having fun* trumps just about everything else in her life until she creeps into age 23 or so. If it's not fun, she's not interested. This is regardless of if she's a single mother or not.

Speaking of single mothers, a decently high percentage of today's VYW are single moms. About 50% of all the VYW I've had in ongoing relationships were single moms. If the concept of dating a younger woman who is also a single mom bothers you, feel free to screen out these women when you're in the dating process, but just remember you are discarding a huge percentage of the VYW population, many of whom are extremely attractive and fun to be with.

Miss Independent – Age 23 - 26

At age 23, a woman finally starts to shed her teenage behavioral model. She stops doing drugs quite as much, cuts way back on the drinking and gets drunk only occasionally, improves her decision making somewhat, starts working more regularly, and calms down on the overall.

The hardcore promiscuity ends, though she still has no problem sleeping with multiple men (only now instead of five or ten guys, it's just two, maybe three). ASD rises a little; she's still very relaxed about having sex but she's not quite the Miss Loosey Loose she was before.

As she hits age 25 and 26, for the first time in her life, she actually starts to avoid boyfriends. Modern-day women in their mid-twenties often want to be "independent" and "free." They often even brag about being "single." They do not want to be "tied down" to some needy boyfriend, remembering all the drama and chaos boyfriends caused her back when she was an irresponsible VYW. Regardless, women this age still love men, fun, and sex. She's going to play the field, enjoy herself, and be independent. It is women in the 23-26 age group who will sometimes literally lecture you after sex about how they don't want anything serious and how they are *not* your girlfriend.

Budding Provider Desires – Age 27 - 32

Women between the ages of around 27 to 32 are just like women in their mid-twenties, except now the ticking of the biological clock has started to ring in her ears, and she's starting to feel like perhaps she should "grow up" and get a husband or serious boyfriend (and kids, if she doesn't have any yet). They will carefully shed their no boyfriend rule and will get into relationships again, though their standards are higher than when they were younger.

At around age 28, if she still doesn't have any children, she'll often suddenly want a baby, right out of the blue. 28 really is the age for this; it's the most amazing thing and I've seen it happen many times.

It's also during this time frame that she'll have the worst day in a woman's life: her 30th birthday. She'll spend most of her 29th year being depressed and her 30th birthday crying, complaining about how "old" she is, even if she's just as attractive as she was when she was 25 (and many women at age 30 are).

Interestingly, this perceived increased age does nothing to lower her standards with men. Indeed, it starts to raise them even more than when she was younger (and, in her opinion, hotter).

ASD Spike / Provider Hunter – Age 33+

At or around age 33, a woman goes through a profound change. Her ASD spikes into the stratosphere. No longer will she have sex with guys on the first or second date (unless she already knows them, or they're really good-looking younger men with no money). No, that's back when she was "stupid" and a "slut." She's "a lady" now, and she "doesn't do that anymore."

Things like enjoying herself, being happy, having fun... that's all gone except for special occasions. Those are all silly things she liked when she was younger. She has responsibilities now. You can't go around having sex and enjoying yourself when you have kids and bills to pay! She's "had her fun," and now it's time to buckle down and slog through the pain and drama that is a woman's thirties, the worst decade of a woman's life.

If you're on a first or second date and actually try to have sex with her, you're in for an interesting experience. She'll whip out a 300-page book called "Dating Rules and Regulations," and follow it to the letter. "Let's see... we're on our second date... so we can't have sex yet, but you can touch one of my boobs... that would be okay. If we make it to the third date I might let you take my shirt off. Maybe. We'll see how well you do on our next date first."

If she's actually powerful enough to overcome the vast rivers of ASD flowing in her system, and you actually succeed in having sex with her reasonably quickly, over the next few weeks she will pressure you for monogamy or pair-bonding in ways younger woman never have. Extra work, frame, and relationship management on your part are required.

As I said, the thirties is the worst decade for unmarried, modern-day women, by far. At this age, a woman has gone through all kinds of failed relationships, financial problems, divorces, legal battles, cheating boyfriends, horrible first dates, asshole male bosses, and likely, stressful kids.

Men are no longer fun to her. Rather, men have become the enemy (at worst) or a necessary evil (at best). When she was 21, dating was fun. Now, it's one of the worst things in the world, and she dreads every minute of it. She needs a provider / boyfriend / husband, but utterly hates the entire process of finding one.

She likely has a job she hates, bills she can barely pay, kids that stress her out, and all kinds of life overhead she never had when she was younger, and she doesn't have the finances to keep up with it all.

On top of all that, when she looks in the mirror, she sees little wrinkles, bits of cellulite, a few gray hairs, and boobs that are possibly starting to sag, and her depression worsens. Single women in their thirties are big, walking balls of stress.

Things get a little better as she enters her forties, but not much. She gets depressed once again on her fortieth birthday, although she's accustomed to being "not young" anymore and it's not quite the shock it was when she turned 30. She also has cleaned up many of the messes from her twenties and thirties, and has a higher income to pad things a little.

She still has very high ASD, however now her sex drive has increased and she's much hornier that she was when she was 35. This actually works to your advantage, particularly in relationships.

If she still is very pretty and has maintained her looks into her forties, she now considers herself a queen, and demands to be treated that way by men who meet her. If she's just cute or average, this aspect is watered down a bit.

Types of VYW

If you're reading this book, it's most likely you are interested in dating VYW, regardless of your age. (And if you aren't, don't worry, this section addresses you as well.) When it comes to older men, not all VYW are the same. They break down in to three very distinct categories. This is something that really confused me when I started dating VYW, and when I finally figured it out, my results soared. The three types of VYW is such a critical concept that I'll be referring back to it often throughout this book. Once you understand and internalize these three types, your results with younger women will improve dramatically, and you'll save a ton of wasted time.

VYW break down into Type Ones, Type Twos, and Type Threes.

Type One VYW

Type One girls are VYW who are disgusted at the thought of being sexual with an older man. The thought of having sex with a man more than about four or five years older than her literally repulses her and produces a visceral, negative reaction.

Usually, this is because of the age of her father. VYW with comparatively younger fathers view having sex with an older man as "fucking my dad." This is particularly true if her father is young and still reasonably good looking.

This is a generalization though, and not all Type Ones have young dads. Some Type Ones are unusually picky girls, and visualize the "perfect man" as being someone in her age range. Others are immature for their age, thus only attracted to men their age, and can't process the concept of having sex or a relationship with an older guy.

A Type One VYW will not have sex with an older man, period, even if he's good looking, and even if he offers her money. She just can't bring herself to do it. She's just too disgusted by the idea, for whatever the reason.

About 40% of VYW are Type Ones. They are the norm. Your goal with Type One girls is to:

1. Identify them as quickly as possible.
2. Stop communicating with them as quickly as possible so you can move on to Type Twos and Threes.

Once you determine a VYW is a Type One (we'll discuss how in future chapters) you need to drop her *immediately* and move on. There is no way she's having sex with you, no matter how good-looking you are, how strong your game is, how drunk she is, or even how much money you offer her. She's not going to have sex with you, period. (Though I admit there are some very rare exceptions.) Spending your time trying to seduce her or change her mind is a complete and total waste of your time. Don't do it. Drop her like a hot potato and *move on.*

This is why Type Ones are good, at least in my opinion. I love Type Ones because they never waste my time. As soon as I determine a VYW is a type one, I thank her for her time, drop her out of my life, and move on to other women. You should do the same.

Type Two VYW

Type Twos are my favorite and will be yours as well. Type Two VYW are the polar opposite of Type Ones. While Type Ones are disgusted at the thought of older men, Type Twos are *only* attracted to much older men, and powerfully so.

The thought of getting fucked by a much older guy gets a Type Two wet. She's always been this way, usually starting at puberty. This is the girl who sat starry-eyed in her algebra class in high school, quietly lusting over her 43-year-old teacher, while all the other girls were flirting with the jock football players. These are the girls who had constant sexual fantasies about their teachers, next-door-neighbors, father's friends, and/or dads who hire them for babysitting jobs.

Since they don't want to be made fun of by Type Ones or Type Threes, most Type Twos keep these desires secret to all but their closest friends (and sometimes not even them). There are rare Type Twos who are more than open regarding their desire for older men, and actually can't wait to show off their forty-something boyfriend to their other teenage girlfriends, but these are the exception to the rule.

Type Twos often feel stuck, since they don't have access to older men the way other girls their age have access to younger men (though the age of online dating and sugar daddy game has certainly changed this for many of them). Most Type Twos are turned off by boys their age, and avoid dating them if at all possible, unless they feel they "have to" because they have no other choice.

If a VYW's last few boyfriends have all been way older than her, this is a telltale sign she's a Type Two.

Obviously, Type Two VYW is the type of woman you're going to be dating and having sex with the most. As long as you do everything right, these women are easy, and I mean that in every sense of the word, not just sexually. You are, hopefully, the non-creepy older man she's been dreaming about her entire life. She is just waiting for you to come into her life and sweep her off her feet in a confident, non-needy, and non-creepy way, that magical way the boys her age are incapable of doing.

Sadly, Type Twos are somewhat rare, representing only about 15-20% of the VYW population at very most. That means the vast majority of VYW you approach are *not* going to be one of them. That's okay. 15-20% is more than enough as long as you're putting in the numbers (which we'll talk about in detail soon).

The good news is that, because of all the cultural trends I talked about back in Chapter 1, the Type Two population is actually increasing as a percentage of VYW in society. It's increasing slowly, but it *is* increasing.

Type Three VYW

Type Threes are a little complicated.

Type Threes are VYW who don't really care about men's age one way or another. They really have never thought about it, either positively or negatively. When they see a man, they are focused on attributes other than his age. If he's attractive to her and does all the right things, she'll go there, regardless of his age (more or less). If not, she won't. It's that simple.

However, that does not mean that Type Threes are easily datable like Type Twos. Type Threes present several obstacles:

1. Like all women, Type Threes are very concerned about what other people think about them. Dating a man 20 years older than her might be okay with her, but she may feel it might look weird to her friends, family, or parents. This may cause serious resistance to the concept of dating an older man.

2. Very unlike most Type Twos, the vast majority of Type Threes have zero experience dating or having sex with older men. If you have sex with her, you'll likely be her first older guy. That means it's outside of her comfort zone. For this reason, Type Threes require more work and game to get to the point where they will have sex with you, much less date you in any sort of relationship context. They are not the "do everything right and it's a slam dunk" the Type Two is.

3. Unlike Type Twos, Type Threes *do* enjoy dating men their own age. That means there is far more competition for these women; both younger and older men are after them, and they'll happily take either. With Type Twos you have far less competition, making it easier for you.

    Every time I'm done dating a Type Three, she always goes right back to dating the young boys her own age. A Type Three will date a 22-year-old just as readily and eagerly as she'll date a 39-year-old.

    I devote an entire chapter in this book on how to close on Type Threes (Chapter 19). They require a little more patience, work, and time than Type Twos.

Type Threes represent about 40% VYW in modern society. However, they are a very fast growing younger woman demographic, growing far faster than Type Twos. I predict that in 20-30 years, this 40% will grow to 60% or higher.

THE DIFFERENT TYPES OF YOUNGER WOMEN

To review, here are the three types of VYW and your default actions with each:

Type Ones –Identify and drop as fast as possible. Zero odds of success.

Type Twos – Proceed strongly. High odds of success.

Type Threes – Proceed carefully, gently, and slowly. Medium to low odds of success.

The Three Types As It Applies To Women Over Age 23

Do the three types of VYW apply to women over age 23? The answer is somewhat, though the differences between the three categories are not as stark and definite, and the women in these categories are a little more flexible.

For example, a Type One 36-year-old woman will still be a little grossed out at the idea of having sex with a man who is 50, but a 50-year-old guy who has taken good care of his health and fitness and has strong game *does* have a chance with her. In the same way, a Type Two 36-year-old woman will be able to be wooed by a 36-year-old man even though she may prefer a guy who is 50.

Speaking in general, the three types do loosely apply to older women. So as always, you want to focus on Type Twos and Threes of any age.

Chapter 4

FRAMES AND MINDSETS NECESSARY FOR YOUNGER WOMEN SUCCESS

In my primary dating book, *Get To Sex Fast**, I talk about how important the twin qualities of *confidence* and *outcome independence* are to your ability to attract and keep women your life. As an older man working with much younger women, these traits are even more important than when working with women your own age.

The good news is that likely, as an older guy with more life experience and success under your belt, you already should have a decent quantity of both confidence and outcome independence, at least more than the typical younger man. Over the past ten years I've worked with and communicated with literally thousands of men on the topics of dating, seduction, and relationships, and the difference between men in their early twenties and men in their late thirties or forties is often night and

---

* http://www.gettosexfast.com/

day. Younger men are often raging with neediness, loneliness, drama queen behavior, extreme outcome dependence, and a strong need for acceptance. (Again, I'm generalizing here. Not all younger men are like this, but a hell of a lot are.) Older men often have these negative traits as well, but not nearly as many or as intensely.

As an older man, you need to take all of your experiences and successes and hone this into a powerful sense of confidence and outcome independence. It is absolutely critical you demonstrate these two qualities as much as you can with younger women, or most of the techniques you learn in this book won't be very effective.

In addition to confidence and outcome independence, you also require a third trait that men dating within their own age range don't need: non-creepiness. As a man much older than her, she's going to be hypersensitive to "creepy" older man behavior from you. You must ensure you don't demonstrate any of this, or else your odds of success go down.

The Life of the Hot Younger Woman

VYW live a different life than older women. I'll use an example by comparing a typical hot 30- year-old with a typical hot 18-year-old.

From the outside looking in, the smoking hot 30 year-old woman and the hot 18 year-old Girl *Appear* to move through life in about the same way. They're both attractive, and they know it. They both dress sexy and present themselves well. They both get an extreme amount of attention from men.

However if you look deeper, strong differences emerge.

The 30-year-old gets hit on by men all the time, sure. But men are not throwing themselves at her, propositioning for sex constantly. They can't, because usually these are men in the workplace where they'd get fired if they pulled that. Other men around her are going to be her age or older, which means their moves towards her are going to be more indirect and less overt.

Her access to men is usually compartmentalized only into those times when she's not working on her life responsibilities. Most of her time is taken up by her job, family, school, the gym, and her children if she has them (which, statistically speaking, she most likely does). Any dating or sexual activity has to come *on top of* all those areas.

The hot 18-year-old's situation is completely different. Unlike the hot 30-year-old, the hot-18 year-old is constantly surrounded by horny younger men who are constantly telling her how hot she is, how big her tits are, how beautiful she is, how much they want her to be their girlfriend, and how much they want her to move in with them. Her social media and online dating apps are plastered top to bottom with young, horny, drooling beta males who are slathering her with complements about how hot she is. The hot 30-year-old woman doesn't have as much of this, and in many cases, would be offended to hear it, but the hot 18-year-old drinks this shit like fine wine, begging for more.

On top of this, she is getting a constant barrage of sexual propositions from these horny bastards. She is being asked for sex on almost a daily basis, and by multiple men. Since younger men usually have very poor game, often she's even *begged* for it.

While the 30-year-old is at work, or college, or the gym, or taking care of children, the 18-year-old is hanging out at malls, flirting with guys downtown, going to underage clubs, smoking weed with friends, and having sex with guys at parties. Unlike her 30-year-old sister, men are constantly around her, complimenting her, groping her, and kissing her ass.

The hot 30-year-old would never tolerate this behavior. She's used to men fawning all over her and, while sometimes she likes the attention, often she tires of it and it annoys her. If a man actually makes a sexual comment, she will often actually get upset.

The 18-year-old? Hell no! She loves all this immature attention from needy younger men. It's all new and exciting to her, and she drinks it up with relish. This is even more intense if she's a late bloomer, and a *lot* of attractive VYW are. I've dated many 18 and 19-year-olds who were ugly ducklings at age 15 and then suddenly blossomed, getting big boobs, losing weight, growing out their hair, and going blonde. By the time they hit 18, they're suddenly gorgeous. These women absolutely love every bit of immature, stupid sexual attention they get from men (even if they complain about it).

In the middle of all this comes you. You are out on a date with a hot 19-year-old, and you start telling her how pretty she is, how cool and fun she is, and how she should "just come back to your place." Will that work? Are you being any different than the last 50 guys who have tried to fuck her?

The answer is, of course, no. Kissing a woman's ass like that might work if she's an older woman and you're willing to wait a few dates, maybe. But if she's a cute VYW, she'll just place you in the "just like everyone else who tries to fuck me" category, which is a roundabout way of saying she will not have sex with you.

Men vastly underestimate the world that attractive, younger women live in. You're allowed into this world, but only if you demonstrate the following five traits:

- Confidence
- Outcome independence
- Non-creepiness
- Maximized physical appearance
- At least an average amount of dating/game skill

Older men thinking they can just "wing it" when it comes to younger women, or think they can game VYW the same way they game 42-year-olds are going to crash and burn (unless they get lucky, which I admit sometimes happens). Even if all you're going to do is sugar daddy game, where you're actually giving women money, these traits are still required to a degree (though granted, to a lesser degree).

This book will cover all five of these traits, in detail.

When Exactly Is A Woman "Younger?"

If there is a difference between normal game / relationship management and game / relationship management with a much younger woman, how much younger does she need to be for you to shift from "normal" style to "younger woman style?" The answer *is if you look like you are 10 years or more older than her.* If you're 35 and she's 27, she's not a "younger woman" by my definition and you can proceed as normal. If you're 35 and she's 23, now she's a younger woman and you need to treat your gaming approach and relationship management from that vantage point.

Sometimes, men look younger than they appear. That's good news for you. If she's 27 and you're 40 but easily look 35, then you don't need to change very much in your approach, since she's going to view you as a 35-year-old man, within 10 years of her, and thus "normal."

This changes a little bit with online dating, however. With online dating, she can see how old you are in your dating profile. As a matter of fact, your age will often be the second thing she looks at right after your photos, even before she looks at your income (if you're on a dating site/app that shows that information). So, what happens if you're 40, it says you're 40 on your dating profile, but you clearly look 35, and a hot 27-year-old is checking out your profile to see if she's going to respond to your opener? Are your younger looks going to carry you to the point where you don't have to use younger woman game? The answer is, partially.

If you look younger than your age, but a woman already knows how old you are, and she's still 10 years or more younger than you, then no matter what, she's a "younger woman," and that style of game will be required. However, as we'll talk about in Chapter 6, your odds of success go way up. Obviously, a young-looking and fit 45-year-old man is going to do much better with younger women than an old-looking, chubby, dorky-looking 45-year-old man, assuming their confidence, outcome independence, non-creepiness, and game skill are identical. Regardless though, *both* men will need to employ younger woman game, not normal game.

This also brings up the issue of whether or not to lie about your age to women, either in person or on your online dating profiles. We'll discuss that issue in Chapter 11.

Confidence and Outcome Independence

If you have already read my dating book, *Get To Sex Fast[1]* or my Alpha Male 2.0 lifestyle book, *The Unchained Man[2]*, then you are probably already familiar with the concepts of confidence and outcome independence, and you're welcome to skip this section and proceed to the next section on non-creepiness. Otherwise, I will summarize these two concepts briefly here.

Confidence means you are self-assured in your abilities, and strongly believe that you can rely on yourself to handle literally any situation when it comes to women of any age. It means that when you spend time with beautiful women, you are relaxed, happy, calm, not nervous, strong, and have no problem stating preferences to women or saying no to them. It means your body language and eye contact is strong but relaxed. Confidence is demonstrated by actions such as speaking strongly and deeply, slow movements, solid eye contact, a relaxed, kicked-back demeanor, laughter, a big smile, and a strong but relaxed posture. Confidence is not about acting cool or tough. Confidence is being relaxed, at ease, in control, and in charge.

Outcome independence means that you **literally do not give a shit** how any interaction with any individual woman ends up. Even if you're on a first date with the most beautiful woman you've ever seen in your life, you don't care *at all* about how it might end up. If you end up having sex with her, great. If she calls you an asshole and storms out of the coffee shop, also great. If she tells you you're the most amazing man she's ever met, also great. You don't care one way or the other. Regardless of what

---

[1] http://www.gettosexfast.com/
[2] http://www.alphamalebook.com/

happens with this one woman, you know there are thousands of other hot women out there, right around the corner, and if she doesn't work out, you're on to the next hot babe on the list.

This indifference radiates out from you via everything you do or say. You're a nice guy and you're polite, but every woman who encounters you can clearly tell that you just don't give a shit.

Outcome independence is, without question, the single, most attractive non-physical quality a man can have to women. Moreover, *the more attractive a woman is, the better it works.* Think about it. Imagine a first date with that super hot 18-year-old from the above example. She's accustomed to excited men drooling all over her and kissing her ass, and here you are, totally relaxed, talking to her in a completely chill way, not complimenting her at all, not kissing her ass, not offering anything to her… just enjoying yourself and clearly not giving a shit about how the interaction ends up.

With the drooling men, she's turned off. But with you, she is suddenly strongly attracted, *and she doesn't even know why.*

Outcome independence is critical for the older man seeking to date much younger women. The hotter the women, and the larger the age difference, the more important it becomes. If you want more detail on outcome independence, read *Get To Sex Fast* or *The Unchained Man.*

Non-Creepiness

When there is a significant age difference between a man and a woman and the woman is the younger one, there is obviously an age difference "barrier" to having sex and/or initiating an ongoing sexual or romantic relationship. This age difference barrier comprises three factors:

---

[1] http://www.gettosexfast.com/
[2] http://www.alphamalebook.com/

- The Creepy Factor
- The Social Acceptance Factor
- The Fear of the Unknown Factor

The social acceptance factor and the fear of the unknown factor we'll cover in future chapters. For now, I'll show you how to overcome the creepy factor. The creepy factor is when a younger woman has her radar up for any "creepy older man behavior" from you. Most younger women have, unfortunately, been a victim of ugly older men hitting on them in very uncalibrated or downright scary ways, as well as making lewd, sexual comments. They've also heard many Type Ones complain about "gross" or "creepy" older men for years.

Because of this, most younger women, even many Type Twos, are going to be hypersensitive about anything "creepy" you do with them pre-sex. The funny part is that many of these "creepy" behaviors would not be considered "creepy" if a man her age did them, just if *you* did them; a man much older than her. It's not fair, it's just the way it is.

If you follow pick-up artist advice, you may have heard the advice to "risk creepy" when trying to seduce a woman. Normally, that's good advice. In *Get To Sex Fast** I talk about things like touching a woman (kino), sex talk, and strongly and confidently escalating to sexual activity as fast as possible (at least in most scenarios). *Under normal conditions*, you should do this, even if you think touching her "this soon" or talking about sex might make you look "creepy." However when you're an older man and there's a large age difference with a younger woman, the conditions are not normal, for the reasons I just described above. An older man can *not* do anything perceived as creepy with a younger woman until after he's had sex with her twice and she's fully comfortable with him.

This is especially true of Type Threes, who are already out of their comfort zone by spending time with you in a dating context already. Even Type Twos have their limit of perceived creepy behavior, and their limit isn't very high. You can't push the envelope on this.

---

* http://www.gettosexfast.com/

The problem is that, as I've talked about in *Get To Sex Fast**, you need to have a sexual frame for normal dating/seduction to work. With younger women, you'll have to be sexual without being creepy, which is something that will take a little practice.

Here are some examples of *sexual*:

- Asking her a question about her sexual history.
- Answering questions you are asked about your past relationships, but doing so in a sexual context.
- Talking about sex in a very casual way, like it's no big deal.
- Confidently talking about how you like bigger asses on women and hate smaller ones. (Obviously you would not do this if she had a small ass.)
- Casually joking about sex or sexual issues, but your sexual jokes are witty and funny, not crude or childish.

Here are some examples of *creepy*:

- Asking her if she wants to pee on you. (Yes, older men say this kind of crap to younger women all the time.)
- Clearly and verbally complimenting her tits or ass.
- Saying something like "I bet you like big, thick cocks!" and then winking at her.
- Sending her a dick pic.
- Talking about fringe sexual stuff like BDSM, fisting, or sex with animals.
- Talking about you and her having sex before you've ever done it, particularly when you use specifics.
- Leering at other women while on a first or second date with her.
- Talking about more hardcore stuff during sex that you love, i.e. talking about how much you love anal sex or threesomes.

---

* http://www.gettosexfast.com/

Hopefully you see the difference. Younger women are instinctively going to have their "creepiness radar" on full-blast when they first meet you. You need to dial down the creepy, needy, sexual stuff as best you can. The good news is once you have sex with her twice, you can get as kinky as you like (within her comfort level, of course).

Another way to describe this is to be sexual, but not horny. Horny men are a turn off, and as a cute younger woman she's more than accustomed to horny men. Sexual men, on the other hand, are extremely attractive, and younger women have little to no experience with sexual men, which is why being sexual and not horny or creepy is so powerful. This alone will differentiate you from all the other men who have tried to have sex with her.

A horny guy is leaning forward, leering at her, getting a boner in his pants as he's talking to her. A sexual guy is leaning back, relaxed, smiling, and talking about sex and sexual experiences in a way that engages her imagination.

I honestly can't tell you the sheer number of younger women, many of whom were extremely attractive, who had sex with me after saying no to other older men, many of whom where better looking than me and/or wealthier than me, strictly because these other guys were creepy, and I was comfortable, relaxed, and nice. The non-creepiness factor in dating much younger women cannot be overstated; it's a make-or-break thing.

Everything you do with younger women, particularly before you've had sex with her twice, including every technique you're going to learn throughout the rest of this book, must come from a place of confidence, outcome independence, and non-creepiness. Otherwise, your results will be very spotty no matter how honed your technique is.

Chapter 5

ACT YOUR AGE, JUST BE THE BEST FOR YOUR AGE

If I had only one sentence to answer the question "How can I attract much younger women as an older man?" it would be this:

Be the man the boys her age are not, and be the best version of that man.

It's common for older men to go out of their way to dress younger, act younger, engage in "young guy" activities, and lie about their age to make them seem younger than they actually are. I realize there are scenarios where this might help, but it's usually if you're a pretty young older guy, as in younger than age 35. The problem is that acting younger will actually harm your results over the broad range of numbers of younger women you will meet or date.

Remember that your primary target market are Type Twos, not Type Ones, and not even Type Threes. The vast majority of younger women you're going to have sex / have relationships with will be Type Twos. The entire reason a Type Two is going to like you, be attracted to you, want to be with you, is because of how different you are from the young guys her age, not because you're the same. By acting younger, *you are actually destroying the one quality that will make it most likely for Type Twos to be attracted to you.*

It's a key point and a lot of older guys misunderstand this. Just think about it; does any 21-year-old girl on the planet want a guy who looks 38 but acts like he's 25? No. If that were the case, she'd just go for guys who act 25 and really are 25. That would be far easier for her.

Lying about your age or trying to act younger is a technique that is geared towards dating Type Ones. But as we talked about in Chapter 3, Type Ones aren't going to have sex with you no matter what you do. Lying about your age or acting younger might work on a Type Three, but Type Threes only make a smaller percentage of the women who are willing to give you enough of a chance to get them into bed. Calibrating your entire younger women approach to appeal to Type Threes is not a path to success. Instead, you must focus on Type Twos and get a sprinkle of Type Threes when you can.

Type Twos don't want older men, nor do they want older men who act like younger men. They want the things that make older men different from younger men. This means you should not only not try to act younger, but instead you should play up the qualities that older men have over younger men. This includes:

- Confidence
- Strength (I'm talking about mental and personality strength, not physical strength, though physical strength can help too.)
- Motivation and drive
- Success
- Being more focused
- Organization (having your shit together)
- Being more controlled
- Having a cool head
- Not tolerating any drama or crap

These are powerful qualities that are ridiculously attractive to Type Twos (and to other women as well). It will even make many Type Threes give you a second look. It's hard for younger men to have those qualities, but it's much easier for you to have them and demonstrate them.

Given that advice, you might be tempted to act *older* than what you actually are. This is a mistake. As we'll talk about in more detail in upcoming chapters, most older men come across as the "dad next door" or even as grouchy grandpas. Too many older guys dress like old, married beta males, complain about things like "that stupid rap music," and get confused when a younger woman talks about something like Snapchat. While you don't want to act like one of her young guy friends, you also don't want to act like her dad, uncle, or grandpa either (though there can be slight exceptions to the dad thing; we'll talk about that later).

Instead of acting like you're older or younger, you want to act like the most amazing man of your age she's ever met. If you're 45 years old, when she meets you in person, and throughout your relationship, you need act 45, but to be the coolest, most fun, most chill and relaxed, most badass, and yes, best-looking non-celebrity 45-year-old she's ever personally spent time with. *That* will get you laid. As a matter of fact, once you get that nailed, you will be shocked at how much easier it is to date, have sex with, and have relationships with younger women as compared to women your own age, because of younger women's low ASD.

You do this by promoting the good qualities and advantages of your age over younger men while diminishing the few negative qualities of your age (if any!).

Here's how you can accomplish both:

1. Never lie about your age, unless you're doing so temporarily as part of a greater overall strategy (which we'll discuss in the online dating chapter). If you're 52, tell her you're 52 and don't shy away from it.
2. Never try to dress like a man younger than you, but, dress in cool, modern styles, with colors and cuts that make you look the best. We'll discuss this in detail in Chapter 7.

3. Be busy. Work hard on your goals and your Mission. Travel a lot. Do fun things regularly. Have a full life and a busy schedule. Make sure she knows you have things to do. Men her age, even those with jobs, usually have a lot of free time on their hands. You don't want to be in that category.

    Eben Pagan (as David DeAngelo) once said the immortal words, "Give her the gift of missing you." It was one of the most accurate things ever spoken on the issue of seduction and relationships. Give her plenty of opportunities to miss you while you get work done in other areas of your life. Let all the young guys her age constantly bother her because they're bored and have nothing to do.

4. Do not tolerate *any* drama or immature behavior from her, which you are sure to get at least sometimes. Men in her age group will dive right into her drama and will fight, argue, scream, bitch, rationalize, explain, threaten, and justify right along with her, sometimes for hours. As an older man, you need to be above that childishness. If she starts throwing immature drama your way, give her one stern warning. When she acknowledges it, immediately change the subject. If she does it again, it's time for a soft next (we'll cover that in Chapter 24). Gently kick her out of your life and go do something else while she cools off. Drama is for younger men, not you.

5. Try to avoid "young guy" vernacular. If you're over the age of about 32, you should not be saying the word "dude" too often, and I better not ever hear the letters "OMG" fall out of your mouth unless you're clearly being sarcastic. I'm not saying you can't be relaxed. Sometimes I say these younger man words myself, just not all the time.

6. Exhibit responsible behavior. Young guys are irresponsible, older men are responsible, or at least that's how it's supposed to be and that's what younger women are going to expect. I'm not saying you can't booze it up or drive really fast *occasionally*. Just make sure you're doing those things responsibly. You know what

I mean by drinking responsibly vs. drinking irresponsibly, for example. There's a difference between when a 40-year-old guy gets drunk and when a 23-year-old guy gets drunk. Right?

7. Demonstrate your knowledge. Talk about the things you know about in conversations *where they make sense*. HTML code or aircraft mechanics are nerd topics that are never a good idea to discuss with women, since it will turn them off and put them to sleep. But quoting something *relevant to the discussion* about business or politics, or quoting a historical fact, or quoting Shakespeare are going to make many Type Twos swoon.

8. If you have them, don't be afraid to talk about your kids, even if your kids are grown, and even if your kids are older than she is. A lot of older men are frightened of this topic, and there is no reason to be. I have slept with numerous women who were younger than my own children (both of whom are now grown), and all of these women knew I had kids and knew how old they were. Again, if you're doing everything right and the women are Type Twos, not only will they not care, but in some cases of extreme Type Twos, it may even turn them on.

9. Be cool. If you're in a relationship with a younger woman and she wants to go to the dance club with you, go. If you don't know how to dance, learn. It's not that hard. If she wants to go to a Halloween party with you dressed up as something stupid, dress up and go. Have fun. If she wants to smoke weed, let her smoke weed. You don't have to, but you should be 100% cool with her doing it.

The point is to not be an old stick in the mud who "doesn't do that stuff" because "that's for young people." Remember, act your age, but be cool for your age. As we talked about back in Chapter 3, VYW like to have fun, and if you don't like to have fun, you're putting the recurring sexual relationship in jeopardy. (Obviously I'm talking here about MLTR or OLTR relationships; with FBs you would never go out, but you can still have a fun vibe with her.)

Chapter 6

MAXIMIZING YOUR PHYSICAL APPEARANCE

As I've talked about in my other dating and relationship books, a key component of your success or failure with women is your outward physical appearance.

There are two schools of thought regarding this, and they're both wrong.

In one school of thought are those defeatists and whiners who think that if you're not gorgeous or have six pack abs then you have no hope of ever sleeping with an attractive woman. Not only is this false, but I'm living proof of it. Back when I was having the most sex with the most women, including VYW, I was a good 50 pounds overweight and had thinning hair. Yet, I was able to date and sleep with 18-22 year olds, without paying for it, with minimal problems. Granted, I did everything else I possibly could to improve my appearance back then, and I've lost weight since then, but clearly looks aren't the be-all and end-all some men make them out to be.

Another school of thought, one much less common but still one you see with some dating "experts" and pick-up artists, is that looks doesn't really matter at all, and if you have super strong game and frame, you'll get laid even if you look like shit. This is also false. You don't have to look like a model, but if you look like *shit* you're not going to be successful at this. Even paying for sex using sugar daddy game will be a problem for you. Therefore, you *must* maximize your physical appearance as much as possible based on age and your genetics.

I went into great detail as to why both of these schools of thought are wrong in *Get To Sex Fast**. Here, I'm going to cover how this applies to you as an older man when dating younger women.

Here is the absolute bottom line for older men: In terms of overall physical appearance (fashion included), you must set a goal to be in the top 15% of men *your age* and *in your city.*

Here's what I mean. Let's say you're 42 years old and live in Denver, Colorado, USA. Let's also say they randomly pulled 99 other 42-year-old men from the streets of Denver and placed them in a large gymnasium, with you among them.

Then they brought in 100 super hot younger women, we're talking 9's and 10's here; all age 18-22. They told the women to rank every man in the gym from best looking to worst looking (including how the men were dressed), and to line up the men against the wall in that order. The man they voted best looking would be the first guy, the second best looking would be second, and so on, all the way to the ugliest guy at position number 100.

Your goal is to be **in the top 15 of those men**. The good news is that you don't need to be number one. I have never been number one in physical appearance as compared to men my age and I never will be. Frankly, if they did this exercise with me, I would make the top 15, but I'd probably be number 15, mainly because I'm still overweight.

---

* http://www.gettosexfast.com/

However, that's literally the only thing wrong with my appearance. My skin looks great. I look very young and healthy for my age. I'm energetic and happy. I have a full head of hair. My teeth are perfect. I have some decent muscle mass. I know how to dress in ways that make me look pretty good. So if you put me up against 100 men in my American city who are my exact age (age 46 as of this writing), I'll *easily* crack the top 15, though I'll *never* crack the top 10, which is perfectly fine.

Some more good news is that the older you get, the easier it is to be in the top 15%, since most men really start to let their appearance go as they age. They get fat, flabby, bald, dress like dorks, and let their grooming go to hell. That is your competition for those Type Twos, and as older men go, the competition is pretty weak. This is one of the great advantages of older man / younger woman game; once you master the basics, it's much easier than you think.

This is why you only need to be in the top 15% of men your age instead of the top 5% or 10% as others may believe. As long as you're in the top 15%, or even very close to that, you're good. If you're not in the top 15% but are in the top 25%, that's tougher. You can still date younger women, but you're going to have to put in a lot more numbers to get results, and your margin for error becomes much more narrow (if not nonexistent). If you are anywhere below 25%, you need to get your appearance up before you spend too much time attempting to date younger women, unless all you want to do is pay-for-it sugar daddy game (and even then, you'll have serious problems if you're in the bottom 50%).

In this chapter and the next, I'm going to lay out everything you can possibly do to improve your appearance as an older man. (A few of these items are modified versions from *Get To Sex Fast**, adjusted for older men.)

---

* http://www.gettosexfast.com/

Physical Appearance for the Older Man – Overview

In terms of being an older man, your overall physical appearance comprises five areas:

- **Fitness** – Your level of body fat and muscle mass, as well as your body shape. Essentially how your body looks naked from the neck down.
- **Skin** – The youthfulness and tone of your skin, particularly on your face, neck, back of hands, and upper arms.
- **Grooming** – Your hair and/or lack thereof, and how you manage it. This applies to all hair on your head (or lack thereof), facial hair, and body hair, including things like eyebrows.
- **Fashion** – How you dress, namely the colors, styles, and cuts of clothing, shoes, and accessories you wear, particularly on first and second dates.
- **Body Language** – How you move, sit, walk, and carry yourself nonverbally.

Since you need to be in the top 15% of men your age in your city, you need to address all five of these areas and maximize each area as best you can based on your age, genetics, and budget.

That last part is important, since often it will require some money to be spent to address certain problems with your appearance, especially if you're the more typical older guy who's just come out of a divorce or long-term, monogamous relationship and have let your appearance slide. Since you're an older guy, I'm going to assume your income is at least decent for the rest of this book. I don't expect you to spend $100,000 on your appearance, but spending a few thousand dollars on upgrading your wardrobe and addressing one or two cosmetic problems with your appearance may be in order. If that sounds like a lot of money, I understand. I'm a frugal bastard and I utterly hate spending money, but you need to realize that spending money in these ways not only improves your ability to date younger women, but it will also,

- Increase your overall confidence in other areas of life.
- Likely increase your income, particularly if you're in sales or are self-employed.
- Increase your self-esteem.
- Making you an overall happier guy.

Looking better really does make you feel better, and I would know. Whenever I see pictures of myself as a pathetic, traditionally married beta male from 15 years ago, I shudder at how bad I looked even though I was 15 years younger. I feel much better about myself today, and looking better is a huge part of that.

Rate yourself on a 1 to 10 scale for each of the five areas above; fitness, skin, grooming, fashion, and body language. If you aren't sure how you rank in some of these areas, just guess. Put these numbers down somewhere and keep track of them. Update them once every few months, and focus on improving them. You might be surprised how much better you can look in just a few weeks, certainly a few months.

To use myself as an example, when I was in my early thirties as a traditionally married beta male, not giving a shit about how my appearance was, my rankings looked something like this:

Fitness – 3

Skin – 7

Grooming – 3

Fashion – 3

Body Language – 7

I was chubby and looked like crap. My skin was okay since I was only 30, but it was way too pale. My grooming was terrible; I had a stupid haircut, often with hair that was too long and unruly, with obviously thinning hair all over the top of my head, and had scruffy hair all over the back of my neck. I dressed like an I.T. nerd working for Microsoft. My body language was decent, but not fantastic.

Today, after spending many years improving my appearance and living for eleven years as an independent, happy, Alpha Male 2.0, my rankings look something like this, again, as compared to the typical 46-year-old American male:

Fitness – 6
Skin – 8
Grooming – 9
Fashion – 8
Body Language – 10

As you can see, that's a huge improvement, and many of those things were simple tweaks, particularly in grooming and fashion (all of which we'll cover shortly). I'm still overweight, but I'm in much better shape and feel stronger and younger than I did when I was 30. My skin is still pretty damn good, and I fake tan a little so I don't look quite as pale. My grooming is always near-perfect. I now have a full head of hair that looks great and perfect teeth. I now wear clothing and colors that enhance my appearance instead of making me look like a dork. My body language, which was already good, is now powerful, strong, confident, and outcome independent.

You'll notice that only one item in the above list is at a perfect 10 (body language). As I keep reiterating, you don't need to look perfect or like a Hollywood celebrity. You just need to look *good*. I don't look perfect at all; far from it. But I look *good*. When a hot younger woman sees me for the first time in real life on a first date, she's not grossed out or turned off by my appearance, unlike with so many other older men my age. In many cases, many Type Twos actually think I look *good*.

Here's one of my favorite stories from my recent dating life. About two years ago, I met up with a younger woman on a first date. She was 22 years old and exactly my type; petite, blonde, and beautiful. I met her at a local Starbucks, and she had arrived before I did. She was sitting at a table but she was turned away from me as I entered the establishment, looking out the window. I sat down at the table next to her, as she was still turned away, and said, "Hi."

Startled, she turned and looked at me. Her eyes widened, and she said, and I quote, "Wow... you are really good looking."

To be fair, she didn't say it as a compliment. She said it more as a statement of surprise, since she knew how old I was (and I was not the first older man she had met on a date like this). Regardless, it made me feel really good. The work I had put in to improve my appearance, which is less work than I had thought it would be, had really paid off. By the way, we talked for about 20 minutes, then went right to my place to have sex. She became a very fun, long-term FB.

Getting your appearance optimized is certainly some work, but I *promise you*, I promise you it's more than worth it.

Fitness

Let's get this out of the way first; I am no fitness expert. Indeed, of the Seven Life Areas I talk about in *The Unchained Man** (financial, woman, physical, family, spiritual, recreational, and social), physical fitness has been my weakest area by far. I've done a lot of research in this area, and I've managed to lose a decent amount of weight and get my physical health up to where I am one of the healthiest men in my forties that I know, but I still don't consider myself a fitness expert and neither should you. So temper anything I say about health or fitness with that, and please consult a doctor, nutritionist, or personal trainer if you have any questions.

Most men under the age of 35, at least in my opinion, don't really need to pay attention to fitness for *physical appearance* reasons unless fitness is a hobby they enjoy. All human begins should pay attention to fitness for *health, stress,* and *longevity* reasons, but I'm only talking here about fitness in terms of your physical appearance.

Once a man hits age 35 or so, negative aspects of aging begin to appear. A man often starts losing his hair at around this age (if it hasn't started already), his skin starts to look worse, crow's feet and other

---

* http://www.alphamalebook.com/

wrinkles begin to appear, and both testosterone and metabolism levels start to drop, causing easier fat gain and retention. Add this to the typical Westerner's poor diet (particularly Americans), and years of eating pizza, beer, and cheeseburgers, coupled with perhaps some cigarette, marijuana, or other drug usage. All of this crap starts to take a toll on the body in ways it never did in when he was in his twenties.

You should consider age 35 as the magical line you cross to old age, where fitness and maintaining your skin, appearance, weight, and health become a priority, even if you never did anything prior to age 35 to maintain these things (which you probably didn't).

When a man crosses over into age 40, this gets even worse. Now, fitness and health activities take enough time equivalent to a part-time job. Let me say that again; if you make fitness and health apriority post-40, which I think you should, it's like taking on a part-time job. This will include things like:

- Regular exercise
- Regular exercise prep
- Increased grocery shopping for fresh, healthy food
- Increased food prep time
- Increased kitchen cleanup time
- Purchasing, managing, and consuming regular vitamins and supplements
- Research
- Experimenting (trial and error to figure out what your body reacts well to)
- TRT (optional, more on this below)
- Increased grooming time (more hairs growing in more places that need to be managed)
- Increased hair management time (unless you shave your head)

This all takes a shitload of time. I don't love it, but I do it, and do it all, since it is my goal to:

1. Stay as healthy as humanly possible throughout the rest of my life, even well into my very old age.
2. Stay out of hospitals and doctor's offices and maintain the highest possible quality of life.
3. Always be in the top 15% in physical appearance for a man my age, again, lasting well into my very old age, so access to younger women is always easier.

4. Live for as long as I can, with the highest quality of life that I can. I live a wonderfully fantastic life, and I want to keep this party going for as long as I can.

Therefore, the part-time job you take on managing your health and fitness post-40 is, to me, worth it. I'm one of the happiest men I know at my age, and I intend on keeping it this way. I'm able to have sex with younger women with ease, feel great, and have high amounts of energy. The time it takes in my physical life to maintain all this is irritating to say the least, and I'm still overweight, but it's still all worth it. I don't even consider it a choice. *It must be done.*

If you are an older man intending on dating younger women, especially if you're nonmonogamous like me and will be doing this in some form or fashion for the rest of your life, this healthy fitness lifestyle is also not a choice for you. It must be done.

To be clear, I'm not saying you have to be ripped like Wolverine. I'm certainly not and I probably never will be. I'm not saying you can't be overweight at all. I am a little overweight, but I'm not anywhere near "fat." I'm not saying your appearance can't have any flaws. Mine has many. I'm saying that you need to just look decent… the top 15% of men your age, which, as I said above, is easier the older you are. With my better-than-average-appearance for my age, do you really think I'm concerned at all about the competition from other American men in their forties? Ha! Not at all. (I beat out many men in their thirties.)

This book contains no specific fitness or health advice, since that's not my area of expertise. The internet and your local bookstore are full of health/fitness advice for men, far more than you will ever need. If you're fat, get it under control. If you're sickly, do what needs to be done to get healthy. If you're addicted to dangerous drugs, take care of it. If you're unusually skinny, get some muscle mass. No, none of these things are easy, but they are doable with some time and effort. I lost 40 pounds so I walk my talk here. Take the time, and get it done, even if takes you a few years and costs you some money. There are few things more worthwhile to put your time and money into than your long-term health and fitness.

Testosterone Replacement Therapy – TRT

One of the biggest areas of fitness, health, and motivation, as it applies to older men is testosterone. Testosterone is the hormone in your body that literally makes you a man. It's what deepens your voice, builds your muscles, strengthens your bones, makes you horny, gives you a sense of drive and motivation, keeps your cock hard, gives you a mental edge, keeps your body fat levels lower, and also helps regulate many other of your key bodily functions. As you can see, it's ridiculously important to an Alpha Male.

In a man, testosterone peaks at around age 18 and stays pretty high throughout your twenties. That's why you were (perhaps) more horny, healthy, strong, and had better sexual performance back then.

That's the good news. The bad news is as soon as you hit age 30, your body starts to lose a little testosterone every year. The change is very subtle and gradual, and you won't be able to detect it from year to year. However, many men suddenly realize in their forties that their cocks don't work nearly as well during sex, or their sex drive has gone way down, or worst of all, their motivation and drive for life, work, and Mission is far less than what it was before.

In my very strong opinion, this can *not* happen to you. If you wish to date younger women as an older man, particularly if you wish to do it for a prolonged period of time, and certainly if you wish to live the Alpha Male 2.0 lifestyle that I talk about in *The Unchained Man**, you must,

---

* http://www.alphamalebook.com/

must maintain a healthy level of testosterone for the rest of your life, all the way until the day you die.

There are many ways to increase your testosterone naturally, including lifting weights, having more frequent sex, eating lots of protein and fewer carbs, engaging in intense cardio exercise, getting more sleep, meditation, and various other means that are beyond the scope of this book. You can and should do most or all of these things (I do), and these things *might* be enough to keep your T levels decent if you're in your thirties or early forties. However, once you cross over into 40+, these things will all help, but they likely won't get your T levels back to where they should be, around when you were in your late teens or early twenties.

This is where *testosterone replacement therapy* comes in, or TRT. This is a system by which, under close supervision of your doctor, you replace testosterone back into your body, getting your T levels back to where they should be. It's important to understand the word *replacement* in testosterone replacement therapy. You are *replacing* the testosterone you lost years ago. You are *not* jacking up your testosterone to levels your body was never designed for; that's done using *steroids*, which is extremely dangerous and very stupid.

To demonstrate, when you were 18 years old, your level of total testosterone was at around 900-1100 ng/dl. That's a great T level, right where you should be for maximum happiness, energy, drive, and physical appearance. If you're in your forties or fifties (or beyond), your T level is probably down around 200-400 ng/dl. Way too low, at least in my opinion (and I'm not a doctor, so be aware of that).

Getting your T levels back up to around 900-1000 will make you feel so good you won't believe it. However, steroid users actually blast their T levels to 2,000 to even 5,000 and beyond. This is, of course, insane, and not what I'm talking about here and not what I'm recommending. So if you ever discuss TRT with someone and they accuse you of wanting to use "steroids," that's not what you're talking about.

I am on TRT myself, and I consider it one of the best and most important decisions I've ever made in my adult life. I was already a pretty motivated guy before the TRT, but once I got onto the TRT program,

- My drive and motivation in my business life and other areas of my life increased.
- I started to sleep better.
- I was able to gain more muscle when lifting weights.
- My sexual performance improved.
- My schedule and time management improved
- My average monthly income increased by almost 80% because of my improved activity and focus. This was more than enough to pay for the monthly cost of TRT.

I cannot recommend TRT enough if you are over the age of 35. I strongly suggest that you get a testosterone blood test to see where your levels are. You can do this either through your doctor or do it yourself online for around $80 (just Google "testosterone blood test"). If your total testosterone level is anywhere below about 700 or 800, I *strongly* suggest you at least seriously look into the TRT option. Be sure to work with a doctor who specializes in male hormone therapy and/or anti-aging. Your standard doctor may not be of much help.

Granted, TRT costs money; it will be anywhere from $100 - $500 per month depending on the options you choose. Just remember that your income will likely go up once you're on this program. Often, TRT more than pays for itself.

You can increase your testosterone via TRT through means such as injections, gels, creams, implanted pellets, or supplements. While all of these work to some degree, injections work best. This is what I do. A few times a week I inject myself with testosterone, HCG, and vitamin B, using very tiny insulin needles that are so small you can barely feel them. It takes me less than five minutes. I fully intend on doing TRT, or whatever future version of it will be invented, for the rest of my life.

If you want more information, I thoroughly documented my entire first two years on TRT at The Blackdragon Blog*, Just Google "Blackdragon

---

* http://www.blackdragonblog.com/

Blog TRT" and you'll see "My Journey with TRT" articles, where I cover literally everything I did, what I experienced, and what I did wrong.

If you follow no other advice in this book, but go on TRT, your frame, game, and sex life, both with younger women and women your age, *will* increase. Not to mention things like your overall happiness, zest for life, and income. That's how important TRT is.

However, don't take my word for it. Consult with a doctor who specializes in this area for more information, and only do this under the supervision of such a doctor. Don't do this stuff on your own.

Skin

The next area to address as an older man is the quality and look of your skin. The skin on your entire body is important, but what is most important, and the areas you need to focus on, are those parts of the body that are visible when you are fully clothed. This means:

- Your face
- The front and back of your neck
- The backs of your hands
- Your forearms, starting from the top of your elbow on down

These four areas need to look as young as humanly possible for your age. Tight, colorful, bright, smooth skin is not only attractive but demonstrates youth and vitality as well.

This doesn't mean you can't look your age. As always, I think your goal should not to look younger, but look fantastic *for your age*. Throughout most of my twenties, I had a round baby face that I really hated. Today at age 46, I have a *few* wrinkles around my eyes, and I actually like them. It makes my face look a little more masculine. I'd personally rather look like Clint Eastwood than Justin Bieber. However, even Clint in his heyday during the 1970's didn't look "old." He looked *good*. He had a few wrinkles, but he didn't have a lot, and his face still looked like a youthful, masculine, vital man.

So if you're 50+, sure, a few wrinkles to make you look more masculine are probably okay. Beyond that though, you want to have smooth, youthful-looking skin.

Maintaining good-looking skin is not difficult. It simply requires a few changes in lifestyle. The sooner in your life you make these changes, the better you'll look, and the longer they will last. I started doing most of these things when I was 35 years old; this is one of the biggest reasons why today, at age 46 my skin looks really damn good.

Start and Maintain a Daily Skin Regimen

Maintaining a daily skin regimen is mandatory if you wish to date much younger women. It requires a little daily time and some money. Some of these things may sound a little gay and not very manly, but tough shit. It's mandatory, and it's more than worth the results.

Your skin regimen should include:

- A good moisturizer. This keeps your skin hydrated, which is critical to healthy skin. There are many good ones. I personally use Clinique SPF Superdefense and CeraVe. The latter comes highly recommended by several dermatologists I've spoken to. If neither of those is available where you are, do some research and find out which are the best moisturizers; you want a good one. A good idea is to have two moisturizers; one with SPF protection and one without. (If you don't use one with SPF protection, you'll have to apply sunscreen as well, right after putting on the moisturizer.) You should apply your SPF moisturizer in the morning, right after you shave, and your non-SPF moisturizer in the evening right before bed.
- Exfoliant (scrub). This is used to exfoliate your face, removing the dead skin particles so new ones can grow to replace them. You work the exfoliant into your skin (it feels rough, and is supposed to), wait about a minute, and rinse. Do it in the shower before you shave. Then shave, then apply your moisturizer. You should only use exfoliant a maximum of twice

per week unless otherwise directed by a dermatologist who has examined your skin. Unlike your moisturizer, your exfoliant doesn't need to be fancy; anything you find at your local grocery store will probably do.

- Face wash or astringent. Ideally, you should wash your face twice a day; once in the morning and once before bed, before you apply any exfoliant or moisturizer.

- SPF protection. This is hugely important, as the sun will damage your skin probably more than anything else in your day-to-day life. Ideally, your moisturizer should have decent SPF protection built in (at least SPF 25 or 30). If it doesn't, you should apply SPF protection after you apply your moisturizer. This only needs to be done in the morning, but if you live in a particularly sunny area and/or spend a lot of daily time outside, you will need to carry some around with you and re-apply it every few hours. Also, and this is important, remember that just because it's cloudy outside doesn't mean the sun isn't damaging your skin. It is. You should have SPF protection on your face 365 days a year, period.

Tanning

If you're white/Caucasian, you must avoid skin that is too white or pale. Whenever you're in dating mode (meeting new women) you must keep a decent tan. You can get a real tan or a fake one. I personally think getting a real tan (from the sun or a tanning bed) is a very bad idea; over time the UV is going to take a toll on your skin and make it look like crap. I vastly prefer fake tans, which are fine as long as you don't look orange. Spray tans are fine if administered at a salon, though they cost more money. There are also numerous self-tanning lotions that work well.

I've tried many different methods for self- tanning, and my favorite is self -tanning towelettes. Google "L'Oréal Sublime Bronze Self-Tanning Towelettes." These are disposable wipes and they work great. When in dating mode, I take one and quickly wipe down my face, neck, arms, and sometimes chest right before I go to bed (you can do your entire body if you wish, but I never bother). The next morning I look nice and tan (at least for my pale skin). It lasts about four or five days before I have to use another towelette. Very fast and efficient.

If you have very white skin like I do, realize that getting a full-on tan may not be in the cards for you. I usually don't look "tan" so much as "much less white." Do the best you can. The less white you look, the healthier *and thinner* you look. This is why many Hawaiian men (as just one example) often look pretty good even when they're chubby; their naturally dark, perfect tan allows them to have a little more chub while still looking decent.

Other Skin Enhancement Techniques

Here are a few other things you should do to ensure your skin looks great.

- Number one, top of the list, **make sure you're drinking a lot of water**. The health benefits of drinking water are massive and numerous, but one of the most noticeable ones is your skin will look better and you'll get fewer wrinkles as you age. Moisturizers aren't going to help much if you barely drink any water throughout the day. I drink four gigantic, tankard-sized cups of water per day, every day, sometimes more. If you dislike the taste of water, drink seltzer water (the fizzy kind), or soak lemons or limes in your water. No excuses, just drink it!

- Make sure you're eating plenty of protein. One of the reasons women tend to wrinkle faster and more heavily than men is because women eat less protein. You need to make damn sure your diet consists of lots of protein, preferably full-chain protein like the kind found in whey.

- Sleep on your back, if you can. You will get fewer wrinkles over time if you sleep on your back, since sleeping on your side or stomach means you're constantly pulling at your facial skin all night long. I realize some guys can't sleep on their backs (I usually can't), but you should at least try it if you never have.

- Stop smoking and doing drugs and keep it light on the alcohol. Drugs, cigarettes, and alcohol will absolutely murder your skin as you get older. I see men in their fifties who drink or smoke a lot, and they often look 10 years older than men the same age who don't. Take a look at a recent, untouched-up picture of Jean-Claude Van Damme. He's almost the same age as Tom Cruise, yet because of his skin, he looks at least 15 years older. Drugs will do that. Alcohol and cigarettes are just as bad… sometimes even worse.

- Get any moles, sun damage, or "age spots" on your face, neck, or hands removed. Often these things can be lasered off for $500 or less.

- If you already have more wrinkles on your face than you like, start applying AHA cream and retinol daily. Visit a skin expert (someone who specializes in facials) or a dermatologist to get the exact dosages required for your skin.

Cosmetic Surgery

If you are well over the age of 50 or so, and your skin already looks bad because of past lifestyle decisions, some cosmetic surgery may be in order. Spending a few thousand dollars one time to make the skin on your face look noticeably better is a fantastic return on investment, and will make a huge difference not only with your dating results but your own self-esteem as well. Studies have shown that getting cosmetic procedures done is one of the few things that increase a person's happiness in which the increase stays forever instead of fading away like with most other happiness-creating events.

I myself got a procedure done to fix my thinning hair (that I'll talk about in the next chapter), and it was one of the best decisions I've ever made. I also fully intend on getting some cosmetic surgery done in the future as I age. Not a lot, but a little. I strongly suggest you do the same if you feel the skin on your face or neck looks particularly bad.

Teeth

The older you are, the more likely you are to have problems with your teeth... and women notice. Older guys get teeth that are more yellow or otherwise discolored. Worse, as you age your teeth tend to move around and get into odd positions. Even if your teeth were perfectly straight when you were 20 years old, now you may have weird gaps or crowding in your smile.

Whiten your teeth semi-regularly, about once every six months or so. Over-the-counter whitening strips are fine, though if you really want them whitened within a shorter period of time, purchasing a teeth whitening kit from your dentist or a website like dazzlepro.com is a better idea. If you have more money, you can even get them laser whitened, but that's somewhat expensive and often painful.

If you have crooked teeth or any weird gaps in your smile, get Invisalign. It's a procedure you can get through your dentist where you wear transparent trays on your teeth that straighten everything out. Unlike braces, no one can tell you're wearing them. I did this procedure myself a few years ago to fix a huge gap I had between my two front teeth, and now my smile is perfect. I had to wear the trays for about five months and the procedure cost about $4000. I now wear similar trays at night when I go to sleep that keep my teeth in place so I'll never have that problem again. Therefore, it was a one-time cost, and I'll never need to go back; very high return on investment.

Chapter 7

FASHION AND GROOMING

Most older men look like crap. Seriously. They dress terribly, either like nerd Microsoft employees or like they're about to go to a Super Bowl party with their buddies. They have thinning hair, graying or white hair, out-of-date hairstyles, scruffy or unruly hair in their noses, ears, necks, or chest.

You can't be one of these men. If you are, your results with younger women are going to be near zero (or literally zero). You must be perfectly groomed and well dressed, unless you are in a very long-term relationship(s) and don't need to bring any new women into your life any time soon. Your fashion must be something you wear *on purpose,* not because it's emotionally or physically comfortable or because it's something you've been wearing for 20 years. Your hair, including your head hair and body / facial hair, must be something you manage and take care of, not just "let be."

Too many older guys who are newly divorced or out of some other long-term, monogamous relationship tend to be the biggest offenders here. If that's you, or even close to you, pay very close attention to this chapter and do everything it suggests. Physical appearance is *critical* to your success with younger women (and all women, for that matter).

Baldness / Thinning Hair

Your single biggest challenge as an older man, in terms of grooming, is thinning hair. Everyone understands that men lose hair as they get older. The problem is having a big bald spot or clearly thinning hair makes you look older, heavier, less healthy, and less attractive. If you suffer from any type of baldness or thinning hair, you *must* address this problem if your goal is to date younger women. This is non-negotiable; it *must* be handled.

You have three viable options:

Option 1: Shave your entire head. This is, by far, the simplest and least expensive option. A clean-shaven head looks far better than thinning hair or a bald spot, both to men and women. Unless you have very pale skin or you're very chubby, try shaving your entire head once and force yourself to keep that look for at least a week. Just think of the thousands of dollars in haircuts and hair products you'll save over the course of your life! If you absolutely hate it, you can always go back.

If you shave your head, you must tan regularly unless you already have darker skin to begin with. Having a stark white shaved head looks pretty bad.

The downside is that there are indeed some men who don't look very good with a shaved head. Some facial structures need hair. I am one of these men; I would look terrible with no hair, but every guy is different.

For example, I have several brothers. A long time ago, one of them started shaving his head. He looked really good; he looked far better *without* hair than *with* hair. Then a few years ago, one of my other brothers also started shaving his head (because he was losing a lot of hair). Well, damn, I love my brother, but now he looks pretty bad. He looked far better with hair. He just has one of those faces that need hair.

So bottom line, some guys actually look *better* without hair, and some guys look worse. I wish I could tell you exactly which facial features to look for to determine which category you're in, but I can't. It's just something you have to see. I have a feeling you probably already know just by looking in the mirror. But like I said, you can shave your head and try it for a week, then you'll know for sure. Don't worry... the hair grows back!

If you determine that shaving your head is absolutely not an option for you, you have two other alternatives, but they are going to cost some money and effort.

Option 2: Get the nonsurgical hair restoration procedure. This is the option I chose many years ago and I've never regretted it. I wanted to shave my head, but since my skin is very pale (even with tanning) and I used to be quite chubby, and I have a round face, I knew that shaving my head wouldn't work. I really wish it did, but it doesn't, at least for me.

Nonsurgical hair restoration (NHR) is when they shave the top of your head and permanently attach a mesh that is populated with real human hair that exactly matches your own. Over time, your own hair grows through the mesh. It looks fantastic and real the instant you get it done. There is no surgery involved. It doesn't come off your head like a toupee and is always attached. You can swim with it, be in high winds, jump out of an airplane, have sex, have women pull your hair, and it still looks great. Your real hair grows into the top of the mesh, and the hair on the sides and back of your head is unaffected, since you never lose hair in those regions (unless you have an unusual health problem).

There are two downsides. First, it's somewhat expensive. Getting the procedure done will cost anywhere from $2,000 to $3,500, then thereafter you'll have to spend $200-$600 per month to have them cut your hair and regularly service the system. (This is in lieu of your usual haircuts and color, so you can deduct the cost of these things to offset these costs a little.)

The second downside is minor. It looks and feels real, but if a woman really probes your scalp with her fingertips, she'll be able to tell something is "up." I've had this system for many years now and have never had a woman complain. No woman has ever been able to tell a lot of my hair is fake, I usually just tell women I have it. (Once they're having sex with you, they don't care.) It can also be a little itchy at times, but it's not a big deal.

If you can afford it, I *highly* recommend NHR. It's really fantastic.

Option 3: Get hair restoration surgery. This is a surgical procedure where they transplant hair follicles from the back and/or sides of your head (which are genetically programmed to never go bald) to the top of your head. They usually take a strip of skin from the back of your head, then cut it up into tiny pieces, and place those pieces (follicles) to the areas on top of your head where you're thinning. The procedure takes about eight hours.

I've known several men who have done this and they're usually happy with the results. Unlike with NHR, nothing is "attached" to your head; it's all your real hair.

There are three downsides. First, it's extremely expensive. The surgery will cost you anywhere from $8,000 to $20,000, depending on how bald you are.

Second, your head looks really weird for several months while the new hair grows in. You'll have to wear a hat for a while, perhaps even for a few weeks.

Third, you may have to have the surgery again in ten years. This is because the hair that hasn't fallen out yet can and will still fall out as you age. To keep your head completely full, you'll have to plan on going in for the surgery at least twice; once now, and again about ten years from now.

I personally like NHR better, but getting the surgery, if you can afford it, is still a good option.

Other options: If all those options seem too extreme, or you can't afford them, or your hair doesn't look too bad yet, you can use Nanogen Nanofibres. This is a very fine powder, the color of your hair, that you shake out of a salt shaker-like bottle onto the top of your head. The fibers bind to your hair and your scalp and do an *okay* job of covering up your thinning scalp. The downside is that this powder can get onto pillows and blankets if you lay down and/or touch your head to anything, which can be a pain. It also doesn't look nearly as good as NHR or the surgery. If you're interested in this option, Google "Nanogen Nanofibres" or "Nanogen hair fiber."

You may be curious about topical hair or scalp treatments such as Rogaine, Nioxin, special laser combs, special shampoos, special vitamin B supplements, and various other treatments to help your thinning hair. In my experience and based on my research, none of these things work very well, and even if they do, they won't make enough of a difference to make you look good.

I think all older men who live this lifestyle should simply plan on shaving their heads, getting NHR, or getting the surgery eventually, perhaps using nanofibres as a temporary measure until one can afford a better option.

The entire point here is to not simply "put up" with thinning hair. You will look far healthier and more attractive with either a fully shaved head or a full head of hair. Do not tolerate clearly thinning hair or a bald spot.

Hair Color

The issue of whether or not to allow gray into your hair depends entirely on the age of the women you're after.

Women over the age of 33 often *like* gray hair. Many really like it, particularly if your natural hair color is somewhat dark. Some like a lot of gray, others like flecks of gray. Even if a woman over 33 isn't attracted to gray hair, having some gray hair on your head isn't going to dissuade them in any way.

VYW and many women in their twenties, on the other hand, can sometimes be turned off by, or at least slightly jarred by gray hair, particularly if they're Type Threes. You might expect Type Twos to like gray hair on a man; sometimes this is true, and sometimes it's not. There are some Type Twos who don't like it or don't react to it one way or the other, while there are other Type Twos who are attracted to it. The problem is that when you first meet a younger woman, you have no idea what category she falls into.

This means that if you're a guy who is way past your thirties and are attempting to date women over 30, keep your gray hair; it will help more than it will hurt. However, if you're a guy of any age going after women under the age of 30, you need to put the odds in your favor and not have *any* gray hair, and need to start dying your hair back to its original, natural color whenever needed.

You may already color your hair for your own personal preferences, and that's fine. I used to like a little gray on the sides of my head since I thought it looked good. One day I had it colored back to my natural hair color, just as a test to see how it looked and found that I liked that even better. I made the decision several years ago that I will keep my hair my natural color for as long as I can, well into my early seventies perhaps. I prefer how it looks and I think it makes me look younger. That can only help my attitude and my game.

Feel free to make your own decision, just make sure to calibrate that decision based on the ages of women you are going after. Having a lot of gray in your hair when you're going after women under 30, particularly VYW, is not a good idea. Your success rates will be much lower.

The easiest way to keep your hair a non-gray color is to have your stylist do it for you whenever you get your haircut. If you only get your haircut once a month or less, and/or if you like to keep your hair very short, you will likely need to re-color parts of your hair (usually the sides) with a home dying kit for men a week or two after your haircut. There are many available at your local grocery store or Amazon. You just brush in some color right before taking a shower, wait ten minutes, and then shower. It works very well.

Hair Style

There's not much to say here other than that you can't have a hairstyle that makes you look like a dork or grossly out of date. Older men can be pretty bad at this. You don't have to have hair like a Top 40 rock star, but you can't look like a dad either.

Shorter is usually better. Really long hair is okay, but you must then make sure you take the time and effort to ensure it looks *really* good; otherwise, cut it. Many guys with long hair often have long hair that looks shitty because they're lazy and just let it go. Also realize that often, long hair may limit the type of women you will get.

Get a decently cool hairstyle. Think edgy. If you have no idea what's cool, a few Google image searches or a quick scan through a current men's magazine like GQ will tell you. Pick a style you like, get a picture of it on your phone, show this to your stylist, and make it happen. It's worthwhile to go to an actual salon (as opposed to the $20 haircut place) and get a professional stylist's advice. You only need to do this once. Once you've got the style down you can always go back to the cheap place and duplicate it.

Facial Hair

I've written before that most women are more attracted to men with facial hair than men who are clean-shaven. This is true and is a universal maxim (exception: many regions in Asia). Speaking generally, your results with women will improve if you grow some facial hair if you currently have none.

However, this takes on a very different flavor when we're talking about older men dating much younger women. While facial hair is a male gender cue and attractive to females, having facial hair also makes you look older than your numerical age. This is true of both younger and older men. If you're 40, you will likely look older than 40 if you have facial hair. Without facial hair you may look 40, or 37, or 35.

Thus, my general advice to older men dating much younger women, particularly if those women are VYW, is to err on the side of caution and go clean-shaven whenever you're in dating mode meeting new women. Feel free to grow facial hair once you have some established relationships.

This is not a hard and fast rule though. Many men do indeed look good, or better, with facial hair. Other men really like having facial hair. If you really want to keep facial hair despite the minor negative of it possibly making you look older than you are, you are free to do so. The one hard rule you *do* need to follow with facial hair is that *you can't have any gray in it*. If you have any gray in your facial hair whatsoever, your odds with younger women plummet, no matter how good looking you are or how many other things you do correctly.

Therefore, if you choose to have facial hair, you must regularly dye it using a beard dye kit. Google "Just For Men Mustache & Beard" for a good one, though there are many others. You may need to do this as often as once a week. Make very sure the hair color matches the color of the hair on your head, or it's going to look very weird.

Also, as always, your facial hair must always be tight, clean, sharp, and neatly trimmed. Unruly facial hair, tangles, big curls, and hair sticking out of the side of your sideburns or goatee looks really bad. Keep your facial hair nice and tight, or just shave it off.

When I say "clean-shaven," some stubble or five o'clock shadow is acceptable if you have a trimmer, skinny, or chiseled face. If you have more of a round face (like me), you should have *no* stubble and must be 100% clean-shaven. Also, if you have stubble, it can't be gray or white! It must be black, brown, or red (if you're a redhead) and nothing else. Dye it if necessary (yes, you can dye stubble) or shave it off.

Body Odor

Be aware of your own body odor. Some guys are really bad at this, especially older guys who have been married for a long time. Being aware of your BO is difficult, because usually, you can't smell yourself. Also, radical shifts in diet or lifestyle can improve or worsen your BO without your knowledge.

For many years, I had no BO and didn't even wear deodorant. No women complained. Then, to lose weight, I shifted to a low-carb, high-fat, high-protein diet, and suddenly my armpits began to smell during activities like sex. Women suddenly started to complain about my BO for the first time in my life. So, I reluctantly had to start wearing deodorant. Just be aware of your body, and use cologne, deodorant, body wash, lemon juice, vinegar, or whatever you need to offset any odors.

Don't be afraid to ask the women you're having sex with about this. Seriously, ask them how you smell during sex. If they say you smell great, then you're probably okay, but if they say anything negative, or they refuse to answer, or they start to look uncomfortable, that means you're a stinky fucker, and you need to address it.

On the flip side, there are some men who overdo the cologne. They spray the damn stuff all over their body and all over their clothing like they're in a damn car wash. Do not do this. One or two sprays under each armpit and/or on your wrists is all most men need. Perhaps you can do one or two distant sprays on your shirt right before you go out on a date. Anything beyond that is usually too much.

Body Hair

I'm sure I don't have to tell you that once you hit age 35, you start growing hair in places that don't look very good. You need to have a regular body grooming regimen once every one to four weeks, depending on your personal preference and the amount of body hair you have. For this, you require four items above and beyond your usual face razor:

1. A personal groomer shaver/clippers. This is a tiny electric razor that is much smaller than a normal razor, used for shaving small areas like your ears. There is a wide selection on sites like Amazon. The cost less than $20 in most cases.
2. A nose hair clipper.
3. A Mangroomer. Just search this on Google or Amazon. It's a long, cordless back shaver and it's fantastic. I highly recommend it.

4. A set of clippers. These are the razors the hair stylists use. You
    can set them to various lengths and just shave right over hair
    without shaving it completely off.

Once armed with those four things, here's what you need to do
whenever you engage in your body grooming regimen:

- Shave the back of your neck. Just use your usual razor and
  shaving cream.
- Shave your nose hairs. When done, look at yourself in a hand-
  held mirror facing upward. You should not see any hair visible
  to the naked eye inside your nose. Men forget that since women
  are shorter than us, women look up at us, right into our nostrils.
  Nose hair is a turn off.
- Carefully shave the edges of your eyebrows. Comb them upward
  and then trim anything that goes above the natural upper line of
  your eyebrow with your personal groomer. Also, shave off any
  "orphan" hairs near or around your eyebrows that aren't actually
  in your eyebrows.
- Color your eyebrows if you need to. If you have normal or
  thick eyebrows, you probably don't need to worry about this
  (unless you have gray in them). If you have very light or very
  sparse eyebrows like I do, you should use a beard dye kit (that I
  mentioned above) and color them once a week right before you
  take a shower. It only takes about 3 minutes.
- Use your Mangroomer and shave your entire back (unless you
  literally have no back hair whatsoever). There are videos on
  YouTube that demonstrate how to do this. Do it in the shower
  with no water running to prevent messes.
- Shave off any hair that grows on the front or sides of your neck
  (if any), and any chest hair that pokes through your collar.
- If you have any, shave off any hair that grows on your shoulders,
  upper arms, feet, and toes. You can also shave the hair off the
  backs of your hands, but that's optional.

- Use your personal groomer and shave off any hairs in and around your ears. You want your ears, both inside and out, to be completely bald.
- Use your clippers and shave down your chest hair. Set it to a one, two, or three (depending on how much chest hair you have and your preferences) and methodically run it over the entire front of your torso. This may sound weird, but trust me, you will be amazed at how much better you look. I don't have a lot of chest hair, but when I did this myself as an experiment years ago, I was sold. Note that I said shave your chest hair *down*, not *off*. Surveys and my own anecdotal experience show that the majority of women actually like a little chest hair on men. Shaving chest hair completely off looks bad, feels weird to a woman touching it, is itchy as hell, and the effect only lasts a few days until it looks weird again. Unless you have the body of a ripped, professional bodybuilder, shave *down*, not *off*.
- Everything I just said about chest hair applies equally to pubic hair (including your balls!), armpit hair, and hair on your arms. You can use your personal groomer or your clippers, depending on the region. As always shave it down, not off (though you can shave ball hair off). I've had more than one woman tell me stories about men they've slept with who had shaved off *all* of their pubic hair. In every case, the woman considered it a turn off. Shaved *off* looks weird. Shaved *down* looks really good.

Fashion

I'm no fashion expert, thus I can't give you any specific fashion tips. I just know what's bad and avoid it. You don't have to wear amazing clothes. You just need to wear clothes *that make you look good*.

Unless you're purposely going for a hipster look, make sure your clothing adheres to modern, current styles. Older men are *really* bad at this since men tend to stick with whatever styles they wore in high school, which was a very long time ago. **Your goal should be to dress with the times for the rest of your life.** You can never look out of date with your

THE ULTIMATE YOUNGER WOMAN MANUAL

clothing ever again. Men can be really stubborn about this; I was at one point myself. Regardless, if you want to have sex with lots of hot, younger women, you don't have this luxury. Do whatever is necessary to ensure that you wear clothing that is modern and in style, at least when you know you'll be meeting or spending time with younger women.

It is perfectly acceptable to ask women for fashion advice, including and especially younger women. (Do *not* ask women *any* other advice regarding dating or relationships!) If this isn't an option for you or something you don't want to do, spend $100-$200 and work with an image consultant; they're great.

Your clothes must fit your body perfectly. Usually, this means you need to get a tailor to customize your shirts, and sometimes your pants too. Put together two or three "date outfits," which comprise a cool shirt, a cool pair of pants, a good belt, and a good pair of shoes (with shoe lifts if you're under about 5'10").

Use Google Maps and locate a local tailor. Have him/her adjust these shirts and pants so that they fit you perfectly, both when you stand *and* when you sit down. Men have a tendency to wear clothes one or two sizes too big; this looks bad and women notice.

Lastly, and this is important, find out which colors look best on you. Women's eyes and brains perceive color far better than we do. There are certain colors that look great on you and ones that make you look terrible. These colors are based on your skin tone, eye color, and hair color. You must know what these colors are so you can wear more of your "good" ones and avoid your "bad" ones.

Again, you can ask women for their opinions, but the best way to determine this is to go to that local image consultant and have them tell you which colors are best to wear and best to avoid. Even once you know this, it's usually best to always have a woman with you (preferably one under age 35 or so) whenever you go shopping for new clothing. While there, have her put different solid-color shirts up to your face and get her opinions about what colors she thinks work for you. Women also usually have really good opinions regarding which styles of shirts and coats to wear. Again, this is one of the very few times I will ever recommend you take a woman's advice about anything dating related.

Examples of How to Look

If you are naturally fashion impaired like I am, some visual images should help you understand how older men can look really good when they take care of their five key appearance areas: fitness, grooming, skin, fashion, and body language.

On first and second dates with younger women, I will often wear nice jeans that fit me well (not the baggy, wrinkly kind nor the "skinny" kind), nice, shiny business shoes, and a very nice button-down shirt (usually blue or purple, two of my allowed colors) that has been tailored to fit my body perfectly.

Sometimes I wear a suit jacket or normal but nice jacket over that, colored dark gray (but not black, since I can't wear that color). I look good, and I look my age. Most importantly, I dress in modern styles and present well, like I know how to dress and what I'm doing. These are all the images I want to convey.

A perfect example of this is this picture of Colin Ferrell, taken when he was 40.

He's wearing pretty much what I'm talking about, although with the extra added bracelet and some other bad-boy bling that wouldn't be congruent with my personality, but it's very congruent with him.

Sometimes I will even wear a full-on business suit to the first date if I have a feeling that would turn her on. This is very common with the Type Twos. Guys in suits to Type Two VYW are like girls in cheerleader outfits to us, so use this to your advantage (unless "Suit Wearing Guy" isn't congruent with your natural persona).

Let's look at an older guy, a little known actor named Thomas Pescod:

Obviously he's violating my no-gray-facial-hair rule, but if he wasn't focusing on VYW and only targeted women in their thirties, he'd be fine since his face is so chiseled that he can pull it off. His skin is also fantastic. You don't need to bare your chest like he is here... as a matter of fact, please don't, but pay attention to the quality, cut, and colors he's wearing, as well as his body language. It's tough and Alpha without being intimidating or scary. Good stuff.

Speaking of great body language, here's my favorite picture of Daniel Craig. I had to scan it from a magazine; the original picture is not even available over the internet.

Notice how he looks supremely confident *and* relaxed at the *same time*. Fantastic. He's completely age appropriate and classy while also looking cool. Also notice how well his shirt and slacks fit him; they've been tailored for an exact fit. Even if you don't have the body of Daniel Craig (few of us do), your clothes can be tailored to fit you this well.

This look is what I call "business badass." He's dressed in nice, classy business attire, but notice that his two top buttons are unbuttoned and his sleeves are rolled up. I absolutely love this look. If it works for you, copy it.

Here is another fantastic, classy-but-badass look that I've appropriated from men who know fashion much better than I do:

Again, a fantastic look for an older guy. Cool hair, cool facial hair (stubble that's colored dark), nice shirt, good jeans, and a vest with a color that looks good for his skin tone. He looks classy but isn't wearing a tie (though a tie would look fine with this outfit if you wanted to class it up a bit) and all of his clothes are just a little wrinkly… not too much, just enough to look not too pressed and anal.

By the way, this guy is Aaron Marino, and he runs a YouTube channel called Alpha M. It's all about fashion and grooming for men, and I highly recommend you watch a few of his videos. He really knows his stuff and you'll learn a lot from him. (I get no money recommending him; he's just good).

If you want a more casual style, Idris Elba is usually a good example:

He's clearly dressed casually and relaxed but he still looks good. His shirt is casual, but you can tell it's *a nice shirt*, made of nice material that fits him well. His faded jeans but amazingly polished shoes present a very nice and in-style contrast. I personally dislike brown shoes (I prefer black ones), but brown works great on him, and they may look good on you as well.

If you're over 50, I can only hope I look as young as Liam Neeson does when I'm in my fifties. Go back and watch his fantastic movie, *Taken*. People don't realize he was 56 years old when he did that film back in 2008. The way he was dressed and the way he carried himself in that movie was part of the reasons he looked so damn good for his age. Here are two pics of him taken while he was in his late fifties, one classy one and one very casual, cool look. Notice his slight but *dark* facial hair; he's following my advice about no gray.

Notice that all of the men in the above photos are taking pretty much all the advice I laid out in the last two chapters:

- They didn't get fat. They're not ripped or perfect, but they didn't let their healthful appearance go.
- They have great body language.
- They clearly all maintain a good skin regimen.
- They aren't bald; they don't even have a bald spot visible.
- They're extremely well-groomed.
- They dress in current, modern, cool styles.
- They have cool hairstyles.
- I strongly suspect that they're on some form of TRT or other testosterone program through their doctors, nutritionists, or physical fitness trainers. Most older Hollywood celebrities are.

By maximizing your physical appearance as we discussed in the last two chapters, your odds and your success ratios with younger women will go way up... you may even be surprised at the difference.

As importantly, you'll also feel better about yourself, feel more attractive, confident, and powerful. You'll also have fewer health problems and probably live longer too; always a nice bonus.

Chapter 8

OVERCOMING YOUR OWN DOUBTS

In coaching and communicating with hundreds of older men throughout the last ten years on the subject of dating much younger women, I have found that the biggest obstacle for these men in dating younger women is not their level of game skill or their appearance. Often those things are problems that need to be addressed, but the biggest problem is that *they don't believe it's possible or appropriate to date or have sex with much younger women.*

This is a mental block you can't afford to have. I've seen men robotically do many of the things this book advises, only to fail because mentally they can't fully accept the concept of dating a 25-year-old or having sex with a 19-year-old (or whatever specific goal they have).

If you have any concerns or lingering doubts about the appropriateness or morality of dating women who are much younger than you, this chapter will help lay those to rest. I'm quite serious about this; if you have doubts about this, it *will* harm your results.

Some older guys sometimes have thoughts such as:

- I shouldn't date a woman that young. It's just not right.
- No woman that young would ever be attracted to a man my age.
- Everyone will think I'm shallow if I dated a woman that young.
- How could a relationship with a woman that young ever work? We're in completely different places in life!

These are all thoughts that come directly from *false* Societal Programming, emphasis on the word false. I shall examine each one.

"I shouldn't date a woman that young. It's just not right."

This is a societal trope that is perpetuated by jaded older men who can't have sex with much younger women (but who want to), and by women over the age of 33 who are terrified about younger women being competition for them. These people install a false belief that a man dating a much younger woman is somehow doing something wrong, immoral, immature, abusive, dishonest, or unseemly.

The reality is that there is absolutely nothing wrong, immoral, or unethical about dating a much younger woman provided these three conditions are all true:

1. She is of legal age of consent where you both live.
2. The relationship is 100% consensual on her part.
3. You are always 100% honest with her, and never lie to her or lead her on.

If you're being completely honest with her, and she's willing, and she's legal, go for it! Date all the younger women you want. There is nothing wrong or immoral about it. Only when one of those three items above is *not* true do we start having serious problems, such as when she's legally underage, or you're deceiving her in some way, or if you're lording power over her somehow. Obviously those are bad, but they would be bad regardless of a woman's age.

So always check ID, always be honest, always make sure it's 100% consensual on her part, and be rewarded with a clear conscience.

"No woman that young would ever be attracted to a man my age."

Incorrect. I already covered Type Two women back in Chapter 3. While Type Twos are statistically the smallest group of VYW, there are still literally millions of younger women out there who are dying for a confident, non-creepy, much older man to sweep them off their feet. They're all over the place, and I'm living proof of this, as are many other older guys all over the world.

As I mentioned back in Chapter 3, Type Two VYW have a rough time. They sit in class all day long fantasizing about having sex with their teacher or dad's best friend, but they can't tell any of their family or their girlfriends because of the ridicule they'd receive. These gals hope beyond hope that someday they can find a (non-creepy!) much older man to fulfill the fantasies they've had all their lives.

Just under 50% of *all* the women I've had sex with since I turned 35 years old (not a small list) were under the age of 22 when I first had sex with them. I'm 46 years old now and this has not let up one bit.

Believe me, Type Two women are out there, and the population of these women is *growing*. There are more than enough for you to date (unless you live in a very tiny town).

"Everyone will think I'm shallow if I dated a woman that young."

Yes, due to today's false Societal Programming, *some* people *may* view you in a negative light if you parade around with a much younger woman. As Bill Maher once observed, if a 50-year-old public figure came out as gay, he would be applauded today. But if he came out and said he had a 20-year-old girlfriend, everyone would be horrified and he would be reviled. Older men dating much younger women is the last politically incorrect taboo left in Western society, and it's not going away any time soon.

Many women over the age of 30 are going to be particularly judgmental about it, since men in their age range dating younger gals is the greatest threat to these women, and it's frightening for them to see.

Some of the typical men your age, married to old, overweight, nonsexual wives may also be upset because of their own jealousy. (They would love to date or have sex with younger women if they could.)

My response to this is threefold.

Firstly and most importantly, who gives a shit about what other people think? I certainly don't. A key part of outcome independence is not caring at all about what other people think about you. If some angry, forty-something shrew glares at you when you walk down the street with your 22-year-old MLTR, or if the wife of your best friend gives you some shit about hooking up with 19-year-olds, why is this your problem? Is this going to negatively affect your sex life? Income? Health? Long-term goals? Of course not. Then it shouldn't matter. If people don't like it, that's their problem, not yours.

Moreover, the playing field is indeed level. Older women are more than welcome to have sex with much younger men if they want, and some of them do (cougars). If/when they do, her forty-something girlfriends will give her high-fives and talk about how independent and liberated she is. It's all hypocrisy, so seriously, don't worry about it.

Secondly, that no one said you need to get *serious* with much younger women. If you simply want a younger woman as an occasional FB, go ahead. Getting into a serious relationship with an 18-year-old isn't a great idea anyway, as I'll discuss in future chapters. Don't assume that "date" means, or should mean that you're having an ongoing serious relationship with a younger woman. You may choose to just have casual relationships with younger women, as needed. Or, you may choose to primary date women your age, but play around with younger women on the side (this is what I do today). Or, if you do want to have a serious relationship with a much younger woman, you can do that as well, provided you don't go too young (we'll discuss age parameters for relationships in the next chapter). Date younger women in whatever capacity you desire.

Lastly, if, for some reason, you really are concerned that if people found out you were dating or having sex with much younger women *and* it would somehow adversely affect your income or other long-term goals, then you are more than welcome to keep your younger-woman-dating a secret. I don't live my life like that (again, I'm outcome independent), but you certainly have that option.

"How could a relationship with a woman that young ever work? We're in completely different places in life!

First, remember what I just said about not having to get serious with younger women if you don't want to. That being said, I can tell you from vast experience (both my own and other people's) that "being in different places in life" has absolutely nothing to do with how happy a man and woman will be in a relationship, provided the man and woman are attracted to each other and have compatible personalities. Here are a few random examples from my life over the past ten years:

1. As of this writing, the longest consistent relationship I have ever had with a woman outside of my nine-year marriage was a five-year relationship with a woman who was 17 years younger than me. We started seeing each other as FBs when she was 19, later I upgraded her to high-end MLTR, and we stopped seeing each other (amicably) until she was almost 25.
2. One of the most mentally rewarding relationships I ever had was with a woman I dated for about two years, while she was 19 and then 20. She was extremely intelligent and amazingly mature for her age, and we had many long, detailed, philosophical discussions that were the equivalent level of discourse as many women in their thirties and forties I've dated.
3. I have had several MLTRs or FBs who were 20 to 23 years old, who lived in their own homes, owned their own cars, had their own full-time careers, did not have any kids, and paid most or all of all their own bills. While this is certainly not the norm for

that age range, there are many women out there like this. I have really been blown away by the quality of many younger women out there. "Younger woman" does not necessarily mean "dumb bimbo." (And yes, many younger women are indeed dumb bimbos. Great, keep those at the FB level; they're fun too. Some of the most fun FBs I've ever had were in the young, dumb, bimbo category. They were fantastic relationships and they were wonderful people.)

Moreover, I personally know many very long-term couples of extreme age differences, where the man is 15, 20, 25, or more years older than the woman, and they are both very happy.

I agree that being in a similar place in life is an advantageous thing to have in a relationship, particularly a very serious one with long-term expectations. However, it is by no means a requirement. What's required are two people with compatible personalities, similar long-term objectives, and who get along with each other without a lot of drama and conflict. Being "in a similar place in life" is not required for any of those things. Indeed, I've seen mountains of *failed* couples and marriages of people who were in the *exact* same place in life (same age range, same intelligence, same socio-economic levels, same basic outlook on life, and so on) and who were absolutely terrible in their relationships/marriages.

So stop worrying. There is nothing wrong with any of this. Go for it!

Chapter 9

RELATIONSHIP PARAMETERS

As I've talked about in my other books*, you need to have clear objectives for your woman life. Do you want to just have fun and get laid? Do you want ongoing relationships? Do you want serious or casual relationships? You must know the answers to all of these questions regardless of the ages of women you want to date in your life, but dating younger women presents a few additional wrinkles to this.

Older men generally date women in one of the following four configurations:

1. Playing around with younger women casually, via one night stands or brief, FB relationships.

---

* http://www.blackdragonsystem.com/productsservices.html

2. Sugar daddy arrangements, where the men are helping to financially support the younger women in some way. These relationships are almost always FB in nature (and in my opinion, should be), but are sometimes more serious than that.
3. Playing around with younger women "on the side." This means the man already has a primary girlfriend or wife (in an open relationship, or he's cheating), and he has one or more younger women as FBs on the side.
4. In a serious, long-term relationship, monogamous or open.

Obviously, dating younger women via one night stands or casual relationships (as FBs or low-end MLTRs) is perfectly fine, regardless of if they're "on the side" women or all the women you're dating. Sugar daddy arrangements are also fine, provided you do them correctly. We'll discuss those in great detail in Chapter 17.

If you want to date much younger women in more serious relationships, a few challenges can arise, so you have to make sure you do the correct things, as well as set expectations accordingly based on her age.

Monogamy Expectations

I don't give advice to men in monogamous relationships, or even those men who want such a thing, since I think absolute sexual monogamy is a terrible idea and fundamentally against both human biology and psychology, and is essentially unworkable for most people under the age of 60, outside of brief spurts.

That all being said, it's very important to understand that *VYW are fundamentally incapable of monogamy or sexual loyalty of any kind.* Women under the age of 23 almost always get laid outside of relationships they are in, even when they date men their age. If they're monogamous, they cheat, and if they're not monogamous, they almost constantly play the field, at least a little. This is regardless of how much they like or love you or how attracted they are to you. They have not developed the maturity to stick with one sexual partner, *and* they live in a sexually permissive society (the modern-day Western world), *and* they have numerous sexual options as presented by the internet and their social circles, *and* this is true even if their appearance is below average.

All of these things combined means that she will have sex with other men while she's having sex with you, at least eventually, regardless of what she promises or what you make her promise. Expecting monogamy from a woman under the age of 23 is just stupid, so never make that mistake. Younger men and older men who date VYW are constantly getting furious at these women when they catch them cheating. It's gotten so bad that open relationships are now getting to be very common with women under the age of 23, where they get young beta male boyfriends but clearly tell these men that they're going to play around with other hot guys or older sugar daddies.

"Normal" women of age 23 and above can be monogamous if that's what you want (or at least can be monogamous for longer periods of time), but as I said above, I can't advise you on this beyond that simple statement. I'm just making it clear that you should never expect monogamy from any woman under the age of 23.

Teenager Behaviors

I've noticed a new trend in the last 5-10 years of more older men dating younger women. This is a good trend for both parties. The bad news is that I've also noticed a trend where older men get into very serious relationships with very young women, then these men are shocked and angered when the very young women act like very young women.

If all you want are one night stands or very short-term relationships, then you don't need to worry about any of this. If you want longer-term, ongoing relationships with younger women, particularly if they're serious relationships but casual ones as well, you need to set your expectations according to the ages of these women.

After dating numerous VYW and older women in scores of ongoing relationships, as well as observing hundreds of other men do the same, here is an axiom that you can reliably depend on:

Women act like teenagers until around age 23.

Men seem to assume that just because the first digit in her age goes from a "1" to a "2" that suddenly a woman is no longer a teenager. Untrue. Men also seem to assume that because society says it's okay for a woman to consume alcohol at a certain age (usually 21), that suddenly means a woman is no longer a teenager. Again, untrue.

Some men even think that some 18 and -19-year-old women are exceptions to the rule and "don't act their age." While it's true that some of these girls are smarter and more mature than their peers (like the 19-year-old I mentioned in the last chapter), these girls are still teenagers, and will act accordingly.

I have observed absolutely *no* difference in behavior or thought processes between 22-year-old girls and 18-year-old girls. If she's under the age of 23, she's going to act like a teenager, period.

- It doesn't matter how smart she is.
- It doesn't matter how mentally strong she is.
- It doesn't matter how educated she is.
- It doesn't matter how smart her parents are.
- It doesn't matter if she has kids or not.
- It doesn't matter how tall she is or how mature she looks (many men make assumptions about those things).

Think about this: how many 20-year-old women do you know who live on their own, in their own house or apartment, don't live with family or friends, and pay 100% of their own bills without any help from government, family, exes, or child support, and maintain the same full-time job for more than 12 months?

I've literally never seen a 20-year-old girl do that. I'm sure they're statistically out there somewhere, but I've never seen it. I've never seen a

21-year-old girl do that either. Or a 22-year-old girl. But 23? Yes, I've seen a small number of 23-year-old women pull that off. Not many, but some.

When I say "act like a teenager," I mean she'll do things like:

- Drink way too much, get too drunk, and/or get drunk when it isn't appropriate.
- Get pregnant by accident. (If not by you then by someone else.)
- Get STD's.
- Do drugs to excess. (This one is less common but is still a reality, especially now with opioid and heroin addiction on the rise.)
- If monogamous, have sex with other men even if they promise monogamy to you (which you should never believe from a VYW).
- If in an open or nonmonogamous relationship, have sex with too many men, or have sex with men in inappropriate situations, often mixed with drinking, which means they may not know these men well and won't confirm these men are wearing condoms during sex.
- Dump you very fast, and leap in and out of "serious" relationships with various men very quickly. This includes marrying men, moving in with men, and/or having babies with men, very fast, often within just a few weeks of dating them.
- Get into obviously dangerous situations (and sometimes paying the price).
- Make very stupid financial decisions with long-term, negative ramifications for her life.
- Get into various kinds of serious trouble, like getting into car accidents, getting kicked out of their homes, etc.
- Throw extreme drama at you for the dumbest, lightest reasons.
- Have horribly disorganized schedules. That means a lot of flakes, cancels, and reschedules, sometimes with either zero notice or very short notice.
- Lie, a *lot*.

- Get into all kinds of extreme drama and arguments with other girls, both in real life and over social media. In some cases this stuff gets physical.

I'm not saying all VYW do all of these things. I've had many relationships with VYW over the years and most of them have been very enjoyable. Yet, most of these women engaged in many of the above actions, often as a pattern of behavior. You need to be prepared for these kinds of things so that you're not surprised or insulted when they happen. They're just teenagers; it's what teenagers do. I'm sure you did a lot of stupid shit when you were a teenager (I know I did), so just remember that.

The good news, as I've said, is once a woman climbs into and over age 23, a lot of the teenage behaviors start falling away from her regular behavioral pattern, and usually (though not always) most or all of this stuff is gone, or greatly alleviated, by the time she turns 25. I've personally seen women go through this kind of growth and sometimes the transformation from stupid teenager to normal adult is quite amazing. (Women at age 25+ are still women though, so all the usual woman issues and problems remain; I'm just saying they aren't *teenage* women anymore.)

Minimum Ages for Serious Relationships

This brings up the topic of the best minimum age for a relationship you consider serious. Dating a 19-year-old is one thing, but is it a good idea to get serious with her?

Obviously, dating VYW as FBs or MLTRs is perfectly fine (provided you remember that she's a teenager of course). I've done it many times and never had a problem. However, when you want a woman under the age of 23 as something more serious, such as an OLTR, monogamous girlfriend, or heaven forbid, an actual wife, the scenario gets much more complicated.

Where exactly is the cut-off age for women who are acceptable for a long-term, serious, in-love relationship? I don't think there's a definitive, objective answer. I don't think anyone can point at a specific age and say

"Any woman over age X will be okay, any of them under that age is a bad idea." Regardless of what age you choose, it's going to be arbitrary.

Regardless, I can give you *my* answer. It's certainly a subjective answer, but it's from a guy with a massive amount of dating and relationship experience who has dated (in long relationships, both casual and serious) women of all ages, from 18 to 50+. I've had to give this a lot of thought, because twice in my life I found myself in "serious" relationships (nonmonogamous ones of course) with women who were much younger.

It's not an issue of how "serious" things are. Rather, it's whether or not you have expectations of the relationship lasting a long time. For example, years ago I bashed celebrity actor Doug Hutchison for getting legally and monogamously married to a 16-year-old. Unlike everyone else who was horrified due to false, anti-sex Societal Programming, I had no problem whatsoever with the age difference. If she's legal, cute, and consensual (she was all three at the time), then go for it if that's what you want. The problem I had was with the fact that he actually expected a relationship to last a long time with a damn 16-year-old girl.

They were legally separated in less than two years (of course!). Since then, they've been back and forth with mountains of drama and chaos. Again, of course, a teenage girl is not someone who's going to stick around in your life in any stable way.

Bottom line, it's a terrible idea to get into a serious relationship with long-term expectations with a VYW under the age of 23. I don't care how smart she is, or how much she "gets you," or how good the sex is. Date her, have her in an MLTR if you like her, but don't expect her to be around longer than a year or two. The odds are minuscule she'll stick around very long, *even if you marry her and have kids with her.* Guys who do that are just asking for a divorce.

What about age 23 then? This is a gray area. I still wouldn't get into a serious relationship with long-term expectations with a 23-year-old unless she was an amazing exception to the rule. True, 23 is when women start to get their shit together, but that doesn't mean I can trust her to stick around consistently for five or ten years just because she's no longer a teenager.

How about age 24? Still a gray area, but I'd be much more confident about 24 than I would 23.

How about 25? Yes.

So there you go. It takes all the way until age 25 for me to give a solid "yes" to the question of eligibility for a serious relationship with long-term expectations. Provided she's passed all the other requirements for an OTLR or similar serious relationship (you've been dating her for at least six months, preferably a year, and you've had zero or near zero drama or jealousy), then I think an older guy getting into a serious, long-term relationship with a 25-year-old or older is perfectly fine. Go for it. Below 25, beware.

Minimum Age vs. Ideal Age

If 25 is the *minimum* age for something long-term and serious, what would be the *ideal* age for this? If 25 is the minimum, the ideal age would obviously have to be older than 25. In other words, if you were actually out screening (something I never do and a concept I'm opposed to, as I describe in *The Unchained Man*) for the ideal, long-term girlfriend or wife, you would probably not go after a bunch of 25-year-olds.

The problem on the other end of the scale is that dreaded Age of Doom, age 33, where a woman's ASD spikes into the stratosphere. If you're a much older guy, or you prefer women in their thirties or forties, then you'll probably have no major problem with that. Other men are going to have a hard time dating these women because getting to sex with them the first time to start that relationship usually involves more work, time, financial expense, and compromise than you may be willing to put up with. Every man is different about this though, so you may fall into either category. (There are also exceptions to this rule as well; my OTLR wife is in her late thirties.)

Therefore, unless you prefer (or don't mind) the ASD of women over age 33, that means we're dealing with an ideal range of 25-32.

That's as close as I can get to giving you a solid number for the "ideal" age. For most high sex drive Alphas, it's indeed somewhere between 25 and 32. I've always had the number 27 rolling around in my head as "ideal" for a long-term serious relationship, but that's completely arbitrary. A 25-year-old would also be fine, perhaps even a 24-year-old. Going the other direction, a sexually liberated, low-ASD, over-33 woman would be perfectly fine with me as well.

If She's Really Young, She's Not Done Changing

There's yet another aspect to long-term relationships that men often forget. That is that *a VYW is not yet the woman she will eventually be.* Young people, men and women both, go through a lot of changes in their early twenties. This is a biological fact. People think puberty ends at around age 14, but that's not true at all. Puberty doesn't actually end until the brain is fully formed and the body stops producing human growth hormone, and that's age 25. For example, if you think back to when you were young, you'll remember that you probably didn't really start to grow hair on your chest until you were older than age 18.

The same concept applies to women. Moreover, this change is not just physical, but psychological as well. This means that what she wants at age 21 or 23 may *radically* change when she hits age 25. I have personally seen this happen with women many times. The type of relationship that may excite her and fill her with happiness at age 22 might not be the kind of relationship she wants at all at age 24. This also includes issues such as what she wants to do for a living, where she wants to live, whether or not she wants children (or when she wants them), and other significant lifestyle choices.

As I talk about in *The Unchained Man*, women are dynamic, in that they are always changing their minds about major issues and desires. It's

---

* http://www.alphamalebook.com/

part of being a female. However, when dealing with a woman in her early twenties, this fickleness magnifies about 10X until she settles into full adulthood at around age 25.

This is yet another reason why establishing any kind of relationship with long-term, consistent expectations (even if it's casual and she likes it that way!) with a woman under the age of about 25 is usually not a good idea.

Side note: None of this applies to the roster concept I describe in my *Ultimate Open Relationships Manual**. Under that model, young women will leave you, and come back, and leave you again, and come back, over and over again, for a long time. They just won't stay with you *consistently*, so don't expect them to.

---

* http://www.haveopenrelationships.com/

Chapter 10

HOW AND WHERE TO MEET YOUNGER WOMEN

Meeting younger women presents several challenges for an older man.

The first one is that older men tend to have busy, full lives. You likely have a strong work life, possibly have children, possibly travel regularly, have to devote regular time to your physical fitness, and so on. Younger men tend to have more time on their hands to meet women; this is often not the case with us older guys.

The next problem is that you are not very likely to meet a lot of younger women in your day-to-day life. Even if you do meet lots of women through your social circle or work, it's more than likely these are women within your own age range and/or women who are already married. Unlike younger men, who are often around single younger women to begin with, an older man must actively seek out younger women.

The final problem is that we older men need a mechanism to meet younger women that is both legally safe for us and comfortable for the women we meet. You don't want to be a creeper; I'm sure the last thing you want is to be ejected from a store or a mall by security guards for hitting on younger girls.

Whenever we talk about meeting women (of any age), we have to talk about game styles. As I've talked about in my other books*, every method of meeting women within a dating context occurs within one of four different game style categories:

- Night Game: meeting women at bars, dance clubs, and similar.
- Daygame: meeting women during the day at "normal" locations like malls, grocery stores, and so on.
- Online Dating: meeting women using online dating sites and/or apps.
- Social Circle Game: meeting women through social activities or mutual friends.

A fifth possible category is speed dating, where you're a part of a group of men who meet women under an organized, structured, group meeting environment. Sugar daddy game is another game style, but I consider that a subset of online dating, since that's where older men meet younger women under that system (which we will cover in Chapter 16).

Each of these game styles takes on unique properties when you're an older man seeking much younger women. Over the next several chapters, I'm going to cover these differences and how you'll have to modify your approach for each of these game styles for maximum odds of success with younger women.

This book can not, and will not, give you detailed, step-by-step instructions on how to execute each of these game styles if you're a complete beginner. That's what my other books are for. As I talked about back in Chapter 1, the next few chapters "stack" with the proven systems and techniques outlined in my other books. If you are a beginner at

---

* http://www.blackdragonsystem.com/productsservices.html

dating, or are very out of practice, I strongly suggest you get one of these books that most closely reflect the game style that interests you the most.

Online dating is covered in *The Ultimate Online Dating Manual*[1], which explains exactly how to get dates via online dating sites and apps. *Get To Sex Fast*[2] covers exactly how to get to sex as fast as possible once you have a first or second date scheduled with a woman you met via online dating, daygame, and in some cases, night game and social circle game.

Your mission is to choose one style of game from the four types and focus on that style until you get good at meeting younger women using that style. A common mistake guys make is focusing on many (or all!) of the four game styles at once. *I do not recommend this.* The fastest way to mastery is focus, not a scattershot approach. I became a full-blown expert and guru at online dating specifically because I concentrated on it like a laser for about two years straight before I started to dabble in daygame and social circle game. I strongly recommend you do the same; pick one style and get really good at it before you start looking at other styles.

I will describe specific techniques for these game styles in the next few chapters, but here's an overview regarding the viability of each game style specifically for older men desiring younger women.

Daygame

I have done daygame and I've made it work. I have met and had sex with VYW using daygame, primarily through meeting younger women at malls. I know of other older men who have successfully done the same, so daygame is a viable way to meet younger women, particularly VYW.

The biggest upside to daygame is that you see exactly what you're getting, unlike with online dating where you can only see a picture of her face and maybe upper body. Often with online dating, you've got your

---

[1] http://www.onlinedatingsuccessnow.com/
[2] http://www.gettosexfast.com/

fingers crossed as you drive out to that first date, hoping that her body and face are as physically attractive as you assume they are. Sometimes this isn't the case. Not so with daygame though, since you're right in front of her and can see her in all her glory.

The downside with daygame is that it's quite grueling. Online dating is easy, in that you can do it at home in your pajamas whenever you want. Social circle game is also somewhat enjoyable because you're usually having fun while doing it. But daygame is *work*. Finding the women you like, opening women (which is hard, even if you're a confident guy), having the conversations, getting the phone numbers, following up, getting repeatedly blown off... daygame is a grind. Regardless, it works if you put in the work. Some of the best-looking women I've ever had sex with I found via daygame.

I recommend daygame for older men who are under the age of about 50 and don't like online dating. Men over 50 can do daygame as well, but the difficulty bar is raised because of your appearance and because you'll have to open older women (many over 30) who have higher ASD, but it can still be done.

We'll discuss daygame in detail in chapters 12 and 13.

Night Game

I have no experience with night game and thus cannot give any advice regarding it, other than what to do the next day once you have a woman's contact information and want to continue the interaction (which is covered in *Get To Sex Fast**).

That being said, I do not recommend night game for older men, and here are the reasons.

1. Successful night game, where you are actually getting laid, usually requires you to stay out late into the evening, many

---

* http://www.gettosexfast.com/

nights a week. Most guys who get laid via night game are having sex at 2am or later. That's fine, but as an older guy, you probably have responsibilities the next morning, like a job and/or children. It's likely that staying out until 2am several weeknights a week is probably not conducive for your lifestyle. It certainly isn't for mine. It's for this reason that night game is mostly for the realm of men in their twenties.

2. You may look too old for hanging out in a dance club while picking up chicks, even if you've followed the advice in prior chapters and look really good for your age. Once you hit age 35 or 40, you're going to start to look a little out of place in clubs and parties populated by people mostly in their twenties. Am I generalizing? Sure. Are there lots of exceptions to this rule? You bet. Some older men look really good, are really extroverted, love the club scene, and can actually have sex with younger women even when they're well into their forties. Some cities are more conducive to this than others, but it can certainly happen. It's also possible you're a musician, minor celebrity, movie producer, or other "personality" where you can get away with this.

    These are all the exceptions to the rule though. If you're well over the age of 35 or 40 and are the typical guy like I was, I would forget night game and focus on daygame, online dating, or social circle game instead.

3. Most older guys tend to dislike dance clubs and loud bars. Personally, I hate the loud music, the inability to carry on conversations without screaming, the horde of sweaty bodies pressed up against me (who are often men), drunk people screaming at me (happily or angrily makes no difference) and the drunken morons stepping on my feet or jabbing me with their elbows. When I was younger, this stuff was fine. Today, it's just irritating.

Since I'm always dating younger women, sometimes they drag me to the clubs. I will go just to be a nice guy, but you'll never see me going to clubs or bars with the objective of meeting and having sex with brand new women.

If you're a more extroverted, fun guy, night game option that may work better for you is quiet lounges rather than dance clubs or loud bars. They are much quieter and have a more relaxed atmosphere. They are much less common and harder to find than typical bars/clubs, but if you can find a few where younger women frequent, those are an option if you really want to give night game a try.

I have no chapters in this book regarding night game, so if that's something you wish to try despite my warnings, by all means, don't let me stop you. You'll just have to find another night game resource with which to combine the other techniques in this book. I have no night game experience so I can't help you there.

Online Dating

If you didn't already know, I'm one of the foremost experts on online dating and this is the primary method I've used to meet and have sex with women over the last eleven years, much younger women included. For older men seeking younger women, online dating is one of the best methods to use. Because of the age difference, your response rates to your online openers will always be very low, but the few women who respond to you will be Type Twos, and will be very excited to meet you and very excited to have sex with you quickly (provided you do everything correctly, of course). The general rule with online dating and the older man is that younger women are harder to get out on a date, but once you get them on that date, getting to sex is *very* fast and *very* easy. Older women (including women your age) are the exact opposite; it's very easy to schedule first dates with these women, but getting them to have sex with you *quickly* is extraordinarily difficult.

Online dating is also good because it's the most time management friendly game style by far. You can do it whenever you want, any time of day you want, from your own home or on your phone, anywhere you are. Yes, you have to go out on real-life dates, but you schedule those to match your schedule, when you want. Very nice for older men, who tend to be busier and have fuller lives than younger men.

The downside of online dating is that, as I already mentioned above, you never know fully what you're getting until you actually go out on that first date and see her in real life. Older men tend to be pickier, so they are more likely to complain that the women they meet via online dating aren't exactly what they advertise.

Another downside is that online dating tends to be more difficult and tedious for more extroverted men or men who aren't naturally organized.

We will cover online dating for older men in Chapter 11. We will also cover sugar daddy game, a subset of online dating, in Chapters 16 and 17.

Social Circle Game

Social circle game is meeting and having sex with women you already know or have recently met via other people you already know. Just like the other game styles, there are many subsets of social circle game, including college game (which probably won't apply to use as an older man), work game (which I do *not* recommend) and referral game (which is fantastic, and which we will discuss in detail in Chapter 15).

The advantage of social circle game is that there is no cold approach at all. There's never any need to go up to a complete stranger; everyone is already friends, at least to some degree. It's much more natural than any other game style. If you already have a large social circle or are a very social person, social circle game can be near effortless.

The disadvantage is the women in your social circle already know you, the good and the bad, or at least they will be close friends with women who already know all of your dirty laundry. This is a serious drawback, especially if you've had any bad experiences or drama with other people in your social circle.

The dreaded friend zone is also extremely common with guys who run social circle game, and in my strong opinion, friend zone is *extremely* harmful to your frame, game, outcome independence, and self-esteem.

Another disadvantage of social circle game is that, unlike the other game styles, it's very hard to systematize. It's great when you have a bunch of cute girls in your social circle, but once you've hit them all up, now what? Where are you going to meet new women? You're going to have to add them to your social circle. Do you know how to do that in a way where you have a constant inflow of new women? Some men do, most men do not.

My general advice for guys interested in social circle game is to treat it in two stages.

Stage one would be the "bleed it dry stage." This is when you make a list of all the attractive women you know in your social circle(s), and then use your skills to try to have sex with as many as you can. I did this myself right after my divorce many years back. I made a short list of every attractive woman I knew, and went to work on them. These were not younger women; most were in my age group, but I was able to have sex with most of them.

The second stage is the "forced growth stage," where you've exhausted all the women in your circle and must consciously increase your circle to include more women. I can't advise you on how to do this, since I've never done it, but I know of many extroverted men who do this via hobbies and activities they're interested in, including using websites like Meetup.com to constantly meet new people.

There is one very effective way to get laid with VYW using a certain type of social circle game, and that's referral game, where you start a relationship with a VYW, then proceed, with her help, to have sex with her cute friends and family members. It can only be done with low-ASD women under the age of 23, but it works very well. It's so powerful I've devoted an entire chapter to it (Chapter 15).

What I Did

If you're curious about what path I chose in terms of game styles, when I first started out, I followed my own advice and chose online dating. Outside of that initial social circle list I made that I mentioned above, I focused 100% on online dating and did nothing else. My goal was to get very good at it, and after about two years, I hit that goal.

At that point, I started branching out into daygame and social circle game, specifically referral game. I dabbled in daygame for just under a year, focusing on VYW and malls. It was hard work, but I was moderately successful, and I had sex with several attractive VYW. Eventually, I found that online dating was less work with equivalent results, at least for me, so I stopped doing daygame as a systematic, regular way to meet women, focusing again on online dating. Since then, I've used my daygame skills (and I don't consider myself a daygame expert) only "on the fly" when I'm out for other reasons and run into an attractive woman.

Referral game worked out much better, so much so that I was shocked at how easy it was. Some of the fastest meet-to-sex events I've ever had in my entire life, as well as some of the hottest women I've been with, have been via referral game. Via referral game, many times I'd be having sex with a new woman *in less than an hour of meeting her*, and with zero money spent.

I kept with online dating through the years, though several years later, as I got older, busier, and made more money, I started experimenting with sugar daddy game, and made that work as well. Today, my game is online dating and sugar daddy game, with occasional referral game thrown in.

Again, choose one style you find most appealing for you, and get to work on it with the younger women until you achieve regular results, then feel free to branch out to others if you wish.

Chapter 11

ONLINE DATING WITH YOUNGER WOMEN

Consider this chapter as an official add-on to my online dating book, *The Ultimate Online Dating Manual**. If you have chosen online dating as your primary mechanism to meet new younger women, and you have not gotten a copy of this book yet, I strongly suggest you do, since the vast majority of the techniques in that manual apply to women of all ages, including the younger ones. Many of the techniques in this chapter will also make more sense if you've already read that book.

This chapter covers specific changes and adjustments that an older man must make if he's targeting much younger women online. You can't simply leap into online dating doing all the normal stuff men who are dating women within their own age range do; some changes and tweaks are required for maximum odds of success. And the older you are, the more this is needed.

---

* http://www.onlinedatingsuccessnow.com/

Online Dating vs. Sugar Daddy Game

Before I get started, I need to make a distinction here between normal online dating and sugar daddy game, which is also done using online dating sites ("sugar daddy dating sites"). There are a lot of similarities between these two types of game, but also some very strong differences.

For the purposes of this book, online dating means you meet up with younger women using normal online dating sites and apps (like OKCupid or Bumble) and attempt to have sex with those women as quickly as possible and for the least amount of money spent. Sugar daddy game is where you meet younger women from sugar daddy dating sites (like Seeking Arrangement) and either attempt to have sex with them with no money spent but with the *implication* that you are, or flat out just paying them for sex after negotiating the monetary aspect as low as you can without pissing them off.

I am proficient with all three of these styles and I will be addressing all of them in this book in separate chapters. Just realize there is a clear difference between online dating and sugar daddy game. As always, you should choose one, stick with it, and get good at it before trying the other one. As an older guy, you probably have the financial resources to make any of these types of game work. In Chapter 21, I discuss the decision-making process of how much money to spend on a woman.

The remainder of this chapter covers normal online dating, as defined above. Sugar daddy game is covered in subsequent chapters.

More Numbers Are Required

Right off the bat, the first thing you must understand and emotionally accept is that as soon as you venture past age 30, your online response rates with women under the age of 23 drop like a stone. They don't drop to zero, but they still drop, and drop hard. These response rates continue to drop every decade, whenever the first digit in your age changes. This is true even if you're very good looking and do everything correctly. If you're a good looking 42-year-old and do everything right, you'll be able to scoop up dates online with women in their thirties with no problem at all, getting response rates of 20% or higher. But, as soon as you start messaging 19-year-old's, that 22% response rate will instantly drop to 3% or even 1%.

This is normal, natural, and nothing to worry about. You need to relax and be cool about this, and I'll explain why in a minute. A lot of older men get extremely discouraged with online dating when they see their response rates drop to a tiny fraction of what they were accustomed to or expecting. Don't let this shock or depress you.

I personally get response rates this low with VYW all the time, but I still get first dates and still get laid with literally every online dating blitz I do. This is because, as we've talked about in prior chapters, despite the fact it's harder to get VYW out on first dates, it's *easier* to get from that first date to sex.

Using that hypothetical decent looking 42-year-old man again, he could easily schedule ten first dates with women in their thirties or forties with no problem, but actually getting to sex very quickly and cheaply with these women (as in within one or two dates with $25 or less spent total) is going to be damn near impossible and a huge uphill battle.

However, if he gets just **one** or *two* first dates with a VYW, he'll probably get to sex with her blindingly fast, on the first or second date, with little to no money spent. As a matter of fact, most older guys are shocked at how sexually easy VYW are (I certainly was when I started dating women this young). It's night and day.

This is why you don't need high response rates in order to be successful with younger women online. Yes, getting those first dates is going to be harder, require more numbers, and more of your time. But once you're on that first date, your odds of getting to sex quickly and cheaply are ridiculously high (assuming you do everything correctly, of course).

This is because of the dynamics I described back in Chapter 3. Most VYW are not Type Twos, but if you actually get a Type Two out on a first date with you, she's demonstrated that not only is she a Type Two, but she's probably attracted to you already on some level. Because of her near absence of ASD, the only thing preventing you from getting to sex fast is you doing something stupid.

Because of all this, you need to send double or triple the amount of online openers you normally would for women your own age. This still means you need to follow the 24/24 Rule that I talked about in *The Ultimate Online Dating Manual**, which means you send a maximum of 24 openers per 24 hours per dating site. If you're using a swipe app, you'll need to swipe right on more women than you normally would. Just plan for this extra workload in advance.

Dating Sites / Apps to Use (and Avoid)

Here is a list of popular dating sites and apps that most people use, and whether or not they're good for older men dating much younger women. (Obviously, every country is different, so if you're well outside of the Western World you'll have to do your own research.)

Match.com: *Waste of time - Don't use it.* Match.com is mostly for provider hunters and divorced women over 30 looking for their second husband. Match is fine for dating within your own age range, but if you're an older guy looking for younger women, Match is a complete waste of your time. In ten years of online dating, I have never gotten a date with any women on Match.com under the age of 26. Other men have reported similar results.

A possible exception to this rule is if you are well over age 50 and are looking for a serious relationship with a girlfriend who is much younger than you but over 30. Match will work for that kind of scenario, but not for VYW.

Bumble: *Usable.* Nothing special here; Bumble will work but you'll have to swipe a lot of women.

Plenty of Fish: *Useable, but there are problems.* POF can work for finding much younger women, but they have age controls where they prevent your messages from getting to any women younger than 10-14

---

* http://www.onlinedatingsuccessnow.com/

years than you, regardless of your settings or theirs. This means that you can set up a profile, make your age 25, and just say in the profile that you're "obviously older." This will damage response rates, but it will work (I've done it successfully many times and so have other older men).

Tinder: *Waste of time – Don't use it.* Don't use Tinder. The attention-whoring culture of Tinder makes it near impossible for a guy over 40 to consistently hook up with younger women on Tinder. Don't bother with it at all; leave Tinder to the younger guys.

OKCupid: *Usable, with a few tweaks.* OKCupid is probably the best overall place for normal online dating for older guys and younger women. However, you need to pay their optional monthly fee, which opens up all the prettier girls. Also, OKCupid has implemented age controls lately, though they're not as stringent as with Plenty of Fish (yet!), and they don't seem to be enacted for all regions. If you get any errors or warnings that your messages aren't going through because OKCupid thinks you're too old for the women you're messaging (sigh), then cancel your account, delete your profile, re-create a new profile with a different email address, make your age 25, and use the technique I mentioned above for Plenty of Fish.

Zoosk: *Usable.* Zoosk is highly location-specific. In some places it works fine and in other places it's worthless. I suggest attempting it and giving it a shot, and if after some good effort you get no dates from it, forget it.

Badoo: *Usable.* Like Zoosk, it works better in some cities/countries than others. Give it a shot if there are a lot of users in your region; lots of younger women on there.

Christian Mingle and J-Date: *Usable, with some problems.* Strangely, these religious-specific sites can work just fine for older men seeking younger women. Many young women from more religious families are going to be more comfortable with dating a much older man. The problem is that these same women tend to be young provider hunters; they'll want a serious relationship with you, if not full-on marriage and kids. But if you're willing to navigate all that, these dating sites can work.

Hinge: *Possibly usable.* Similar to Tinder, Hinge works off your Facebook friends list. If you have a huge friends list on your Facebook profile that includes a lot of younger people, then go for it. Otherwise you should probably pass.

eHarmony: *Waste of time – Don't use it.* This site is for old provider hunters only. Stay away.

Coffee Meets Bagel: *Waste of time – Don't use it.* Since the app matches you instead of you being able to search women, it's useless for us older men going after much younger women.

Ignore Overtly Negative Responses from the Type Ones

As we talked about back in Chapter 3, many of the women you message will be Type Ones. These lovely ladies are going to be disgusted and upset at even receiving your opener. You are definitely going to receive some negative responses from some of these girls. "Dude what the fuck are you thinking I'm 19!?!" and similar. Again, this is perfectly normal and nothing to get discouraged about. Plan on getting these kinds of messages in advance so you won't be freaked out when it happens. These women are Type Ones, so they don't matter anyway. Just ignore them and move on. Delete her message, don't give it another thought, and keep on sending out openers. As they say in sales training, every "no" you receive means you're closer to a "yes."

This brings up the topic of possibly getting flagged or banned from dating sites for messaging younger women. In ten years of regular and intense online dating, I have literally never been flagged or banned from any dating site, ever. This is because I follow the rules I laid out in *The Ultimate Online Dating Manual**, in that I am not sexual at all in my profile nor my openers. I have found that men who get flagged/ banned from dating sites tend to be guys who either get sexual in their conversations way too fast, or who argue with or troll women on these

---

* http://www.onlinedatingsuccessnow.com/

sites. Don't be sexual and don't be a jerk, and you'll never get banned. Use normal, friendly openers (as I talk about in Chapter Nine in *The Ultimate Online Dating Manual**), and if a woman is a bitch to you, don't respond. Just move on. Trying to convince her or turn her around will be a waste of your time.

More Time Before Date Pitch

Under my usual online dating system, I stress that you need to pitch the date as fast as you can, much faster than most men. Using a dating site like OKCupid, this means pitching on the date after two or three exchanges. Using a dating app like Tinder, this means pitching the date after about ten minutes of back-and-forth text banter at the most. This is because going into conversation-mode with a woman online just raises the odds of you not actually meeting her in real life.

However, as you might imagine, being a much older man talking to VYW online requires a little more care than with women in your own age group. The fast date pitch approach often does not work with VYW and older men, particularly with Type Threes (but even many Type Twos as well).

If there is more than ten years age difference between you and her, and she knows this or strongly suspects this, particularly if she's a VYW, I suggest a light conversation of about 15 minutes of back-and-forth texting or other instant messaging (via the dating site or some other messaging/texting app is fine) before actually pitching the date.

This is not always needed, but it usually is. Meeting a much older man online is threatening and scary, even for many Type Twos, so usually she'll need a little more comfort building before you actually pitch meeting her in real life.

Obviously, if she suggests meeting up before 15 minutes, don't keep talking; schedule a meet right then and there!

---

* http://www.onlinedatingsuccessnow.com/

Low-Pressure First Date Pitch and Venue

Do not use the word "date" when pitching or scheduling the first meet-up with a VYW online. At this point, you're probably not sure if she's a Type Two or Type Three, and you don't want to push the envelope. Even if she's a Type Two, you may be the first older man she's ever met in a dating context in her life, or online.

As I talk about in *The Ultimate Online Dating Manual**, normally you want to meet up at a cool bar for just 60 minutes, perhaps buy her a drink and yourself one, then get the hell out of there and schedule the second date where sex is going to occur.

With VYW, your first date… let's call it first "meet," needs to be even more casual and low-pressure than that. Moreover, it's possible she'll be under the legal drinking age, which precludes the possibility of meeting at a bar.

Therefore, you need to frame it as not a "date" but just "hanging out" and "having fun." Low-pressure, low-risk, and no big deal. Meeting up with a stranger over the internet for the first time is scary enough. Meeting up with an older guy is even scarier. You need to make this as easy and as safe for her as possible.

Here's an example of a very low-pressure date pitch that I've used successfully with many VYW:

> *"You seem fun. We should meet up. Something simple like at the food court at the mall. Just for like 30 minutes. If anything, you could end up being a cool friend."*

With this date pitch, I'm accomplishing several things that all work in my favor:

1. I put the word *fun* in there; that's on purpose. Remember, VYW are all about fun. It's their favorite word.

---

* http://www.onlinedatingsuccessnow.com/

2. I pitched a place that she probably already knows very well, the food court at her local mall. Far less threatening than a bar, or even a coffee shop, which these days has a very "first date" vibe to it.

3. I'm saying that we'll just talk for 30 minutes. Very non-threatening. It also shows outcome independence, which is not only attractive but very unlike all the other men on the dating site slobbering all over her. If she comes back and says something like, "Only 30 minutes?" then of course responds with something like "Haha. Of course we can hang out for longer if you want." (Obviously, this kind of reaction from her is a very good sign.)

4. I'm doing a little takeaway at the end by suggesting that I might put her into friend zone if I don't find her attractive enough. This shows that I'm not desperate for her, have massive outcome independence, and I'm not looking to have sex with her immediately. This helps both attraction and comfort.

The majority of first meet locations with VYW that I've had that resulted in fast sex were mall food courts, classy delis, bookstore coffee shops, and normal coffee shops. If weather permits, outdoor parks also work very well.

Malls are a good place to meet up with a VYW. Malls are fun and familiar places for younger girls. You never have to twist a 19-year-old girl's arm to go to a damn mall. One possible problem with malls is that she may get uncomfortable if it's a mall where a lot of her friends hang out. She might not want her cohorts seeing her with an older guy. Therefore, be sure to make it very clear that you are flexible and that if she doesn't want to meet at a mall, you're happy to meet at a deli or coffee shop.

The best place in the mall for a meet is the food court. The second best would be at a bookstore coffee shop within the mall. In either case you can even get up and walk around with her a bit once you're done talking.

Another extremely effective place for a first online VYW meet is a classy deli. Not a standard deli, but a nice one. I define "deli" as a restaurant that is not bussed by wait staff; i.e. you can just walk in and sit down at a table and no one will bother you. If you want food, you go up and get it yourself. (Panera Bread is an American example.) Check around your local area for some nice delis. Sometimes upscale stores like Nordstrom's have small, quiet, classy delis inside and these work *very* well.

The third best option would be your standard coffee shop like Starbucks. Consider this your fallback option if a mall or classy deli is unavailable to you. There's nothing wrong with coffee shops per se, but they don't make you look as fun, classy, or relaxed as a mall or classy deli. Also, they tend to put more pressure on her since a coffee shop isn't quite as "fun" as a mall. People are also getting to the point where they know that the coffee shop is the default place for meeting on online first dates. We want to avoid this stigma if at all possible.

Another good option for first meets, if you can make it work, is outdoor parks. I have had several first meets with VYW at parks that have resulted in sex. It sounds crazy, but trust me, it works. Of course, there are some logistics involved with parks. The weather needs to be nice, they can't close too early if you're there in the evening; you don't want them too crowded, and so on. Regardless, they're certainly an option.

Should you meet at a bar if she's of legal drinking age? You can, but I usually do this with drinking-age VYW. Bars are fine if she's 23 or older, but if she's under the age of 23 I always try to get one of the above locations to work. If she clearly indicates that she *wants* to go to a bar, then by all means do so.

Odd Hours

Unlike older women, many younger women work or go to school at odd hours and are often only available to meet at late hours or in the morning. I've had many first dates with VYW that were at 10pm, 11pm, sometimes even midnight, as well as 10am. Be open to this, because many women will want to meet you at those hours. It will not be the norm, but younger women, VYW in particular, will sometimes ask to meet up with you at odd times.

I've always had a personal rule that I will not stay out too late to have sex (which is one of the reasons I never did night game, where staying out until 2am or beyond is often required). However, if you follow the dating model I lay out in *Get To Sex Fast*[1], you'll keep the first date to one hour or less, therefore meeting her at 10pm or 11pm isn't any big deal, particularly if it's an unusual thing.

This also means you must know of several convenient locations that are open that late. Check around and make a note of at least two different 24-hour restaurants in your general area. That way, when that cute 19-year-old wants to meet up at 10pm tomorrow night but has no idea where or what will be open that late (and bars won't be an option because of her age!), you'll immediately know exactly where to go.

Social Media

As I'm sure you're already aware, most younger women are consumed with social media. Constant communication with friends as well as attention whoring is a literal non-stop activity for these girls. Most women under the age of 26 or so will be on one or more sites/apps like Facebook, Instagram, Snapchat, Twitter, and numerous others. Many younger women also treat dating apps like Tinder and OKCupid as de facto social media sites to get attention from men (not dates, but attention).

If you have no idea what Snapchat or Instagram is, you need to get up to speed fast. You don't necessarily have to be a regular user of these services, but you should at least be reasonably familiar with them. You do not want to be on a date with a hot 20-year-old and ask "What's Tumblr?"

A decent Facebook page, at a minimum, is highly recommended. As I talked about in *The Ultimate Open Relationships Manual*[2], having

---

[1] http://www.gettosexfast.com/
[2] http://www.haveopenrelationships.com/

your younger women as friends on your Facebook page is good way to get in touch with them to re-establish the relationship. Younger women constantly get new phone numbers and change phones. A Facebook page, amazingly, has become a more stable way of keeping in touch with someone long-term than an actual phone number.

You also need your Facebook page to look decent. It can't have a bunch of boring stuff or "dad" stuff on there. That's not attractive. You also can't repel women away from you with its content.

Here are the parameters of your viable Facebook page:

- Have some pictures of you doing some fun and interesting things. Traveling, having fun, parties, outdoors, indoors, etc. You don't need piles of these kinds of pictures, but you do need some, and they need to be prominently displayed.

- Ideally, if you can get it done, have lots of positive, funny, witty comments from you with responses from your friends, preferably cute women. This is social proof.

- Have at least 100 friends in your friends list. Most VYW have over 700 Facebook friends, some have well over a thousand; many have several thousand. If you have less than 100, it will look strange. If you're starting from scratch, send out friend requests to absolutely everyone you know, as well as the people who know them. Getting to 100 Facebook friends isn't very difficult. On the flip side, you don't want too many friends on your Facebook page either (unless you are a public figure or have a very public job). Most people have figured out that people with bazillions of friends on Facebook are often people with no real life. You don't want to be perceived that way (yes, even if *she* has tons of Facebook friends). I've been on Facebook for ten years, and I'm a public figure with literally millions of readers, and I have a grand total of 338 friends on my personal Facebook page. That's about right.

- Important: Avoid any and all political content on your FB page. If using Facebook as a dating and relationship management tool, you should never post any political opinion you have on there.

Doing so instantly alienates, and possibly angers at least 50% of your younger women prospects. We live in a hyper-political era where normal, everyday people fly into a rage whenever they read something on social media they disagree with politically. You can't do this on your Facebook page (or Instagram page, or whatever). That cute 21-year-old may have the opposite political opinions from yours, and if she sees those viewpoints on your page, she's gone. If you absolutely must express yourself politically, there are a hundred other ways to do that online besides your friggin' personal Facebook/Instagram/Twitter page.

You should get into the habit of adding every VYW you meet or date to your Facebook page, whether successful with her or not. If you're uncomfortable adding her as a friend, or if you feel she wouldn't like it because she has a boyfriend or something, simply bookmark her page instead. I've had many long-term FBs and MLTRs with younger women where I communicated with them via Facebook without ever actually adding them as a Facebook friend.

Lastly, and most importantly, with younger women and social media, **don't become one of her attention whoring male e-orbiters.** Never, ever, *ever* post any compliment on her social media pictures or comments. Doing so will murder any attraction she had for you, and will cause her to mentally place you in the category of one of the hordes of men on her social media who are drooling over her and whom she'll never have sex with (or never have sex with again). Any time she posts a sexy picture of herself on her social media, just glance at it and move on. Do not comment on it. Don't even leave a teasing or sarcastic comment. Just click away. Let all the guys she'll never have sex with compliment her and play with her on her social media. You want to be the one *having sex with her,* not commenting on her stupid social media page.

Younger Women Over 30

If you're a much older guy seeking to date much younger women who are over age 30, the online dating dynamic changes a little. Women in their thirties are quite different from VYW, as I explained back in Chapter 3, and they can't be treated exactly the same. The fact she's more than ten years younger than you doesn't change this.

If she's over 30, all the techniques I talked about above regarding waiting a little longer to pitch the first date do *not* apply. Feel free to date pitch on the second or third exchange (if using a dating *site*) or within just 10 minutes or less after some back-and-forth banter (if using a dating *app*). You also can pitch a normal date at a cool coffee shop or bar (obviously) and don't need to worry about malls or other "safe" venues.

Here are the dating sites/apps listed above, this time calibrated for younger women over 30:

Match.com: Usable, with a caveat. Match.com is great for women over 30, but just be aware these women will be mostly provider hunters, meaning higher levels of ASD you'll have to overcome, and they'll desire serious relationships. If that's what you want, go for it.

Bumble: *Useable, but there are problems.* Bumble will work but you'll have to swipe a *lot* of women.

Plenty of Fish: *Useable, but there are problems.* Again, the age controls, as I already described above.

Tinder: *Waste of time – Don't use it.* Again, Tinder is fine for dating women your own age, but not much younger women, regardless of their age. Avoid.

OKCupid: *Usable, with a few tweaks.* OKCupid is usable as long as you do what I recommend in the OKCupid listing at the start of this chapter.

Zoosk: *Usable.* Zoosk is highly location-specific. In some places it works fine and in other places it's worthless. I suggest attempting it and giving it a shot, and if after some good effort you get no dates from it, forget it.

Badoo: *Unknown/varies.* Like Zoosk, it works better in some cites/countries than others, and so results will vary greatly with women over 30. As usual, I suggest trying it if there are a lot of users in your region.

Christian Mingle and J-Date: *Usable, with some problems.* Similar to Match.com, in that they will work, but there are more provider hunter type women on there.

Hinge: *Possibly usable.* If you already have lots of Facebook friends, then go for it.

eHarmony: *Waste of time – Don't use it.* There are many over-30 women on there, but the site is too unworkable for our purposes here. For example, you can't even search for new women; they send you "matches" only every once and a while, not when you want them. Not good.

Coffee Meets Bagel: *Possibly usable.* I've received some reports from older guys (men well over age 45 or 50) successfully dating women in their early thirties using Coffee Meets Bagel, so give it a shot.

There are many other differences between VYW and younger women over 30, but they involve real-life interactions outside of online, so we'll cover those in future chapters.

Chapter 12

DAYGAME WITH YOUNGER WOMEN - PART ONE: LAYING THE GROUNDWORK

I have to tread lightly here. I have personally done daygame, I've achieved results from it, and I've had sex with much younger women (as young as 18) using daygame in my past. That being said, I do not consider myself a daygame expert, and just about any experienced daygame guru on the internet is going to be light-years better than I am regarding daygame on my best day. (I'm an online dating guy.) These days, I only do daygame on rare occurrences when I'm out and about doing my usual thing, *and* I see an attractive woman, *and* I'm feeling and looking really good, *and* I have plenty of time. In other words, I don't do daygame very often. It's been many years since I did daygame in any concentrated fashion.

That being said, since daygame is an effective way to meet younger women, and since I have technically done it, I've included this chapter and the next one just for the sake of completeness. Once you've read these two daygame chapters, if daygame seems like the path you wish to take, I highly recommend you seek out more qualified daygame experts like

Tom Torero, Krauser PUA, and Good Looking Loser (just Google those guys) and get more daygame techniques and data, calibrating what you learn with the data I'm giving you in these two daygame chapters for younger women.

This is not a book on daygame, this is a book regarding younger women and older men. Therefore, in this chapter and the next, I will only be talking about daygame as it applies to older men and VYW specifically. That means meeting younger women in a non-creepy, fun way, getting their contact information, then contacting them later for an actual meet. I'm not saying this is the only way older men can bring much younger women into their lives via real-life cold approach; I'm sure there are probably many others. I'm just saying this is the way that I know works.

Daygame, despite its downsides, is an extremely effective way to meet younger women if you put in the time and effort. Younger women have far less ASD and social inhibitions than older women, and are often very pleasant to talk to during cold approaches.

As we discussed back in Chapter 10, one of your biggest decisions is which game style to focus on (online, daygame, night game, or social circle game). I'll cover the pros and cons of daygame as I see them.

Daygame Pros and Cons

There are a lot of great things about daygame that make it better than other game styles, and there are some problems with daygame as well. Here's how daygame compares to other types of game, particularly as it applies to the older man seeking much younger women.

The Pros of Daygame Over Online Dating

1. You see exactly what you're getting. When you approach a woman via daygame, you see exactly how she looks in real life, head-to-toe. Online dating's biggest weakness is that often, you have no idea how a woman really looks (particularly her body)

until you meet up with her on that first date. Not a problem with daygame.

2. You can establish rapport much more quickly. Many men are more compelling in real life than online with a profile and a photo. I am certainly in that category. If you have a compelling look, personality, or presence that does not convey well online, daygame is likely the place for you.

3. It's more enjoyable for more social or extroverted men. If you have a more social personality type, daygame is going to be much more enjoyable and less tedious for you than the online stuff. Really extroverted guys often tend to hate online dating.

4. It builds confidence and woman skills faster. Nothing will build your own personal confidence levels than getting into the habit of walking up to a complete stranger, a very attractive woman you've never met before, and just start talking to her. This is literally one of the hardest and scariest things a man can do. Get past this, and your overall confidence will grow faster than just sending out online openers.

To be fair here, it's not like online dating doesn't build confidence either. You need to be a confident, outcome independent guy on that first date. Yet, I agree that real-life cold approach will build your confidence levels faster.

The Pros of Daygame Over Night Game

I can't say much about this since I have zero night game experience, and it's unlikely you're going to choose night game as your game style if you're an older man. (Do you really want to hang out at dance clubs when you're over 40? I don't.) Regardless, the big advantage daygame has over night game is that it can be done during the daytime. Night game usually requires you to stay up late into the night in order to be successful, and as an older man, that probably isn't very appealing to you, nor is it likely to be compatible with your lifestyle.

The Pros of Daygame Over Social Circle Game

1. You'll never run out of women. The biggest problem with social circle game is that you run out of women way too fast. This will never be a problem with daygame; you can meet new girls literally every day if you wish.

2. Daygame girls don't know you. This is usually a good thing, not a bad thing. You're a blank slate and can present to her only the best aspects of you. Women who already know you usually know too much, including the bad or unattractive things about you. Friend zone is never a problem in daygame.

The Cons of Daygame

Daygame is great, but there are some problems with it you need to be aware of.

1. It's much more scary. It takes serious courage to walk up to strange women and start running game. Some guys can do it. Many guys can do it, but do it badly because they're so nervous or awkward. Many guys can't or refuse to learn. Online dating and social circle game isn't scary at all.

2. It's a grind. Seriously. Daygame is hard, hard work. You need to open lots of girls, and each open is going to take a decent amount of time; not just the time you're talking to her, but also the time walking around looking for women attractive enough for you to approach. If you live in a city like Los Angeles or Miami, you've got plenty of hot girls, but most of us are not going to be so lucky.

   In addition, most of the women are going to ghost you when you text them back, forcing you to go out again and meet more. It's tough.

3. It's not nearly as schedule-friendly as online dating or even social circle game. This is the main reason why I chose online

dating over daygame years ago. With online dating, you can do literally whenever you want, at any hour of the day, anywhere in the world, and you don't have to go anywhere or even get dressed or take a shower. With daygame, no. You have to take all the time to get ready, look great, then go somewhere, hang out there for a long time, talk to lots of girls, and so on. And you can only do it at certain hours.

4. It's harder to put in large amounts of numbers very quickly. I can sit down and blast out 50 openers to new women, or swipe hundreds, all of whom I find attractive, and do it all in far less than an hour. I've never seen anyone put in these kinds of numbers in such a small period of time using nothing but daygame (unless you're a maniac approaching every woman you see, including the ugly and average-looking ones).

    However, this disadvantage can be mitigated if you don't mind having sex with more average-looking women or if your positive response rate from daygame is extremely high because you're such a compelling guy. One could argue that though the number of openers is higher with online dating, the response rate will often be lower, so keep that in mind.

5. It's slightly more dangerous. I don't mean physically dangerous, I mean culturally. If you live in Asia, Central or Southern Europe, or South America, this won't be any big deal. But if you live in a more sexually uptight culture with a puritanical past (like the USA or Canada) or a post-feminist culture (like the UK or in Scandinavia), you can get into real trouble if you start hitting on much younger women excessively in one location. Men have been escorted out of malls by security and banned from certain locations because they were hitting on younger women in creepy or uncalibrated ways. If you follow the advice in this chapter and the next, this shouldn't happen to you, but I have to admit that you're taking *some* risk doing this... yet you'll never have this problem with online dating or social circle game.

I'll repeat that online dating, social circle game *and* daygame are all valid ways to meet younger women. The choice you make is will be largely dependent on your personality, lifestyle, and schedule. Choose one style to focus on and get good at it. Then consider the other game styles something to occasionally dip your toe into.

Daygame Pre-Scheduling

If you want to get good with daygame, or any other skill, you need to consistently focus on it and do it repeatedly, many times a week over the course of many months. There's a lot of daygame advice online that implies you can just do daygame "whenever you feel like it" or as you "go about your day-to-day life." *That advice is only for men who are at an advanced level of game already.* If that describes you, then fine, but if you consider yourself a beginner or intermediate at daygame, you need to ignore this advice.

Instead, your goal should be to go out and meet women *at least* three times per week, every week (unless you're taking a week off as a break) until you start getting the results you want. Each outing should be a minimum of an hour, though two hours is better, and longer is even better.

This is not a book about time management (I address that in *The Unchained Man*), but as a time management consultant, I can tell you that your best course of action is to sit down once a week and map out when your daygame times will be for that week, then stick with those appointments. (We'll talk about the best days and times to do this in a minute.)

For example, on Sunday night, you may decide to go out and meet women Tuesday night at 6:30pm for one hour, Wednesday night at 4:30pm for two and a half hours, and Saturday at noon for three hours.

---

* http://www.alphamalebook.com/

If you stick to a schedule like that, you *will* get good at daygame, given a few weeks.

It's important you stick to this schedule. Guys who are serious about daygame go out and meet women when they've decided they should *even if they're not feeling like it.* I did this myself, and I've heard the same from daygame gurus when they first got started. Sometimes I really didn't feel like going out, but I forced myself to anyway. Often, those were some of the best days I had in terms of results. During one day in particular, a Saturday, I *really* didn't want to go out, and wanted to read a new book I had just purchased instead. Yet, I made myself a weekly commitment that I had to go to one of the local malls on a Saturday for at least two hours to practice my daygame.

So, grumbling, I made myself get ready, dress nice, and go out. That day at the mall, in a sunglasses store, I met a very hot, blonde 19-year-old who had just graduated from high school. Less than a week later, we had sex. She was one of the best-looking women I've ever had sex with. Getting out there and making things happen, especially when you don't feel like it, works.

The Best Places for Daygaming Younger Women

Younger women are everywhere, obviously, but for daygame, you need to find places where the numbers are concentrated so you have the highest odds of meeting the type of women you like. Here are the best times and locales for meeting younger women.

Malls

In my opinion, malls are hands-down the best places to meet VYW, for obvious reasons. Most of VYW I had sex with via daygame resulted from a mall meet. I will still occasionally meet women at malls in my normal day-to-day activities, especially during the summer when younger women are out of school.

When I say "mall," I'm specifically talking about the big shopping malls, and the bigger, the better. I'm not talking about small malls or strip malls. Also, fancier, upscale malls are not as good for younger women daygame, since younger women don't have the money to shop at these places. The best malls for younger women are big malls that are the standard type that cater to the middle or even lower-middle class. If you have any of these within easy driving distance to your home, that's the mall you want to use.

If you live in a larger city, you'll likely have several malls to choose from. If that's the case, go spend time at all of these different malls, and pick the best one. Because of the demographic differences in neighborhoods, different malls in the same city will indeed have different amounts of hotter, younger women. It's your job to determine the best one. For example, of the two malls closest to my house, each mall about 25 minutes away from each other, one is very hit-or-miss, with a random smattering of attractive women, while the other almost *always* has *lots* of hot girls whenever I go.

The overall best place to meet younger women at a mall is the food court. That's where everyone in a mall tends to congregate. Regardless, you can successfully daygame at malls anywhere within the mall.

You want to go to the mall when it's the most crowded and when the most younger women tend to be there. Generally speaking (though there are always exceptions) usually these times are best:

Non-summer months:
Tuesdays – Thursdays, 6pm-8pm
Saturdays – Sundays, 1pm-5pm

Summer months:
Tuesdays – Thursdays, 1pm-7pm
Saturdays – Sundays, 1pm-4pm

In addition, during the Monday to Friday weekday, especially during summer months, the food court will be packed with women between noon and 1:30pm. In malls that are large enough, often you can just work the food court during the lunch hour and forget about the rest of the mall.

Be careful when doing any daygame at a mall. Always be very nice, polite, courteous, and low-key to everyone you talk to there, including the women you meet, but everyone else as well. If you turn into a spastic approach-machine, or if you act pushy or creepy, you risk being ejected or even banned from the mall. If you follow my advice in the next chapter, this won't happen to you (it has never happened to me), but just make sure you do so.

Downtown Congregation Areas

Every downtown area has one or more areas where younger people congregate. It could be a city park, city square, a particular street, or similar. There will almost always be large amounts of people hanging around, talking to friends, eating, or shopping, particularly when the weather is nice. As I describe this, you're probably already visualizing where this place (or places) is in your city.

If you're not aware of where this place is, I promise you your city has one (or several), unless you live in a small town. Ask around or drive around and find out where this place (or places) is if you don't already know.

If you work downtown, live downtown, or spend a lot of time in your downtown area, this is probably the ideal place for you, particularly if you set your own schedule during the weekdays.

Best times to meet younger women at downtown congregation areas are:

Non-summer months:

Monday – Thursday, 1pm–7pm.

(Why not weekends? Younger women are around, but often they're "away" on weekends doing something else. I've found that usually, the downtown daytime congregation areas are not where VYW hang out on weekends, though your city may be different.)

Summer months:

Any day of the week when the weather is good, any time after 11am.

College Campuses

I have no personal experience in meeting younger women at college campuses, but I know for a fact these are fantastic places to meet them under certain conditions. Other men I personally know and have communicated with have had much success there.

The best places in campuses are college libraries, food courts, or outside congregation areas, at just about any time of day before 6pm.

If this is an area of interest for you, it would behoove you to pick the largest college campus near you and scout it out at different times of the day and different days of the week to get an idea of when the most women are available. In all seriousness, you could make an entire daygame "career" at just your local college campus.

Again, like with malls, be very careful and low-key when doing any daygame at a college campus, particularly as an older man. Also, if you live in a more extreme left-wing region (such as Scandinavia or California) I would probably skip colleges altogether; it's too culturally dangerous to do daygame there in my opinion.

Lunchtime Game

One type of daygame that I came up with, and that worked for me, was "lunchtime game." This can only be done at large, downtown areas. The system is to hang out at common places the downtown employees go to buy food and coffee during lunch on the weekdays and meet the women at the restaurants, delis, food courts, and coffee shops during their lunch break. Between 11am and 1:30pm, these areas are jam-packed full of cute women; a very high concentration of not only women in their twenties but women in their thirties and forties as well (if these are younger women to you).

Depending on your location and schedule, you could literally do 100% of your daygame this way, picking three to five days a week to go down and do lunchtime game during your own lunch break.

Coffee Shop Game

I have never done this, but I know a lot of guys who have made this type of daygame work. The system is to bring a book or your laptop down to your local coffee shop, plant yourself in a location where you can see everyone, and just work from there for a few hours. Whenever a cute woman sits down in your vicinity, you strike up a conversation. This is a more slow-churn form of daygame that takes much longer and requires a lot more patience, but you can actually get work done while doing it, so you're not exactly wasting time, making it a good daygame option for certain men.

Places *Not* Suitable For Concentrated Younger Woman Daygame

Daygame can be done anywhere, and if you see a hot Girl And want to talk to her, do so, regardless of where you are. That being said, in terms of concentrated daygame, there are some places that aren't worth the effort (unless your city is very unusual).

Street Game

Street game is for hardcore daygamers only. It's when you literally see a hot girl walking down the street, and you actually go stop and interrupt her to start up a conversation. While I know this kind of game can work, I generally do *not* recommend this for older men seeking to date much younger women. It's just too aggressive. Younger women, particularly VYW, will be much more frightened and reluctant during street game than if you meet them at a quiet clothing store at a mall while they're relaxed and standing still.

If you really want to give street game a try, feel free to do so, but I don't recommend it for older men. Leave street game to the younger guys.

Grocery Stores

Yes, there are sometimes really hot VYW at grocery stores, but on the rare times you see them there, they're always with their mothers or boyfriends. Think about it. How many VYW do you know who like to go to grocery stores by themselves? Or with their cute girlfriends? You see my point. Grocery stores are not a good place for concentrated daygame for younger women.

The one *possible* exception to this is the smaller, downtown grocery store where everyone stops by on their way home to get food. During the hours of 4pm-6:30pm, you may be able to meet younger women at these, depending on your city and neighborhood.

Bookstores

I love bookstores, but they present the same problem as grocery stores; just not enough cute women are there. Sometimes you'll get lucky, but usually you won't. The exception to this is bookstores with large coffee shops attached; focus on the coffee shop end, not the bookstore end.

Chapter 13

DAYGAME WITH YOUNGER WOMEN - PART TWO: EXECUTION

Once you've determined exactly where, when, and how often you're going to actually get out there and daygame for younger women, now it's time to execute. This chapter will overview the process of what I've done in the past that works, mixed in with a little of what I've been told works by other older men who have been successful at this. Again, I strongly recommend that if daygame becomes your primary game type focus for meeting younger women, you check out the resources from full-time daygame experts whom I listed in the prior chapter.

I'll walk you step-by-step through the entire process, listed in order. Failure to do any one of these steps means that you'll waste your time with daygame, so all of these steps I consider mandatory.

Your Appearance

Before you go out to daygame, you need to look your absolute best. When I say "absolute best," I'm speaking literally and I mean it. Your appearance needs to be maximized as best you possibly can. Before you leave your home, you need to look at yourself in a full-length mirror and ruthlessly evaluate yourself from head to toe. If you don't look as perfect as you can, based on your age and genetics, go back and correct it before going out.

Review Chapters 6 and 7. Even better is to review the appearance checklists I have in Chapter 16 in *The Unchained Man*[1] or (even better) Chapter 7 in *Get To Sex Fast*[2]. If you have neither of those books, I strongly recommend them for this. Anything you can possibly do to look better, including your fashion and grooming, will increase the odds of your success with daygame (or any game for that matter, only with daygame it's even more important because of the completely cold approach aspect of it).

Looking your absolute best is not only important for your odds of women being attracted to you, but for your own confidence as well. You'll carry yourself better and with greater confidence and (hopefully) outcome independence if you know you look good.

Your Mental Frame

After your physical appearance check-up, you need a mental frame check-up, which is just as important. Review all the concepts and frames we talked about back in Chapter 4. Confident. Outcome Independent. Funny. Relaxed. Non-needy. Non-creepy. Your frame must be well defined and crystal clear in these areas or very little of this will work for you.

Pump yourself up. *Feel* good. *Feel* strong and confident. Remind yourself about how you're the man these Type Twos have always been

---

[1] http://www.alphamalebook.com/
[2] http://www.gettosexfast.com/

looking for, for their entire lives. Remind yourself about the edge you have over younger men, who aren't as confident as you, have less money than you, are more emotional and needy than you, and have less game than you.

I used to put affirmations on my phone and read them aloud right before I went out to do daygame. They were silly and corny, but they helped me get into a good mental state, which helped a lot. "I am strong! I am good-looking! I'm the classy older man these women crave! Women love me!" And so on.

Do whatever works for you, but do it. Get into a peak, positive emotional state before leaving your home. Look *forward* to meeting attractive women; don't view it as a chore.

Your Objectives For The Day

This is extremely important and I see a lot of guys screw this up. You can't just go out to do daygame to "meet women" or to "get laid" or to "get phone numbers" or whatever. *These are not goals.* These are empty, generic statements or hopes.

Before you leave your home, you must have *specific and clear* objectives for today's daygame excursion. They must be defined in terms of specific actions or results, always with numbers attached.

If you're new at cold approaching women, younger or otherwise, some examples of some goals would be things like the following:

- Say "Hi" to five younger women who you find *very* hot, at least an eight on your personal one-to-ten attractiveness scale. That's all you have to do; just say "Hi" and then walk away. If you say "Hi" to five women who are very hot to you, you've done your job, you've hit your goal, and you can go home.

- Start up at two conversations with two different women, of any age or attractiveness, even if you consider them ugly, which last at least five minutes.

Baby-step goals like this are perfectly fine if you're new at this. Pick a goal like that, and do it for at least two weeks, going out three to four times per week as we discussed in the last chapter. After two weeks, you can increase your daygame objectives to something more meaningful, such as...

- Start three conversations with three really hot (personal eight or higher) younger women. Each conversation must last at least 30 seconds.
- "Contact close" at least one woman of any attractiveness. That means you get at least one woman to give you her phone number, even if you think she's lying.

Once you get the hang of this, you can move to the third level, and set daily goals like...

- Do not leave the mall (or wherever you are) until you've had at least three quality conversations with three younger women that lasted at least five minutes.
- Do not leave the mall (or wherever you are) until you have three phone numbers or social media links from three hot younger women.

The above goals are just examples. Please feel free to design your own based on where you think you are with this. The point is to not just "go out to meet women." *Every single time you go daygaming you must have a very specific, numerical goal that you must hit before you go home.* Daygame takes too much time and is too much work to just wing it with fuzzy objectives.

The Opener

If you didn't already know, an "opener" is the first set of words you say to a woman in order to start up a conversation. There's been a lot written in the seduction community / dating industry about openers and pickup lines. Frankly, most men put too much importance on the opener even tough it's actually the least important part of the entire process (and that goes for online dating as well as daygame). Openers don't and won't get you laid and never will. It's the interaction that goes on *after* the opener that will make or break you. The only issue with openers is that they can't be *really bad*. The good news is that trite, boring, or "plain" openers can work just fine as long as you do everything else correctly. (I've had sex with hot women I've met via daygame using just "Hi" as an opener.)

"Really bad" openers, in terms of older men meeting much younger women, means that you are acting stupid, weird, creepy, sexual, or too direct. Most of those things may be obvious, but the "too direct" issue is something that's particularly important for older men.

There is a big debate in seduction circles that you may have seen before regarding "direct game" versus "indirect game."

Direct game means you walk right up to a girl you've never met and tell her that you think she's attractive and that's why you came over to her. Example: "Hey. How are you? I just saw you and thought you were cute so I decided to come over and say hi."

Indirect game is when you open a woman by saying something that has nothing whatsoever to do with the fact that you find her attractive. Instead, you just talk to her like you're being friendly and platonic. Then, a little later in the conversation, you can indicate that you might be interested in seeing her again and ask for her contact information.

The debates over whether direct game or indirect game is best get very heated among pick-up artists. I know for a fact that they both work, but I'm not an expert enough in daygame to tell you which one works best, or for which scenarios. However, I *do* know one thing with 100% certainty, and that is this: if you look ten years or more older than the woman you're opening during daygame, you *must* use indirect game.

There is no debate about this. If you start opening much younger women in a daygame scenario using direct game, you will just waste your time. (If using social circle game, that's different, and I can't speak about night game.)

As an older man meeting much younger women, you *must* use indirect game, period, end of story. This means your opener cannot be a "direct" one where you tell her she's cute or attractive. Instead, your openers must be very simple, friendly, and safe.

Here are several opener methods I know work well with much younger women.

1. Ask her a question about something she's wearing. It can be clothing, shoes, jewelry, a hat, whatever. Examples:

   "Hey, where did you get those shoes? My ex-girlfriend (or sister, or whomever) wore those same shoes!"

   "Is that hair tie made out of silk?"

   "Nice pin." (and then smile)

   "Those shoes/boots are funky. Where did you get them?"

2. Ask her a question about whatever it is you're both looking at in the store (or coffee shop or whatever). This one is my favorite (in situations where it's applicable). I will typically play the "dumb masculine guy who doesn't know anything about female fashion" card. I'll ask very simple questions about female fashion, which is easy since I really don't know much about it.

   I have had sex with VYW by just asking about the sunglasses we were both looking at in the store.

Examples:

   "So, how do you tell which of these sunglasses are for men and which are for women?" I've used this one many times. It always starts a funny conversation, namely because most sunglasses are unisex.

   <hold up two hair clips> "Hey, I need a woman's opinion. The brown one or the black one?"

   These are really easy since women love to talk about clothing. Noting will make a woman relax, and even entertain her, like explaining female fashion points to a man.

3. Just walk up to her and ask her a completely random question. You get slight bonus points if it's a *little* funny. I've walked up to women and asked, in a relaxed, confident manner, "Is your name Suzi?" When they say no, I just keep talking as if we already know each other, like "Oh! Crazy. Oh well. How are you?"

Again, don't worry about these openers seeming boring, trite, or gay. They are, and it doesn't matter. *All you need to do is start a conversation. How you start it really doesn't matter as long as you're not being direct or creepy.*

The Conversation

There are three goals for you as an older man regarding the initial daygame conversation once the opener is done and you're actually talking back-and-forth:

1. Establish safety and non-creepiness. This means that she doesn't fear you and doesn't find you weird or creepy. She can still be a little shy or nervous, that's okay. She just can't be scared, creeped out, or turned off.

2. Establish rapport. This is what daygame guys call the "hook point." This is when she's actually at least a little interested or curious about you. This is usually achieved when she either starts talking *a lot* (very common with VYW) or she asks you a question about yourself.

3. Contact close. This means getting her contact information. Phone number is the best, social media is the second choice though not that great, and email is worst. Later, you'll contact her using this medium and set up an actual meet.

How long should the conversation be? The short answer is, in terms of results, the longer, the better. If you establish safety, rapport, and get a phone number all within three minutes, that's fine, but if you do all of this and talk for 15 minutes instead, the odds of her actually replying to you when you text her later go way up.

The only constraint here is time management. It's going to be harder to meet a large number of women if all of the conversations you have take 15+ minutes rather than three or four minutes. This is why I tend to lean in the direction of shorter conversations, but with more women. But that's just me; I'm a very busy guy and a very anal time management nerd. I'm also accustomed to online dating, where you're sending out hundreds of openers and doing thousands of swipes, so that's just the kind of rhythm I'm comfortable with. If you're more normal and/or have more time on your hands, please feel free to talk longer. Your success odds *do* go up when you do this; it's *not* a waste of time.

You might be thinking about what daygame guys call the "instadate," where you start talking to a woman during daygame and just do a mini "date" right then and there, where you both walk over to a nearby table, coffee shop, or whatever, sit down, and talk. I know this works, but I have never personally done this, so I can't advise you on it. My general advice is to go for this if she's showing a lot of interest and rapport, but don't expect an instadate to happen very often. The vast majority of women you open will either not like you enough to do this, be too nervous, or be too busy.

Conversational Techniques

Years ago, I used to use a lot of canned pick-up artists techniques in my conversations during daygame. Over time, as I got better with women, I just started having normal conversations with them and found that it was just as effective in terms of actually getting to sex.

That being said, I think canned conversational, daygame, or pick-up techniques are good for guys who are complete beginners. If that's you, feel free to use the techniques I'm about to describe, as well as (and especially) those of daygame experts you like. I've noticed that other men go through a similar progression as I did, starting with lots of canned techniques, and slowly moving to more natural conversations as you get more comfortable with daygame and women/dating in general.

Though I don't have the space to re-print the entire chapter here, I *strongly* recommend reading Chapter 14: Conversational Skills in *Get To Sex Fast**. Everything in that chapter directly relates to daygame, and I would consider that chapter as a backbone to your conversations with women during daygame or first/second dates with women, including younger women.

Here, I will quickly run through a few basics that I've used with VYW during daygame that have worked for me.

One of the easiest ways to move a conversation forward with a woman you just met is to follow the two-step formula of A) make an observation about her, followed by B) a question. You can start with the words "You seem…"

> *"You seem really happy. Is it your birthday or something?"*
> *"You seem very educated. Are you in college?"*
> *"You seem a little pissed off. Did you get in a fight with your BFF today or something?"*

Listen to her answer, then ask another question based on what she just said. Keep doing this, then just roll into a very casual, fun, brief conversation. Remember your frames from Chapter 4; confident, outcome independent, non-needy, and most importantly, non-creepy!

Be as *relaxed* as you can. Smile and be funny. Make sure she laughs, or at least smiles at least a little, several times in the conversation. A word of warning though; if you're a more extroverted guy, it's important to not go overboard with the funny stuff and be a spastic clown or a trick monkey. Two or three points of levity in the conversation is all you need. Don't try to be Robin Williams. That will turn her off.

Avoid dangerous questions and dangerous topics. Do *not* talk about politics, religion, or man/woman relations. Do *not* ask her where she lives (too scary a question). Even saying something like, "So do you live

---

* http://www.gettosexfast.com/

around here?" is a no-no. Younger guys hitting on younger women can ask questions like that, but as an older man, you can't. Asking her where she works is okay.

Do *not* compliment her appearance in any way during the conversation. Again, as older men, we need to use purely indirect game. If you really want to compliment her, compliment her energy or her attitude or something like that, never her appearance. I personally wouldn't compliment her on anything at all (and don't).

Be sure to maintain good eye contact. This is especially important if she has an amazing body or big giant boobs that are popping out of her shirt. Control yourself and do *not* look at them. Remember, as a much older man than her, the margin for error into creepy zone is much thinner for you than it is for men in her own age group. They might be able to get caught with their eyes wandering to her chest, but you can't. Just maintain gentle, soft eye contact. Keep a smile on your face and a relaxed expression at all times.

If she asks you any questions, this is a very good sign. That means you've reached rapport, the "hook point." Always answer every question she asks you, and don't dodge any questions. If you do, you'll raise red flags.

Usually, at least in my experience, you will not get asked any questions. Instead, she'll either act cold but polite (which usually means she's not interested in you) or she'll be bubbly and happy but talk about herself a lot (which means she *could* be interested in you).

Once you've reached this point, it's time to contact close her (unless you have plenty of time and want to keep talking to her).

The Contact Close

The contact close is not a big deal. You just ask for her information in a very casual, non-needy way. Here are a few examples of how you can do this:

- "Are you on Snapchat or Instagram?" (Snapchat is better.) When she answers yes, get her Snapchat/Instagram name, whip out your phone, and friend request her right there.
- "Hey, I've got to go. Are you on Facebook?" When she says yes, just say "Cool. What's your email on there?" Again, you can friend request her right then and there with your phone. If you're not comfortable with doing this, then put it in your phone, or write it down, or whatever.
- "You're fun! We should text sometime. What's your number?" Don't push hard for this if she resists, but if she gives you her number, put it into your phone right then and there. If she doesn't want to give you her number, you can then ask for social media as above.
- "You're fun! We should text sometime. Here, put your number in my phone." Then just hand her your phone with the new contact screen already on the phone number field. This is obviously a more aggressive form of contact close, but I've never had a problem with it once I reached the hook point.

Right after getting her contact info, I used to just say something like "Cool! It's been nice meeting you. You're very different. I'll see you later," and just leave. However, most daygame guys have told me that it's better to stand and keep talking for at least another minute or so after the contact close before you leave. I've done this a few times and it *seems* to help, so I suggest you go that route. You still want to leave though; it's very important that *you* terminate the conversation. If she does, your odds go down.

As I mentioned above, some forms of contact information are better than others. Here's the approximate hierarchy of the best forms of contact to get from her, starting with the best and ending with the worst.

1. Her phone number
2. The ID for her texting app, if she uses one, such as Kik, WhatsApp, Line, Viber, etc
3. Snapchat

4. Facebook
5. Instagram
6. Her email address

So usually, you should try to get her phone number. If that doesn't work (or if you're still a beginner and you're uncomfortable asking for it) you can go for her texting ID if you live in a part of the world where those are used more often. If you must ask for social media, Snapchat is the best, since that has a texting feature that a lot of younger women like to use. Facebook and Instagram are options, but the problem with these is that you'll just be one horny guy on her friends list who wants to fuck her; not a great place to be. Lastly, you have email, which many years ago used to be a good way to contact women, but not so much anymore, as social media and texting have taken over many social functions that people used to fulfill with email.

The Half-Routine

Daygame, like all forms of game, is a numbers game. Most of the younger women you contact close, likely the vast majority, will never respond to you in any meaningful way when you follow up with them later. This is normal and to be expected.

The good news is that there is a technique that worked very well for me that dramatically raised the odds of her responding when I texted her later that day or the next day. It's what I call the "half routine." It's not my idea; it's an old technique that started with Neil Strauss a long time ago (sometimes the oldest techniques work best). It involves one or more canned routines that I avoid these days, but it's still effective.

Lots of daygame guys are really good at getting phone numbers but have a lot of trouble getting women to respond when they attempt to contact them. Neil Strauss said, and he was right, that this was because these men never gave the women a compelling reason to talk to them again. They were just being a fun or cool guy, and often this is not enough (unless you're *really* good looking or have some other unusual edge). It's better if she has a clear and specific reason to contact you again, beyond you being cool, attractive, interesting, or funny.

One of the easiest ways to do this, and a technique I have used myself to great effect, is to run a canned pick-up routine on her, but only run the first half of it. Halfway through, you say you've "gotta go" and you contact close her to "continue the rest later." Not only does this give her a compelling reason to keep the conversation going, but it also gives you a convenient excuse (and reason) to get her contact information and a reason for her to give it to you.

The actual routine you use doesn't matter, and there are many to choose from. I'm not going to describe them all here, but I will list the common ones below. Google these, perhaps adding the term "PUA" to them, to get a description of exactly what they are and how to use them.

The Cube

Strawberry Fields

The Lying Game

Reading her palm

The Ring Finger Routine

If you are uncomfortable using a canned routine, or simply don't like using them, you can simply tell her something like, "I need to tell you something I just noticed about you. But I need to go, I'll have to tell you later," then contact close her. Just realize that the odds are lower with doing something like this unless she clearly really likes you.

The half routine really works well with VYW. It's fun, and women under the age of 23 are all about fun. Not only will the odds of her responding to you later be much higher, but sometimes *she* will *text* you saying, "Hurry up and tell me what you were going to tell me!" This happened to me more than once, including with women many men would consider nines or tens on the one-to-ten attractiveness scale.

Following Up

Once you have her contact info, it's time to follow up with her. When is the best time to follow up? The consensus, and one I agree with, is to follow up the next day. Do not wait longer than the next day. Younger women move on to the next shiny object very fast, so if you wait two or three days after you meet her, the odds are she either won't remember you or won't consider you nearly important enough to respond to.

Following up later the same day can be okay if the woman is under the age of 23 or so and it's been at least several hours since you met her. For example, you met her at 1:00pm and you follow up with her that evening at 7:00pm. If you're at all in doubt, contact her the next day (but not after that).

For the initial contact, don't worry about being fancy. This isn't an opener, since you've already opened her. Just keep it simple. Something like "Hey Suzi! It's Joe. We met at the mall today. :)" is perfectly fine. However, I have found that it's better if you end the first statement with a question. This not only raises the odds of getting a response, but it also confirms that if she doesn't respond, she probably doesn't want to talk to you. The best questions to ask are call-backs to something you talked about, like "Hey Suzi! It's Joe. We met at the mall today. :) Did you make it to your veterinarian appointment?" Again, don't worry about being clever or silly unless you really want to. Keep things simple at this point.

If you don't get a response, she's probably out. You could send her one more text later that day or the next day, again, ending with a question (make sure it's a different question, obviously). If you don't get a response to that one, delete her out of your brain and move on. She's not going to happen. There are unusual times where you actually get a response a day or two later, but these are very rare, so don't plan on it.

Don't get discouraged. Again, most of the women you contact close will never respond to your contacts. *Plan on this in advance so you don't get surprised or discouraged when it happens because it's going to happen a lot.* It's part of how daygame "works."

The above assumes that you got her phone number or ID for a texting app. If you instead get her social media information, assume that your odds of actually getting a response to her are lower but still worth trying. If the social media allows you to contact her without adding her as a friend or following, just hit her up with a message like I described above. If not, then add her and, if you can, attach that same message to the add. If the social media platform doesn't allow this, then don't worry. Just add her, and if/when she accepts your add, then send her that message.

This is precisely why if you can only get her social media, you should add her to it right then and there as you're talking to her with your phone. Your odds are much better doing that then adding her as a friend after she's already gone. She may not even know who you are at that point.

The Follow Up Conversation

Once you've got her responding to you, you have essentially ended daygame and have begun online dating. Simply use the same process we talked about back in Chapter 11, using the system in *The Ultimate Online Dating Manual*[1] if you want more info.

To summarize what you need to do, your goal is to have a brief back-and-forth conversation that lasts about 10 minutes or so, then you gently pitch a first date in a very friendly, non-threatening way as we discussed back in Chapter 11. If she balks, just drop the subject, keep talking for a little while, and gently try again. If she still balks, she's probably out. If she says yes, schedule a date and handle logistics (again, as we talked about in Chapter 11).

Once you've scheduled the first date, you're out of online dating mode and now into date game, as I cover in detail in *Get To Sex Fast*[2], as well as in the rest of this book. In other words, I consider daygame as officially "over" once a woman responds to your first contact the next day. At that point, it's basically online dating, then date game.

---

[1] http://www.onlinedatingsuccessnow.com/
[2] http://www.gettosexfast.com/

Hired Guns

"Hired guns" is the term used for women who actually work at the establishments where you daygame. If you see a cute 20-year-old working behind the counter at a lotions kiosk, Starbucks, or clothing store, do you talk to her and get her contact info?

My general answer is yes, provided you will not be hitting that exact same location again often, particularly at that same time of day. For example, if you hit up the cute Girl At the sunglasses store at the mall, and things don't go well (or they do go well but you never hear from her when you contact her the next day), then when you're back there a few days later daygaming once again, things might feel a little awkward for you.

If it's clear this isn't going to happen, or it's clear you will not be at her exact location again soon, then sure, go ahead and hit her up! Often these girls are much easier to talk to since that's what they're trained to do. Plus, sometimes these girls are really bored and are dying to talk to someone.

Talking to hired guns is also a good way for beginners to get started with daygame. If you're new enough where you're still terrified to walk up to a Girl And give her an opener, start with doing this to hired guns, with no expectation of results. Just do it to get practice. It's much less scary to open hired guns, since again, they *have* to talk to you and they *have* to be nice. It's very good daygame practice for new guys.

Here's a silly-but-easy way to talk to cute hired guns and get phone numbers. Feel free to use this technique to either practice or to actually attempt to meet real women. Go into the makeup section of a large department mall store (like Macy's or Nordstrom's), find the hottest woman who works there, and ask her some questions about man makeup. Tell her you want to cover up the dark spots under your eyes, or make your cheeks less red, or whatever, it doesn't really matter. Then sit in one of those makeup chairs and have her put some of that crap on you. While she does it, talk her up, establish rapport, and when done, contact close her. It's shockingly easy, and a little fun too.

Get More Data

Again I want to reiterate that I'm just scratching the surface of daygame here, and only covering the aspects of older guys and younger women. If daygame is your method of choice for meeting younger women, it would behoove you to research the topic of daygame further (starting with the recommendations I made in the last chapter), keeping in mind that regardless of what you learn, you need to keep the older man / younger women frames of confidence, outcome independence, non-neediness and non-creepiness.

Daygame works, if you work it.

Chapter 14

SOCIAL CIRCLE GAME WITH YOUNGER WOMEN

Because younger women, particularly VYW, have much lower levels of ASD than other women, social circle game can not only be effective but hyper-effective in terms of attracting them and getting to sex and relationships quickly.

Most people assume that the opposite is true; that an older man getting with a younger woman via some kind of social circle would actually be more awkward than a guy messaging a younger woman who is a complete stranger on a dating site. That is not the case, provided such a man follows all the recommendations in Chapters 4 through 5 regarding being a type of man that a Type Two or Type Three would be attracted to. Obviously, a fat, disgusting, creepy older guy hitting on 19-year-olds in his social circle wouldn't be effective, but that's not what we're talking about.

The effectiveness of younger woman social circle game and an even more effective type of social circle game called referral game (which we'll be talking about in the next chapter) are the results of a confluence of two factors: extremely low ASD and something I call "social safety."

Low ASD Environment

Most VYW live in a low-ASD world where everyone has sex with everyone else and it's perfectly normal. These women have had sex with multiple men and it wasn't any big deal. All of their girlfriends and sisters have likely done the same. Many of their guy friends have had sex with many of their girlfriends. Many of their ex-boyfriends have had sex with many of their girlfriends. As sugar daddy game becomes more normal and accepted in society, many of these women have either had sex with much older men already (the Type Twos) or they have many younger female friends who have done it, enjoyed it, and even recommend it to others. Outside of the college scene, young women in their early to mid-twenties getting pregnant by accident left and right is a normal, everyday thing, and something even celebrated and envied.

In a world where women are over the age of 33, all of this behavior would be considered insulting, disgusting, and horrific. But in a world where most everyone is under the age of 23, it's perfectly normal and no big deal. If you're a man who is well over the age of 35 and have not had access to this world because you don't spend time with women under the age of 23 (and have no children in that age range), you will likely be shocked at how easy and casual the concept of sex is to people in this age range. As people get older, ASD grows (even with men) and people become more uptight about this stuff. This hasn't happened yet with VYW, and that's to your advantage.

Social Safety

You're probably already familiar with the concept called "social proof." If you didn't already know what this is, social proof is when women see you in the company of, and desired by, other attractive women. Seeing this actually increases your attraction among women, since you have been "social proofed" by other attractive women. If they want you, she wants you. That's why men who are commonly around attractive women, have pictures of them with attractive women having fun, and/or have a reputation for having sex with lots of attractive women actually get laid much easier than men who don't have any of these things. Social proof, as irrational as it is, is a powerful attractor, or at least can be.

"Social safety" is a variation of this concept that only applies to older men dating much younger women. As I've described in prior chapters, the concept of safety and non-creepiness is very important to older men dating younger women, in ways younger men don't need to worry about. As a much older man, you can be perceived as a greater physical and/or sexual threat to a much younger woman, again, in ways she doesn't feel threatened by a younger man her own age.

When a hot younger woman (let's call her Woman A) personally sees you dating or having sex with another hot younger woman (let's call her Woman B) whom she knows at least reasonably well, not only are you social proofed, but you are marked as being "safe." The thought of having sex with you if you were a complete stranger may have terrified her (*even if she was attracted to you*), but now that she sees you having sex with or dating (FB, MLTR, or OLTR) one of her hot younger friends or acquaintances, she assumes that you're safe. You're not going to beat her up, you're not going to be weird, and you're not going to be a creeper. You're going to be a decently cool *safe* guy. This means 80-90% of the heavy lifting in terms of getting to sex with her has already been done for you. It's very powerful and extremely effective. One of the fastest things that will get you laid with younger women is for them to see you in some sort of sexual or dating context with *other* younger women. Seeing you with cute younger women in a platonic but fun context can also help, though not as much, since this is social proof (which is good) instead of social safety (which is better).

Younger Woman Social Circle Game

There are two types of social circle game when it comes to younger women. There is younger woman social circle game, where you attempt to date women you have met in a social context, where the two of you are already in some kind of social group together. Then there is what I call "referral game," where you have sex with one younger woman, and then, often with her assistance, you have sex with her female friends and/or family members. This is a slightly more advanced version of social circle game that only works on low-ASD women younger than about age 23. I will address social circle game in this chapter, referral game in the next.

Younger woman social circle game involves you spending time in circles where younger women (hopefully attractive younger women) inhabit. You enter these circles, spend time in these circles, become acquaintances with the attractive women (notice I said *acquaintances* and not *friends*) and then hit them up for first dates when the buying temperature of these women is highest.

Like with daygame, I don't consider myself an expert on social circle game but I have done quite a bit of it, mostly with younger women, and I've been successful at it. I have never done it systematically as my primary form of meeting new women (I use online dating for that), but I've seen other men do this, and there's no reason you couldn't.

Social circle game tends to work best with guys who have more extroverted personalities or are already involved in certain social activities or want to. If you already have lots of friends or acquaintances, or if you have the type of job where you meet lots of new people, this is also a huge positive factor in choosing social circle game.

Step one with younger woman social circle game is to identify and target one or more social circles where younger women hang out. Here is a very general (and likely incomplete) list of examples of these kinds of social circles:

- Dancing (dance clubs, dance classes, there are many types)
- Colleges (this is a huge world, with lots of subcategories of social circles where an older man would not look weird)

- Strip clubs
- Modeling (particularly amateur modeling)
- Photography
- "Cool" Churches (there has been a slight resurgence in young women going to churches, at least in the USA; these are not the old-school churches, but the new, liberal, "fun" ones; there are at least several in most large neighborhoods)
- Anywhere where drinking or light drug use is common, particularly weed and ecstasy (sadly, heroin is a new epidemic as well, but I don't recommend dating women addicted to *hard* drugs, just the light ones like weed).
- Gyms / Fitness (this is mostly a domain for women over 30, but many younger women are in these circles as well, particularly in larger cities)
- Bars and the party scene (though this borders on or outright becomes night game rather than social circle game)
- Beauty (this means things like makeup, hairstyling, tanning salons, and so on; younger women in this current generation boil or spray their skins to look tan and pile on the makeup to the point where they look like the Joker; use this to your advantage)

I'm sure there are many other younger woman social circles that I don't have listed here; feel free to do your own research (or think back to your own experiences) to come up with more.

The next step is to find these social circles if you aren't in any already. The internet, specifically Google, Google Maps, Instagram, Facebook, and the best social circle site of them all, Meetup.com, are all your friends here. Use these resources and find where these social circles gather in your area. Then go insert yourself into one or more of these, and spend at least once a week in these circles. Ideally the circles you choose should be circles that you're already interested in, regardless of women. For example, dancing is a fantastic way to meet a lot of younger women, so if you've ever thought about learning how to salsa dance, go for it and kill two birds with one stone.

Don't make the mistake many beta males make of spending lots of time in masculine social circles and getting upset there aren't any women there. Amazingly, I have heard complaints from men who spend time in gun clubs, UFC training, cryptocurrency conferences, or go to Comic Con nerd conventions that there aren't any hot women at these places. Well, fuckin' duh, pal. You need to hang out in feminine, younger-woman-friendly social circles, not guy ones. If you can't find any feminine social circles you like, choose one or two you can tolerate and just go with it. If you absolutely can't tolerate any, then you should not choose social circle game as a mechanism to meet younger women, and should go for online dating or daygame instead.

Make sure to spend a decent amount of time in these social circles. I consider once a week a minimum. If you don't spend enough time, you won't meet enough women to hit up, and social circle game is just like any other game in that it's a numbers game. Most of the women you meet up with will never have sex with you, so if you only have two cute younger women because your social circle isn't large enough, or because you don't go often enough, that won't be enough for any level of results (unless you are very, very lucky, but you never want to rely on luck; as I've said before, luck is not a system).

What happens when you've exhausted all of the women you know in any given social circle? Yep, this is the big downside of social circle game; unlike the other three game styles, the numbers in any one social circle game are limited, at least to some degree. Once you've exhausted your pool of women, you'll have to go join another social circle or constantly help recruit new members into your existing social circle, which might be more work than you're willing to do. I have no expertise in doing this, so you'll have to do your own internet research for more data on expanding / growing existing social circles. The one exception to this rule are those few social circles that constantly have a natural influx of new people (and hopefully, new younger women).

Interaction with the Women in the Social Circle

The biggest danger with social circle game is the dreaded **friend zone**. I have noticed that very social guys with big social circles tend to get stuck into friend zone far more often than typical guys. Therefore, during social circle game, you must do everything in your power to avoid this. Friend zone means that a cute girl really likes you as *an entertaining and validating friend* rather than as *an attractive sexual partner*. Always remind yourself during social interaction with women in the social circle that you are there to get *laid*, not *liked*. Being a fun, friendly, supportive, talkative guy is a great way to be beta male and put you into friend zone pretty fast.

Instead, your frame with the women in your social circle is the *very cool but slightly aloof older guy*. When talking to women, you use the same frame that I talked about in earlier chapters, using the same conversational techniques I outlined in *Get To Sex Fast**. You're polite, cool, calm, confident, very outcome independent, and just a little aloof, almost like you're *not* there to make friends. Do not have long, drawn-out conversations with these women that last longer than 30 minutes or so. If you find yourself in such a conversation, end the conversation before then, just as she's starting to open up to you. End it politely, but end it. Remember what I said earlier: hot younger girls are accustomed to men of all ages kissing their asses and wanting to have sex with them. You must do the opposite. Don't indicate at all that you find her attractive in any way. You're friendly and polite, but you don't give a shit. As I talked about in the daygame chapters, **indirect game** is what you must employ.

When do you pull the trigger and pitch a date / meet? The answer is "not too soon, but not too late."

"Too soon" usually means the first or second time you met her at the social gathering. Social circle game is a slower type of game. It's not like night game or even daygame where you can just talk to a girl for

---

* http://www.gettosexfast.com/

a few minutes and then contact close or pitch a date. Yes, you *can* do this and you *can* be successful if there are extenuating circumstances, like you're unusually good looking or have huge status in the social circle. But if these things don't apply to you, you need to build more rapport and mystique about you before you date pitch.

"Too late" usually means after you've had many conversations with her over an extended period of time. At that point, you're in friend zone, and you're probably never going to have sex with her no matter how good you are. She knows you too well now, and you've blown your opportunity window.

In terms of the right time to pitch a date, I can't give you a specific opportunity window, since every scenario is different and different social circles are more conducive to sex than others. For example, you can pitch dates much faster in a dancing environment than you could a business environment. That being said, speaking very generally, the best opportunity window tends to be once you've had three or four different conversations with her, which lasted well more than five minutes, over the same number of meets. This means that if you have three conversations with her in the same day, which probably doesn't count. I'm talking about three different conversations over three different days/meets.

Again, I don't consider myself a social circle game expert, but three to four good-but-brief conversations on separate days *seems* to be the best time to date pitch.

You date pitch by keeping things very safe and simple, just as I outlined in prior chapters. Just say something like, in a *very* outcome independent manner, "You're pretty cool. We should hang out some time." If she responds positively to this, contact close her (ideally get her phone number, which should be very easy at this point; you might even already have it!) just like I talked about in the daygame chapter.

Then, follow up with her the next day, and follow the usual sequence I outlined in *Get To Sex Fast**. At this point, you're officially out of social circle game and into dating game.

---

* http://www.gettosexfast.com/

Multiple Women in the Same Social Circle

Once you get good with social circle game, you will quickly reach a point where you'll find yourself having sex with multiple women within the same social circle. The second downside of social circle game is that this needs to be managed, and it can blow up in your face if you're not careful.

The good news is that if you're dealing with VYW, as I said earlier in this chapter, their ASD is going to be so low that many, perhaps even most VYW won't even mind if they realize you've had sex with other girls in their circle. On the extreme end of that spectrum, some women might even be attracted by this.

If you're dealing with mostly VYW and you're not involved in long relationships with multiple women in the same social circle, there is nothing to worry about other than the usual stuff of keeping things quiet. Don't go around bragging to everyone that you banged Ashley last week. It's entirely likely that Ashley may tell everyone she banged you, but you have no control over that, and if she gets any blowback about that, she has only herself to blame.

If you are dealing with women older than age 23 and/or you're actually carrying on ongoing FB or MLTR relationships with women in the exact same social circle, this is much more complicated. I've said before that regardless of anyone's age, it is usually not a good idea to carry on an ongoing relationship with two or more women in the same social circle. If the women meet only once every few months or so, that's probably fine, but if they meet more often than this, drama is almost sure to develop, and both of your relationships will be at risk.

Therefore, if social circle game is your focus, it is my recommendation that you maintain two or three concurrent but separate social circles, where you are only having an ongoing relationship with one girl in each circle. I realize that represents more work on your part, but that's the only way to keep drama and conflict levels to a minimum. To be clear, it's okay if you've already had sex with more than one woman in a social circle. I'm only talking here about having recurring sex with multiple women in the circle *at the same time*. So you could conceivably have an FB relationship with Girl A in a circle, then when that ends have an MLTR relationship with Girl B in the same circle, and when that ends have a quick fling with Girl C, then circle back to Girl A or B. Multiply this by two or more social circles, and you'll have plenty of women to play with once you get good at this style of game.

Chapter 15

REFERRAL GAME

This chapter assumes that you've already read the last chapter on social circle game, so if you skipped ahead to this chapter for some reason, stop right now and read the prior chapter first; otherwise this chapter won't make a lot of sense to you.

Referral game, if and when you can structure it, is the fastest way to get to sex not only with women, but with younger women. Many of the fastest meet-to-sex times I've had with women in my entire life were from referral game, some as low as under 30 minutes. Also, some of the best looking women I've ever had sex with were from referral game. So referral game is one of the fastest ways, if not the fastest way to get to sex with very attractive, younger women other than paying for it.

Sounds perfect! What's the catch? The catch is that usually referral game just isn't an option, so referral game is not something you can reliably depend upon as a regular system of bringing new younger women into your sex life. Instead, referral game is an every-once-in-a-while play, to be taken advantage of when you see the opportunity. This means you need to be aware of these opportunities if and when they arise (and if you date enough younger women, they will).

Referral game is when you take a younger women you're already dating in an FB, MLTR, or OLTR relationship (we'll call her "Girl A"), and using her help (or at least her permission), you have sex with other women she knows (we'll call her "Girl B"), including her friends, acquaintances, family members, and in some extreme cases, complete strangers she goes and gets for you (and perhaps her, if she likes girls).

Referral game is not only possible, but extremely easy once you get the hang of it. Over the course of my history, using referral game, I've had sex with various Girl A's sisters, cousins, best friends, and in one case, even a mother. As I discussed in the last chapter, women under age 23 have such low levels of ASD and live in such a hyper-sexualized world that this stuff is no big deal, provided you do everything correctly.

As I said above though, it's not a perfect system. There are several limitations, including the following:

1. You can't be in a monogamous relationship. The relationship must be either verbally stated as either open or very, very casual.
2. Girl A must be under the age of 23 or so. It is extremely unlikely, and in most cases impossible, for any woman over the age of 23 to agree to do this unless money is involved. As you might imagine, only women with very low levels of ASD will agree to something like this, and that means VYW, age 23 (or so) or below.
3. Girl A must have some attractive and relatively young female friends or family members who also have reasonably low levels of ASD. If Girl A has no hot female friends for family members, obviously it's not going to work.
4. You have a nonmonogamous EFA already established with Girl A and are able to convey at least some of that to Girl B. This is so Girl A will go along with your plan *and* so Girl B won't feel like she's hurting or betraying Girl A somehow.

5. It's true that in some extreme cases, Girl A can actually go out into the world and bring women back to you, but in order for this to happen, she must be reasonably confident and have strong bi-sexual desires. If she doesn't have both of these things, it's unlikely to happen no matter how badly you want it (again, unless money is involved).

Because of all these limitations, most of the women you date, younger or otherwise, won't qualify for referral game at all. You'll just have to be happy having sex with her and the other separate FBs and MLTRs you go get yourself. (Not that it's a bad thing, of course.)

Instead, as you bring new younger women into your life (age 23 or under) as you get to know them, you can start asking them questions about their social and family life. Does she have a best friend? Does she have a bunch of girlfriends? Does she have a sister? If you're really ballsy, you can ask about her mom, including her age and her appearance, and so on. If she does indeed have cute, young female friends or family members, you pitch to her that the three of you should hang out. From there, you sexually escalate on Girl B, either one-on-one or with Girl A (which would mean a threesome, or close to it).

From there, you can actually repeat the process with Girl B. You can start having sex independently with Girl B, then ask her about other girls *she* knows, and have sex with those girls (Girls C, D, and so on). I know that sounds crazy, but I've personally done it several times.

To give you some specific real-life examples, take a look at this chart.

Referral Game Example

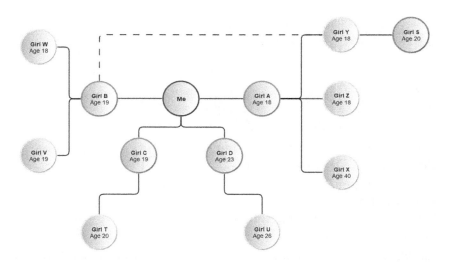

It's an actual representation of what has happened with four particular VYW I dated, colored in pink, Girls A, B, C, and D. All four women were under age 23 and did not know each other. By having sex with these four women and using referral game, I actually ended up getting sexual with a total of *twelve* women instead of just the original four. (And I haven't done this with just these four women; I've done this with more; these particular four are just examples.)

Here's what I did. Using my normal dating techniques (mostly online dating) I met and had sex with four new women, Girls A, B, C, and D. I started seeing them as regular MLTRs or FBs, as I always do (I never do one night stands; I don't see the point). In this particular case, Girls A and B I was seeing at the same time (at least part of the time), Girls C and D I met later.

Using referral game, I made sure to meet other women in their social circles.

Girl A was a friggin' gold mine. She was one of the first VYW I had ever dated. She was 18 years old, extremely extroverted, had lots of cute girlfriends, and just happened to have some really attractive female family members as well. First, I had sex with one of her best friends, Girl Z, also 18 years old. Two years later, I had sex with her mom, age 40, Girl X. One year after that, I had sex with her sister (Girl Y), who by then was 18 years old. Shortly after that, I had sex with one of the sister's co-workers (Girl S). (This was one of the few times I was able to go "two levels deep.") I had sex with all five women just from meeting and having sex with one girl, Girl A.

Moreover, using the relationship management techniques I describe in *The Ultimate Open Relationships Manual**, I had sex with almost all of these women multiple times over a period of several years. Girl A I first met and had sex with when she was 18, but I kept on having sex with her (off and on at least) until she was 26. If you're doing the math, that's eight years. It was similar with Girls Z and S.

Girl B was a 19-year-old Asian girl I dated as an FB, then later an MLTR, then later almost an OLTR, for many years until she was about 25. During that time, I had sex with her best friend (Girl W, age 18) and another of her close friends (Girl V, also 19 at the time). Girl B also was very good at bringing new women to me she met on Facebook, though this is a slightly different type of referral game that I didn't include in the chart and will explain a little later.

You'll notice a dotted line between Girls B and Y. When I wanted to have sex with girl Y (the sister of Girl A), she was a little reluctant initially because she was a Type Three. She liked me but had never been with an older man. I put her and Girl B together, and they hit it off. Girl Y became attracted to Girl B, and soon we all had a threesome, then I was having sex with Girl B independently. Once you're at a higher level of game and confidence, you can do things like this; place some of your women together to improve your results.

---

* http://www.haveopenrelationships.com/

Girls C and D were more typical cases. Each time, I simply had sex with one of their friends. With Girl D (who was *barely* young enough to do this at age 23), I had sex with her best friend, Girl U, age 26, first via a threesome and later independently. With 19-year-old Girl C, I had sex with one of her friends (20-year-old Girl T) once I stopped seeing girl C. Girl T actually ended up being a much longer relationship than Girl C. Thanks, Girl C!

You'll notice that Girl U and Girl X are both well over age 23 (26 and 40 respectively). When I said the woman needs to be age 23 or under, I was speaking only of the referring girl, not the referred girl. You can meet and have sex with a 19-year-old and then get "referred" to her 30-year-old cute family member or co-worker with no problems. But you can't do the reverse; you can't meet and have sex with a 30-year-old woman and expect her to help you have sex with her 19-year-old cousin or co-worker. The 30-year-old has way too much ASD for that and would never agree to such a thing (though yes, there are rare exceptions to every rule), and would be insulted if you even hinted at wanting such a thing.

So as you can see on this chart, I only had to meet four women via normal game, but was able to have sex with twelve women with minimal time and effort because of referral game. Not bad. And again, I've done this with more than just four women. This is the power of referral game, a subtype of social circle game.

What Referral Game Is Not

Referral game is when you actively pursue a woman you're dating friends or family members of, with her permission or active assistance, to get to sex with these new women as fast as possible. I am not talking about meeting Girl A's friends at a party and just start gaming them over time. There's nothing wrong with doing that, but that's just standard social circle game. Instead, with referral game your only objective of the entire interaction is to have sex with Girl B and do so very quickly. It's not to hang out with her and have fun, not to cross your fingers and fantasize about something someday, and not consider her a possible back-up if things with Girl A don't work out.

I am also definitely not talking about having sex with one of Girl A's female friends and then hoping Girl A never finds out. That's cheating, which is always a recipe for eventual drama. Even if you're in an open relationship, having sex with a woman's close friends or family members without telling her first can often lead to problems. As with all of my dating and relationship techniques, I'm here to show you how to *avoid* drama, not create more of it. Referral game is very transparent and above-board. Both Girls A and B are well aware that you have had sex with both of them. How happy they are about that is a different story, and depends on the nature of your relationship with Girl A, as well as the frame you've been keeping with her, but there is no hiding or deception involved in any of this.

Pros and Cons of Referral Game

The negatives of referral game are that it requires all the right parameters and requirements to be in place (that I listed above), and it requires strong game and a directive frame. If you're a complete beginner at dating much younger women, or at nonmonogamous relationships, you should probably wait until you've got a little experience under your belt and consider yourself at least at an intermediate level before attempting referral game.

Another slight downside to referral game is that ongoing relationships with the second level B girls are unlikely, since they tend to view Girl A as your "primary" or your "girlfriend," even if she's only an FB. Most B girls are going to be reasonably brief flings, though there can be exceptions to this (as was the case with Girl T in my example above).

The great thing about referral game is that it's *almost literally no work*. There is no going out and meeting women, no online openers, no phone calls, no messaging, no dates, no number closes, no scheduling first or second dates, no flaking, and no time needed establishing rapport (at least not really, you'd be shocked at how little you need). As long as all the referral game parameters have been met and you're at least somewhat confident and have a strong sexual frame, it's amazingly easy. Honestly, it will be easier than any other type of dating or seduction you've ever done.

It's also very fast. I have no problem declaring it's probably the fastest form of game out there. I've had many referral game lays that were literally under one hour grand total from meet-to-sex. Several were under 30 minutes, and virtually all of them were with literally zero money spent.

How To Do It

Here are the step-by-step instructions on how to do referral game. Just like any other skill, it will take a little practice and you may screw this up the first few times you attempt it. Don't let that dissuade you! Keep at it, and I promise it will work. You'll be pleasantly surprised when it does.

1. *Establish and maintain a strong, nonmonogamous EFA in a relationship with your Girl A.*

   It is critical that you establish a nonmonogamous EFA with your Girl A and stick with it. If you have a normal monogamous relationship with her, or like most men, you *act* like you have one, referral game is going to be effectively impossible.

   How to create and maintain a nonmonogamous EFA is beyond the scope of this book. I lay out exactly, step-by-step how to establish and maintain an open or poly relationship in my book, *The Ultimate Open Relationships Manual**. If referral game is important to you, consider that book as required reading.

2. *Ensure that all of the referral game requirements have been met.*

   The five requirements for referral game that I listed earlier in this chapter must be met before you attempt anything. She must be age 23 or under, she must have reasonably low ASD, she must have at least a few cute girlfriends or family members she's close to, your nonmono EFA must be strong, and if you want her to actively go get women for you, she should have some strong bi-sexual tendencies.

---

* http://www.haveopenrelationships.com/

3. *Start probing about other women in her social circle.*

Start asking her about her female friends and family members, if you haven't already. Just do this as part of any normal conversation. Don't start throwing questions about this out of the blue. Women love talking about other women in your life so this should be easy. In many cases, VYW will even say things like, "Oh yeah, my friend Suzi is hot! Let me show you a picture!"

Encourage this. Once you identify other women in her social circle that you consider attractive, ask her about how close she is to these women, how often she hangs out with them, and so on. If these are women she's close to, comfortable with, and spends time with at least semi-regularly, they're good candidates for Girl B's. If she's not close to them or if they are people she only sees rarely, these are probably not good candidates.

4. *Gently pitch a mutual meet-up.*

Once you've picked a potential Girl B you want to have sex with, pitch a meet-up for all three of you to Girl A. Don't hide the fact you think Girl B is attractive from Girl A. You can simply say something like, "Girl B is really cute! The three of us should hang out next week."

If your sexual frame is really strong and Girl A has lower ASD, you can flat out tell GGirl A that you want to fuck Girl B. "She's hot. I'd have sex with her. The three of us should hang out!"

If she gives you a strong no, ask her why. She'll either have an *internal* reason or an *external* reason. An *external* reason is when she says something like, "Oh no, if we did that Girl B would tell my mom!" or "Girl B is my friend, but she gets drunk a lot and posts a lot of drunk shit on social media, so that wouldn't work." External reasons are valid. If she really feels strongly about it, then forget about this possible Girl B and try again later with a different one.

An *internal* reason for saying no is when Girl A actually gets angry, jealous, or defensive with you. If she reacts this way, you've likely done something wrong. Either your nonmonogamous EFA wasn't as strong as you thought, or her ASD levels are higher than you thought. If she's just a little jealous but not upset, then keep gently pushing the issue and see how far you get; she may just shrug, change her mind, and say okay. However, if she's adamant about her internal reason, then this particular woman isn't a good candidate for referral game, and you'll have to look elsewhere (and ask yourself what you did wrong, because I promise you probably made some kind of mistake in the past with her somewhere).

The timing of when you pitch this mutual meet-up is important. A few parameters around this:

- Only pitch this when Girl A is in a good, relaxed mood. If she's had a bad day or you guys just had an argument, then this is not the time. Wait for a better day. There's no rush.

- Never pitch or say anything like this during sex with Girl A. I know men who have made this mistake, and that will just cause jealousy and perhaps drama, no matter how low her ASD is or how much she likes you. Only talk about this stuff when you're both fully clothed and hanging out casually.

- Do not pitch this if Girl A and B are currently mad at each other. Women, particularly younger women often experience huge ups and downs during their relationships with their female friends and close family members. Sometimes they love them, sometimes they utterly hate them. Be aware of this, and only pitch when Girl A and B are on good terms.

- Do not attempt this when Girl B has a relatively new boyfriend. It's best when Girl B is either single or has had the same boyfriend for at least six months or more.

- If Girls A and B are related, you can still do this, but you need to tread more carefully. You probably don't want to tell Girl A that you actually want to have sex with her sister, but you can instead tell her that her sister "seems cool" and that the three of you should hang out. If she agrees, then just proceed as normal.

5. *Schedule a time for the three of you to hang out.*

Once she agrees, you need to schedule a time for all three of you to hang out. Let her do this, just encourage her to do so. Once she's agreed to do this, don't push her hard to actually schedule it. Just tell her to text Girl B and set up a time. If she doesn't do it right then and there, let it go. It might be a week or more before she gets around to it. That's perfectly fine; as I said above, there is no rush, and if you keep bugging her about it, you reduce the odds of it ever happening.

Make sure the meet-up is only the three of you. Do *not* agree for the meet-up to be a few of Girl B's other friends. **No, just the three of you, or else call off the meet.** Also, ideally make sure the meet-up occurs in the evening (night time is sexy time) and at a location you can completely control, which ideally means your home.

What if Girl A agrees to do this but never gets around to actually setting up the meet? Just make a mental note of it, and use the two-step referral game process that I discuss later in this chapter.

6. *Qualify Girl B.*

Once things are scheduled, or close to being scheduled, make sure Girl B is of legal age (if she's young). Make sure there is no new boyfriend in her life (again, an *old* boyfriend is okay). Try to determine if she's a sexual girl with minimal ASD (most VYW are in this category). If you can, try to determine if she's a Type Two; has she ever had sex with an older guy?

7. *Make sure Girl A is with the program.*

As best you can, make sure Girl A is "on board" with you "playing" with Girl B. Unless you're actually planning to do a threesome, don't go into specifics about what will or won't happen, and don't start talking about threesomes or taking turns or whatever. Just get her acknowledgement that "it's on" tonight. That's all you'll need. (If you are both actually pre-planning a threesome and have verbalized that, of course that's fine too.)

8. *Pre-plan logistics.*

At this point, either you and Girl A are actually planning a threesome with Girl B, or you're planning on just "hanging out." Either way, you need to pre-plan logistics so that sex can occur with Girl B. This means you have several things ready to go, like:

- Condoms
- Lube
- Knowing *exactly* how and where the sex will occur (the bed, the couch, the floor with blankets, etc.)
- Ensuring isolation (just you and Girl A and B, or even just you and Girl B)
- Anticipating any logistical problems that may arise
- Etc.

One of the most common reasons guys screw up things like this is because *they didn't properly plan the logistics.* This is always important when you know the odds of you having sex with any new woman is high; with referral game where two women are involved, importance is even higher.

9. *Hang out with the two girls and have fun.*

Once you're with Girls A and B, relax and have fun. Keep things very light, casual, friendly, and funny. Don't discuss any tough or controversial topics. Keep the conversation on very simple, surface-level subjects. If she's young, use all the techniques and frames in this book.

Also, let the two girls interact with each other. They're already friends, so let them talk, and be cool about letting them talk to each other without putting yourself into the conversation. I've had sex with many Girl B's within 30 or 60 minutes of meeting her even though she literally didn't know who I was or anything about me except that I was dating Girl A. Very similar to a first date, the more talking Girls A and B do, and the less talking you do, the higher your odds of success become.

10. *Have sex with either Girl B, or both of them in a threesome.*

After the three of you have relaxed and chatted a bit, start to sexually escalate on either both women (if you're going for a threesome) or Girl B (if Girl A has left, or has temporarily left the two of you alone). I will cover how to do this in either scenario.

Threesomes

This is not a book about how to do threesomes, and such a topic is outside the scope of this book. However, using a threesome as a mechanism to be successful with referral game does apply to our topic of younger women, so here I will summarize how to initiate a threesome. If you need more detail, feel free to Google this topic or purchase more materials on it.

Remember that 90% of whether or not this referral game threesome will work is based on all the groundwork you've laid up until now. If you've done everything correctly so far, your odds of getting this threesome are very high. If you attempt a threesome and get a hard no from either Girl A or Girl B, that doesn't (likely) mean you attempted the threesome incorrectly. Rather, it means you didn't lay the proper groundwork I described in this chapter. Keep that in mind if you ever attempt this and fail.

1. *Establish the primary and secondary woman.*

The two women you're going to have sex with at the same time are not equal, and shouldn't be. There should always be a primary woman; the woman you're seeing, and a secondary woman; the new woman you're bringing into the bed with the two of you. In this case, it's obvious which one is which. Girl A must be your primary woman, and Girl B must be your secondary.

Even if the two women are both people you're already seeing, one still needs to feel like she's a little more important than the other. Before the threesome ever begins, you need to be mentally clear about which girl is the primary and which one is the secondary. (Don't actually tell the women this, just get it clear in your mind.)

2. *Initiate in the correct sequence.*

If you're a beginner at threesomes, the safest sequence to follow for a threesome is the following:

A. All three of you should play with each other very briefly.

B. Have sex with the secondary woman first (Girl B), and get inside her as quickly as possible. Enjoy her for a while.

C. Switch to the primary woman (Girl A) and finish (orgasm) with her.

If you're still raring to go after you orgasm with Girl A, feel free to play with both women for a while or grab Girl B and go to town on her a second time if she's willing.

This order ensures that you get to have sex with Girl B quickly (to avoid any last minute ASD from her) and that Girl A feels more special, preventing possible jealousy. It's a winning combination that eliminates a lot of problems and works pretty much every time.

3. *Be very strong, and lead at all times.*

Initiating a threesome takes confidence and leadership. You can't be passive. You need to be strong and *lead* the women into the threesome. The two women sitting in front of you are never going to initiate a threesome, even if they're very attracted to you and each other. (The one possible exception is if they're very drunk.) *You* are going to have to initiate everything.

Be commanding, strong, and directive. Tell them exactly what you want them to do. "Get on the floor." "You, kneel down here, and you, lay down here." You get the idea.

Obviously, if either woman says no, then stop immediately. However, if you've laid the groundwork I've described in this chapter, this is unlikely to happen. I've literally never had a woman say no to this stuff once escalation began because I always lay all the necessary groundwork.

4. *Initiate using a proven method.*

   There are two ways I know that work well in initiating a threesome: the direct way and the indirect way.

   The direct way is the method I use. You simply relax for a little bit, talk to the two women while on the couch or bed (not the kitchen table), and get them comfortable. Then, you just start in. Start sexually escalating on the primary woman. While doing this, touch the secondary a little bit. Encourage your primary to start touching the secondary as well. If you've laid all the groundwork I've described above, you won't need to "encourage" your primary to start getting sexual, and the secondary will follow her lead.

   Once things start moving between the three of you, shift your escalation from your primary to the secondary, and have sex with her, while letting your primary touch whomever she wants during this time. And away you go.

   Here's an important point. Remember that there is no rule that requires the two girls to get sexual with each other during a threesome. Many women are down for threesomes but do not want to get sexual with the other woman; both women just want to be sexual with you. This is perfectly fine, and don't push this if you sense resistance. Just encourage both women to make you feel good. You can even end up taking turns if you wish (I often do).

   If the direct method is outside of your comfort zone, then use the indirect method. It's something I stole from Neil Strauss many years ago (I steal a lot of his stuff, don't I?), and it works (again, if you've laid the groundwork). It's not a technique I use since I'm a more sexually dominant guy, but if you're not a dominant guy or if you're a beginner, it's a valid technique.

While the three of you are talking, start talking about how great it would feel to get a massage from two people at the same time, moving their hands on either side of your body at the same time and in the same way. Once the conversation has moved to massage, tell them that the three of you should try it.

Take off your shirt, and lay face down on a large bed or on a blanket on the floor. Tell the two girls to get on either side of you and massage your back, but to move their hands at the same time and in the same way. Have them do this for just a few minutes and then tell Girl A that it's her turn.

Have her take off her shirt and lay face down and start massaging her with Girl B for a few minutes. Then it's Girl B's turn for her to lay face down without her shirt on, and for you and Girl A to massage her.

Massage her for just a minute or two, then start making out with Girl A while you're both still massaging Girl B. All you have to do now is let nature take its course, and within a few seconds you'll be having a threesome.

This method is nice because it "warms up" both women nicely and slowly, gets them accustomed to touching each other, and rolls into sex nicely. (Again, if you're a more dominant or experienced guy, you can skip all this and just get to the good stuff like I do.)

When Girl A Leaves You Alone With Girl B

Sometimes, instead of a threesome, Girl A will simply leave you alone with Girl B. I personally prefer this to threesomes. (I actually don't really like threesomes, since I prefer one-on-one sex; I simply use threesomes as a tool, but that's just me.) Sometimes she'll do this as part of a plan the two of you designed in advance. Other times she'll just do this on a whim or because of some other circumstantial reason. Yet other times she'll do this because it's late at night and she'll just go to sleep while you and Girl B are still awake. There are all kinds of possible scenarios where this happens. I've even had times where, earlier in the evening when I was in the bathroom or something, Girl A literally asked (or flat out told) Girl B to have sex with me, and to expect that later in the evening, Girl A would leave the two of us alone. That's not the norm but it can happen.

Regardless of how or when Girl A leaves the two of you alone, simply talk with Girl B for just a little bit, and then sexually escalate. Do not talk to Girl B for too long. It's possible you may lose your window of opportunity. Talk just for a little bit, and just start to slowly touch her and/or kiss her, using the techniques I outlined in Chapter 17 of *Get To Sex Fast**.

If she says she's worried about Girl A hearing the two of you, or Girl A "finding out," tell her that you and Girl A have already talked about it and she's "perfectly cool" with you and Girl B having sex. It's quite rare you'll get this objection if you've laid all the groundwork, but it's still possible.

If Girl A has actually left the building for the evening and isn't coming back, this escalation with Girl B is even easier, since she won't have that worry. However don't plan on this occurring; usually Girl A will still be in the vicinity.

Two Step Referral Game

The above method of standard referral game will work in most cases. However, some of my referral game successes happened with only the minimal cooperation of Girl A at all. Often, they occurred after Girl A and I stopped seeing each other. I call this "two step referral game." It's still referral game, but a different variation. Here's how you do it.

---

* http://www.gettosexfast.com/

1. *Follow steps one through six in normal referral game, above.*
   Strong, nonmonogamous frame with Girl A, ensure that all the parameters for referral game have been met, then find a qualified Girl B that you meet with Girl A at some point. Then if, for any reason, sex does not occur, proceed with the next steps.

2. *Contact close Girl B.*
   Get Girl B on your social media and, if you can, her phone number.

3. *Maintain light contact with Girl B.*
   Contact Girl B via social media or by texting on at least two separate occasions. You want it in her head that it's "normal" to be communicating with her this way. Do *not* contact her all the time, or even regularly; that's friend zone, and if you do this, the odds of ever getting to sex with her drop like a stone. Just a few times, sporadically, is all you need.
   When conversing with her, just be friendly and fun, nothing too deep or serious. Keep your conversations on the short side.

4. *When you view it as appropriate, pitch a meet.*
   Whenever you're ready and you feel it's appropriate, contact Girl B and pitch a meet. The words "ready" and "appropriate" mostly depends on you and your individual scenario. They vary greatly to the point where I can't give you any specific guidelines on when to do this.
   Many men wait until they stop seeing Girl A to do this, and that's probably the safest move, though your success odds with Girl B will often go down if you wait this long. If the relationship with Girl A is casual enough, you can hit up Girl B while still seeing Girl A; I've done this one or two times and never had any major issues. Use your best judgment here, depending on you, your relationship with Girl A, and Girl A's personality, ASD, and jealousy levels. I would not hide what you're doing from Girl A,

however. Let Girl A know, at least eventually, even if that means I don't tell her until after I meet up with Girl B.

Simply message Girl B and pitch a casual date, simply following the same sequence I outline in *Get To Sex Fast**, except that in many cases you can get right to sex on the first date if you've already spent some time with Girl B and she's comfortable with you. If you've never met her in person, you may have to wait until a second meet, and if so, that's fine.

Be sure to tell Girl B that seeing her is "allowed" in your relationship with Girl A. Hopefully, Girl A has already encouraged you to do it; tell Girl B this if that's the case. Beyond that, it's standard stuff at that point.

Referral Game Used With Sugar Daddy Game

I'm jumping the gun here a little bit, since I'm going to describe how to do sugar daddy game with younger women in great detail in Chapters 16 and 17, but here I'll describe how to manage referral game within a sugar daddy dating environment where Girl A is actually receiving money from you in some form or fashion.

As I will describe in those chapters, there are two kinds of sugar daddy game, one where you don't pay the women and one where you do. If you're not paying the women, then referral game is identical to what I've described above. If you are paying them, referral game changes a bit, in that it gets much easier.

When you are maintaining pay-for-it sugar babies who are under the age of about 26 or so, referral game becomes much simpler. Since the women know they're getting paid, and any cute friends they refer to you are (they assume) also going to get paid, some of these women will actually volunteer their friends without you even asking. This has happened to me more than once.

---

* http://www.gettosexfast.com/

If this happens, immediately ask to see pictures of the girl she's talking about on her phone. Once she shows you, if you like what you see, get her phone number from Girl A right then and there. Then tell Girl A to contact Girl B in the next 24 hours to expect a text from you. Your best bet is to send a picture of yourself to Girl A's phone (make sure it's a damn good picture of you, as I talk about in Chapter Five of *The Ultimate Online Dating Manual**) and have her send it to Girl B so she knows what to expect.

Then wait 24 hours or so, and text Girl B. If Girl A has done her job, all you need to do is schedule a meet with Girl B, and you're in. Your success rate for this is very, very high. (As a matter of fact, I don't think I can ever remember when this *didn't* work.)

Your sugar babies don't need to volunteer their friends; you can just ask them, and you should. Just flat-out ask them if they have any cute girlfriends, sisters, cousins, co-workers, or whatever. Some will say no, but some will say yes. Then look at their pics and proceed as I described above. Just like with normal referral game, sugar daddy referral game is very, very fast, simple, and with very high odds of success.

If you date enough sugar babies, you would seriously get to the point where you could get 100% of your new women supplied via sugar daddy referral game. It's quite possible, though only if the number of women you play around with is decently high (since again, many women won't be able to refer you to anyone, or won't want to).

---

* http://www.onlinedatingsuccessnow.com/

Chapter 16

SUGAR DADDY GAME – PART ONE: MEETING WOMEN

Sugar daddy game is when you meet much younger women, using sugar daddy dating sites, and attract them into your sex life via either giving them money or acting like you might. Sugar daddy game has become quite popular over the last several years, and its popularity is increasing. Rising divorce rates continue to provide lots of older men who can afford it, and the continuing softening of economies all over the Western world, as well as sharply rising prices for college, child rearing, and health care continue to provide a large and ever-growing supply of attractive younger women interested in these arrangements.

If you have absolutely no interest in paying normal girls (college students, young single moms, etc.) to have sex with you, or indicating that you might, then feel free to skip this chapter and the next where I go through the process of sugar daddy game in detail. The downside is that yes, often you need to either give them money or provide more expensive dates (though not always). The upside is that it's extremely fast, efficient, and takes far less time to get to sex with very attractive younger women than with standard game. Moreover, the women on the sugar daddy dating sites are *much* more attractive than on normal dating sites (though this is less true than it was a few years ago). It's also a fantastic option for men who are in open marriages or open relationships with a serious partner, since sugar daddy women (called "sugar babies") don't care if you're already taken, and most cases, actually prefer it.

As always, you need to weigh the pros and the cons. I've done lots of sugar daddy game in addition to normal older man / younger woman game, and I like and can recommend either. If you're over the age of 35 (preferably over 40), and have a decently high income with not a lot of debt, and are a very busy guy who doesn't want to take a lot of time with women outside of sex, I recommend sugar daddy game; it's a viable option for you. It's particularly useful with men like me who have an open marriage / relationship with a live-in wife or girlfriend, since minimal "dating" is required and your special lady will be assured that your FBs are mostly having sex with you because they know they're getting paid (whether or not they're actually getting paid, and whether or not that's the actual reason they're having sex with you).

Sugar daddy game is a subset of online dating. While many of the same concepts apply, there are also some stark differences.

The Two Types of Sugar Daddy Game

There are two distinct types of sugar daddy game, both requiring a different set of techniques.

The first type, the most common by far, is pay-for-it game, where older men hit up the women on these sites, negotiate how much cash they're going to pay the women who respond to their openers, and then have sex with them quickly, paying them either cash per visit or a monthly/weekly payment, creepily called an "allowance." It's essentially prostitution, though most of the women involved are not actual working prostitutes (though some are). Many are single mothers or college students needing cash to support themselves, their kids, or their tuition. This type of game involves the least amount of skill and often takes the least amount of time, but the financial costs are higher.

The second type of sugar daddy *game* is don't-pay game. This is truly sugar daddy game. This is where you present yourself as a wealthier, higher value man who doesn't mind spoiling a girl. You meet up with the women via sugar daddy sites, have a first and perhaps a second date, and have sex with them without paying them anything. Again though, the dates involved are often going to cost more than is typical, so in many cases this is not actually "free" unless you get lucky or you're very good-looking. First and second dates costing $50-$200 are not unusual for don't-pay game, so be prepared for this possibility. Every once in a while you might be able to get laid literally for free (or close to it) like I do with normal online dating, but this will usually be rare and not a repeatable, reliable outcome.

Does some level of game play a role in either type of sugar daddy game? Yes. Even pay-for-it sugar daddy game requires some. If you don't believe me, then picture some disgusting-looking, dumpy, a-hole, extreme Asperger's-ridden guy walking up to a young hottie in a club, slapping down $1000 cash, and saying, "Have sex with me! I'll give you $1000!!!" Will that work? Of course not.

It works the same on the SD sites. Ugly, dumpy, uncalibrated, needy, high-income beta males constantly hit on the women there and throw out huge and insane offers ("I'll give you $8,000 a month!!!"), and most of these guys don't get laid. So, some baseline level of game and physical appearance is required to make sugar daddy game work. *Everything* I discussed in part one of this book regarding appearance, outcome independence, and so on apply here. Less with pay-for-it game, much more for don't-pay game. However, it is true that with sugar daddy game (both types), less game is required than for normal online dating, since your money (or the promise of it) will make up for a lot of your unattractiveness and mistakes... though not all!

Examples of Sugar Daddy Sites

Seeking Arrangement - This is the best-known sugar daddy site and the one that gets the most press, though sugardaddie.com is larger.

SugarDaddie.com - This is the largest sugar daddy site, though the number of women there varies from city to city.

Established Men - This site has more verifications for the men signing up. It leans towards longer-term sugar daddy (i.e. paying) relationships.

Sugardaddyforme.com - A smaller site but one that still works in many larger cities.

What's Your Price - This is a site started by the same guy who started Seeking Arrangement. It's where you actually pay women for first dates. Not for sex (though some women will do that if you're down), but just for the first date. If that sounds horrible, you're right. I don't recommend this site at all, regardless of which category of sugar daddy game you want to use.

The Differences Between Sugar Daddy Sites and Normal Online Dating Sites/Apps

1. **The women are far more attractive.** This is the most noticeable difference. Regardless of your tastes, super-hot women will be available to you on these sites, particularly those under age 25. Once you get over age 35, the numbers on the SD sites start to thin out, though there are indeed women well over 35 present.
2. **Response rates are far higher.** As I talked about back in Chapter 11, on "normal" online dating sites, your response rates as an older man going after much younger women are

going to be extremely low, even if you do everything right, with rates as low as 1-3% not being unusual. On sugar daddy sites, the response rates are easily 30% to 50%, sometimes even 60%. Unlike on normal dating sites, these women know (or think) they're going to get paid hundreds of dollars, so they're more than happy to respond to your openers.

3. **Many women will actually open you.** On normal dating sites, it's rare that women will actually hit you up unless you're very good looking. Even then, most of the women doing so will be the unattractive types (since these women aren't getting as many incoming messages, they must open men cold like we do with women). On sugar daddy sites, particularly if you're not ugly, look clean cut, and have good photos, you will sometimes be bombarded with women opening *you*, including very good looking ones. Many of these women will be from distant cities, but many will be local too.

4. **The site is full of actual hookers and professional sugar babies who will be aggressive about getting their hands on your wallet.** If the first three items above make sugar daddy sites sound like a paradise, this is where reality sets in. The majority of the women on these sites are there to get your cash, and if you're not willing to fork it out, they're not going to be having sex with you, no matter how good your game is or how good looking you are. It's important to understand that the majority of these women will demand this *even if they're legitimately attracted to you*, which is why game or looks don't apply here as much as they do with normal online dating. Over time, this trend has worsened, and I predict it will worsen further as sugar daddy game becomes more mainstream.

There are four types of women on SD sites:

A. **Escorts.** These are actual prostitutes using the site to get business. These sites say they don't allow these women, but the reality is a decent percentage of women are precisely that: hookers. No amount of game will work on these women (yes, there are always ultra-rare exceptions to every rule). You pay, or they vanish fast and move on to the next potential customer. These women easily represent at least 10%-20% of the women on the site, possibly more.

B. **Professional Sugar Babies.** These are not hookers per se, but experienced hooker-like women who have their solid "price," will not negotiate on it (much), and will absolutely not have sex with you unless you pay up, no matter how strong your game is or even if they're attracted to you. If you don't agree to their price they're gone in a flash, onto the next high-income beta male who will agree to their fee. This represents the majority of the women on these sites, making up at least 60-70% of the women on there.

C. **Successful-Boyfriend Seekers.** These women aren't sugar babies in that they won't demand money-or-nothing. Of course they will take money if offered (and most men on these sites do offer, a lot, and these women happily take it). However, making money is only their secondary objective. Instead, these women are hardcore Type Twos whose primary objective is to date a *successful* older man. If you have strong game and do everything right, often you can date and/or have sex with these ladies without directly paying them cash. However, they will still expect you to be older and classier and/or higher income than average. They will often (though not always) expect more gifts, fancy dates, and/or financial support if you continue to see them beyond sex once or twice. This is the smallest category of women on sugar daddy sites, making up less than 10% of the total.

D. **Newbies.** These are the new girls who have never done an "arrangement" before and are there only because they need help with college tuition, supporting their kids, paying their debts, or buying nice clothes. As such, they aren't as jaded or battle-hardened as the other women and are much more flexible when it comes to money. If you have decent game, often you can have sex with them without paying anything. However, if you want to continue to see them beyond sex once or twice, they *will* expect some money, or they'll move on to a beta male boyfriend or another sugar daddy who will happily provide the cash you refuse to give her that she "needs." These women represent perhaps 20% of the women on sugar daddy sites.

When you first start talking to a woman on a sugar daddy site, it's relatively easy to identify which category she's in. If she's an escort or professional sugar baby, she will almost immediately start referring to you by love names, such as babe, hun, sweetie, sexy, and similar. Often they will throw out specific cash amounts before you do. Another tell-tale sign of these women is if they go sexual in the conversation before you do. True-blue escorts often will also sometimes throw around hooker terms like incall, outcall, hosting, or party.

5. **Long-term relationships are generally not an option on sugar daddy sites unless you're willing to pay.** If you're a player out for just one or two night stands, then this doesn't affect you; go for it and have fun. If you're a companion-seeker or a nonmonogamous relationships guy, you may be disappointed. As described above, all four types of women on sugar daddy sites will *eventually* demand money or leave, with rare exception. Women on sugar daddy sites also tend to get boyfriends or other paying sugar daddies *much* faster than women on normal dating sites. So maintaining a longer-term relationship with any of these gals, whether monogamous, nonmonogamous, casual, or serious, is going to be next to impossible (barring the usual exception to the rule) unless you're willing to start paying them on a regular basis in some form or fashion. Just be aware of this. (I'll cover ongoing relationships with sugar babies in the next chapter.)

Differences in Sugar Daddy Game vs. Normal Online Dating

If you want to give sugar daddy game a try, use all the techniques already described in chapter 11 and in *The Ultimate Online Dating Manual*. The vast majority of them directly apply here and will increase your response rates, date rates, and sex-per-date rates. However, use the below techniques to modify and adjust for sugar daddy game.

1. **Go right to sex on the first date if that's what you want.** This is particularly true if you're doing pay-for-it game. If you're willing to pay, there's no need to meet at a bar or whatever. Just have her come right over to your place, or worst case, meet at a coffee shop briefly so she's comfortable and then quickly bounce to your place. You don't have to do this and you may use the two date model I describe in *Get To Sex Fast*[1], but many women coming from a sugar daddy site, particularly the ones under age 23, will be down for sex on the first date if they know they're getting paid. If you're doing don't-pay game, meeting at a bar or similar location then getting to sex on the second date may help; it depends on the woman and your level of dating skill.

2. **It's okay to message women who haven't been online in several days.** Back in Chapter 8 in *The Ultimate Online Dating Manual*[2], I said you should only message women who are currently online first, then open women online within the last 24 hours, then only very reluctantly bother with women who haven't been online two days or more.

This rule of thumb still applies to sugar daddy sites, however because the number of women is smaller and their motivation is higher, it's perfectly okay to open women who haven't been online in three, four, five

---

[1] http://www.gettosexfast.com/
[2] http://www.onlinedatingsuccessnow.com/

days, or even a week or more. It will probably take more time for these women to respond, but often they will. You should still avoid opening women who haven't been on the site longer than about 15 days; those women have moved on to boyfriends and likely won't be coming back any time soon.

Negotiation Skills for Pay-For-It Game

If you just want to get from zero to the sex with hot younger women and you're willing to spend a little money for pay-for-it game (or are at least open to the possibility that you *may* have to pay for it), then a key skill to learn with sugar daddy game is how to negotiate with candidates in order to get your costs as low as possible.

How much does pay-for-it sugar daddy game cost? It's hard to give specific numbers, since these figures will vary from region to region and country to country. Speaking very generally, in the United States, most women on sugar daddy sites will usually *ask* for anywhere from $300 to around $800 for having sex. There are a few odd outliers who will demand $1000 or more, but these are rare in most cities.

This applies only to sugar babies you meet cold on an SD site. Sugar babies you meet through referral game will ask for much less, sometimes as low as $100, and possibly even lower. (This is yet another huge advantage of referral game, even in the pay-for-it realm.)

I emphasize the word *ask* in the above paragraph because what women will ask for is usually not what they'll actually *take*. Most women on these sites are quite negotiable and will drop their asking prices 20-50% just by you engaging in some basic negotiating tactics which I'll explain in a minute.

As I already said above, there are some women who are not negotiable under any circumstances. These are, using the four categories I described above, the escorts and professional sugar babies who have been doing this for quite a while and already have a track record of being showered with cash by desperate older beta males willing to pay their exorbitant prices. These women will not budge on their prices and often will actually get upset with you if you suggest paying them less than what they're offering, especially if you offer them much less (which in most cases, you should). When you come across these young ladies, gently excuse yourself from the conversation and move on. This is not someone you want in your life, and there are plenty of other very hot, younger women on these sites who will not be this inflexible.

The best time to discuss the financial aspect of the scenario is *when she brings it up*. A rule I've found that works best is if she doesn't bring up the issue of money, you shouldn't either. Only discuss the money aspect when she brings it up, and don't worry, she will (unless she's a real newbie or a very submissive successful boyfriend seeker).

Most women will bring this up before you meet. Sometimes they'll bring it up during the messaging conversation on the web site, but more often than not they'll bring it up over phone texts as you're scheduling the first date.

Most women will ask *you* what you "had in mind" for how much you want to give her, or she will say something indirect like she's "not free," or that she "likes a man who helps her out," or that she "really needs money," and so on. When she does this, *ask her what the last guy gave her*. This is very critical, and it accomplishes several things.

First of all, it establishes the number she had in her head all along. After much trial and error (and several angry girls who never saw me because they didn't like the numbers I was tossing out) I have found that sugar babies on SD sites almost always expect whatever the last guy gave them. This is completely regardless of how old or young she is, how attractive or ugly she is, or if the monetary figure made any sense. If she's average looking and the last guy gave her $600 for sex, that's what she'll expect from you. If she's hot as hell and the last guy gave her $250, that's what she'll expect from you. (You will run into both of these examples and many others.) If you throw out numbers that are very different from what she's accustomed to, she may get angry and actually end the conversation right then and there and block you on the site. Yes, it's stupid, but welcome to sugar daddy game.

The second thing this does is that it forces her to say a number first. Rule number one in negotiation is *the first person to say a number loses.* By asking her what the last guy gave her, it forces her to give you a number first. Also, the young girls on these websites have no negotiation skills, so they'll have no idea what you're actually doing when you ask them this number.

Once you have that number, now you can negotiate it downward. Here's a general overview of some negotiation basics for sugar daddy game (that apply to business and financial scenarios as well):

1. React with shock at whatever number she gives you. Say something like, "Wow. 400? Really? Well... I really didn't realize it was that much. Ummmm...." Sometimes you can send just that text and she'll drop it by $100 or more, instantly.

2. Offer her 40-50% less than what she's asking for. Once you express shock at her number, offer her a much lower one. State it very nicely, almost like a question. For example, "How about $200?" Don't be too forceful, such as, "That's crazy. I won't pay you more than $200." The odds of that working are much lower. Remember, these are young, very attractive girls with hordes of hungry beta males just desperate to throw money at them. She really doesn't have to take your offer. So negotiate, but be nice while doing so.

You need to offer her much less than what she's asking for, since, per usual negotiations, you'll end up with a number between what you ask for and what she'll ask for. Therefore, you need to ask for a number *lower* than you're planning on actually paying. For example, if she says $400, you can't say $300, because she'll demand $400 again, or perhaps say $350, saving you just $50. So instead, when she says $400, you'll pitch $200 or maybe $250. This will likely cause her to settle on $300 (or so).

That being said, you *can* go too low. For whatever reason, women on SD sites are very touchy about men offering less than they think "they're worth." If she says $400 and you pitch $50 or $100, she might get very upset and instantly drop you. Again, this can happen. So using a guide of 40-50% of her initial offer is a good guideline to use.

You'll get the occasional woman who throws some crazy numbers at you, like $1000 for sex or $600 just for dinner with no sex. In my opinion and experience, there is no working with these women, just tell her she's too expensive for your budget and move on to other women. To repeat, these numbers have nothing whatsoever to do with how attractive these women are, how fun they are to be with, or how good they are in bed. All they indicate is how desperate, ugly, or stupid the last sugar daddy she was fucking was.

What if she doesn't give you a number at all? This is not the norm, but it can happen. If that's the case, try to get a number out of her as best you can. Remember, the first person who says a number loses. If she absolutely can't or won't give you one, then you'll have to lowball her. I would like to tell you to just offer her $50, but again, that will just piss her off. Instead, play dumb, like you have no idea how this stuff works, and say something like, "Well, I didn't really have a number in mind. I don't know. Like $100?" Or you could offer $150 if you live in a city where sugar babies demand more money. She'll probably still get upset, but she won't end the conversation, since she at least knows you're serious about giving her money. At this point, she'll finally give you her real number, then just use the above techniques to get this number down as much as you can.

What if she doesn't bring any of this up until you're actually together in real life? This sometimes happens, and it's a very good thing when it does. This means she'll actually be more flexible in her numbers. Women (and people in general) always are nicer and more flexible in person than over texts or semi-anonymous dating site messaging. Just use the same negotiation techniques listed above, and stay very nice.

You'll almost always get a better deal if you discuss the money stuff in person, which is why you never want to bring up the money issue until she does.

This covers the price of her "company" the first time you meet up and have sex with her. If you start seeing her on an ongoing basis, you can easily start dropping her price even more. I'll explain how to do that in the next chapter.

Don't-Pay Game

If you have stronger levels of confidence, game, or have higher than average good looks, you can go for don't-pay sugar daddy game instead of pay-for-it game. This means that you're going to meet women on SD sites and present yourself as a successful older man. You will imply that you're "generous" but you're not actually going to agree to any specific numbers.

As I said, don't-pay game requires a higher degree of game, confidence, and/or good looks. So if you're an absolute beginner, I don't recommend pursuing this until you have some other younger women experience under your belt (unless you just want to experiment for fun).

With don't-pay game, if she brings up the issue of money, you strongly but gently tell her that you're a successful man and you're generous, but that you don't want to do anything transactional and you want to just "see how it goes." Tell her that she's welcome to never see you again after you meet up if she doesn't find you to her standards. If she ignores all that and absolutely demands some money, then you have a decision to make. Either you can just move on and forget her, or downshift into pay-for-it game and begin the negotiation process I outlined in the prior section. It's completely up to you.

As you might expect, the number of times you're successful with don't-pay game are going to be much less than pay-for-it game, since most of the women on SD sites aren't going to go for don't-pay game no matter how amazing you are. So, if you're going to stick with don't-pay game, be aware you're going to have to put in a lot more numbers, send out many more openers, talk to many more girls, go on many more first dates, and so on.

When you meet up on the first date, if you're not going straight to sex, you need to really play up the "rich, successful guy" angle. Meet her only at a very, *very* fancy bar. No coffee shop dates or anything like that. Many don't-pay guys actually meet women at fancy restaurants and buy her food (though I've never done this). Dress up very nice; a full on suit and tie is best if you want to maximize your odds, (unless you have fantastic physique, in which case you want to wear some really nice, expensive clothing that really shows it off well). Wear a nice watch. If you drive a nice car, make sure she sees it. And so on.

If this sounds like you may attract a bunch of gold diggers, you're more or less correct. The more wealth and success she smells on you, the less likely she is to demand money when you have sex. As to whether or not she'll demand money from you down the road, I'll analyze that in the next chapter.

All the usual frames and techniques about confidence, outcome independence, and the dating techniques I talk about in *Get To Sex Fast** are all paramount with don't-pay game. You need to be a confident, outcome independent, chill guy who does everything right.

---

* http://www.gettosexfast.com/

Chapter 17

SUGAR DADDY GAME - PART TWO: SUGAR DADDY RELATIONSHIP MANAGEMENT

You may already be aware that I have a comprehensive book on how to create and maintain nonmonogamous relationships called *The Ultimate Open Relationships Manual**. If long-term, nonmonogamous relationships with much younger women are what you're after, I highly recommend you get that book and follow its techniques, since pretty much all of them apply to older men dating younger women.

This chapter is specifically about how to carry an ongoing sexual relationship with a sugar baby, a woman you met and initially had sex with from a SD dating site. The nature of these relationships are a little

---

* http://www.haveopenrelationships.com/

different from standard ones, and you need to be prepared for these differences and mange them so you're not surprised…. or get ripped off.

I have maintained several consistent and off-and-on FBs via sugar daddy relationships over the past two or three years, along with my usual, normal FBs and MLTRs (though today I have a live-in OLTR wife with FBs on the side). There are indeed some distinct differences with sugar baby relationships, as well as a lot of similarities.

The Money Aspect

The biggest difference is obviously the money factor. If you're doing pay-for-it game with an ongoing sugar baby, your goal is to further negotiate her price down as you continue to see her, getting her per-visit price down as low as you possibly can.

The good news here is that it's extremely easy to do this. As I talk about in great detail in *The Ultimate Open Relationships Manual**, once a woman has had sex with you twice, you achieve a point called Lock-In, where she's "locked in" to you now to some degree, and will keep having sex with you without you needing to "game" her anymore. It's at this point where dating/seduction ends, and where relationship management begins.

This applies to sugar babies as well. Just like in non-sugar baby relationships, once a sugar baby has sex with you twice (meaning sex with you on two separate occasions), she will install you in a place of trust within her mind, in that you are a normal, reliable, non-creepy guy she can at least somewhat rely upon. You have officially separated yourself from all the weird, creepy older men on the sugar daddy site she was getting weird messages from (and believe me, women on SD sites get a constant slew of disgusting messages on a regular basis).

It's at this time you can further negotiate her price down. It's a very simple procedure I have done with numerous women. It has literally a

---

* http://www.haveopenrelationships.com/

100% success rate with women under age 23 (meaning it's worked with literally *every* woman under 23 I've tried it on), and a 68% success rate with women age 23 or over. Here it is:

1. Negotiate her initial price down as best you can, exactly as I explained in the last chapter.
2. Have sex with her using this price once.
3. Have sex with her again, on a different day but as soon as possible, using that same price.
4. Schedule sex a third time.
5. The day you're going to meet up with her, before you meet, text her to confirm everything (which is something you should do anyway with VYW). Once it's all confirmed, say, "Okay. BTW I can only give you X today." Give her a number that's around $100 less than what you paid her before. So if you gave her $300 before, tell her you can only pay her $200 today. If you paid her $400, tell her $300, and so on.

If she's under the age of 23, either she'll just say "okay," or she will complain a little bit. Just be nice but adamant and tell her that's the best you can do today. If you've done everything else correctly up until now, she will agree to it. As of now, that's her new price you can start paying her per visit from now on.

If she's over the age of 23, she's going to be much more upset. In most cases, she will complain profusely, much more than the under-23s, but she will likely, though very reluctantly, agree to see you for the reduced price "just this once." Usually, she won't it bring up during your meet, but if she's a more confident or dominant woman, she will, and complain about it some more.

After the meet, she might refuse to see you again or may see you again but only for her original price. At that point, you have a decision to make: keep seeing her at her high price, or dump her and look for someone else less expensive. The choice is yours (I always dump them and find someone else more flexible).

This doesn't always happen with sugar babies older than 23. As I said above, this technique still works 68% of the time, at least so far, so there's only a 32% chance she will literally refuse to drop her price.

This is one of the reasons why, if price is an important factor for you (it is for me; I'm a financial tightwad), you might want to stick with sugar babies who are under the age of 23. These women will be far more flexible about price once you achieve Lock-In, though you "pay" for that reduced price by dealing with all the usual problems of VYW in relationships that I outline in Chapter 20. As usual, the choice is yours.

"Allowance?"

Many sugar daddy relationships involve a thing called an "allowance" that I alluded to in the last chapter. This is when the man pays the sugar baby a flat amount per month with the expectation that she's going to be sexually available for him.

Unless you are extremely wealthy and have money to burn, never, ever, *ever* agree to this. If you're doing pay-for-it game, always insist on a pay-per-visit system. Just about every time I've seen a sugar daddy couple with an allowance, the woman abuses it. She gets her fat paycheck at the beginning of the month, then dumps the guy after two weeks. Or she's always "busy" when he wants to hang out with her. Or she goes on some trip and is gone for a week. And so on. The only time I've seen an allowance work in the long-term is when the two were living together or living in the same building, or she was actually living in an apartment he was renting in his name, or similar arrangement (and I wouldn't do that either).

Giving a sugar baby an allowance encourages her to not see you as often, whereas giving her money on a per-visit basis encourages her to see you as often as she can and to make herself available to you. If you give her an allowance, she may start to actively avoid you, but if she's on a per-visit basis, *she* will often text *you* out of the clear blue so you two can have sex so she can get her cash.

The good news is that I've literally never had any woman complain that she wasn't getting an allowance. As long as you're giving her cash every time you see her and never try to rip her off or fail to do what you promise, she'll be perfectly fine with a per-visit arrangement. It's pretty hard for women to complain about this.

Don't-Pay Game

If you're doing don't-pay game and you're not paying her at all, expect her to start asking for money at some point. The odds are good that she will ask for some financial gifts or support in some way *eventually*, so you need to expect this and come up with a battle plan for when this happens. I'm not saying it always happens; sometimes it doesn't, but it usually does unless the scenario is unusual (like you're extremely good looking, or famous in some area, or her career benefits in some way by seeing you, etc.).

One way to sometimes get around this is to offer mentorship or other career benefits to her. Help her start a business, get a job, get in with a certain company or crowd, set up a web site, do her taxes, assist with some legal issue, and so on. I've done things like setting up web sites for women, given them old laptops I received from my business clients that I no longer needed, and help them fill out their child support paperwork. Often this can sustain a don't-pay sugar daddy relationship for much longer, though it doesn't always work.

As you might expect, the younger she is, the more likely a don't-pay relationship will sustain. These kinds of relationships are much less likely to sustain for six months or more if she's 27 years old, whereas if she's 20 she may stick around for quite a while.

Plan ahead. Come up with two or three things you can offer a don't-pay sugar baby if/when she starts bugging you about helping her out financially. That way, when it happens, you're covered.

FBs Only!

All sugar baby relationships must be FBs only. Keep your relationship to just friendship and sex, and nothing else. Don't make a sugar baby into an MLTR or OLTR. I'm not saying it isn't possible, since I have seen it done. I'm saying that taking a financial transactional relationship and turning into something with real romantic feelings and/or commitment is very likely to blow up in your face unless the scenario is extremely unusual *and* you are an accomplished expert in younger woman game and relationship management. (Even then, I probably wouldn't recommend it.)

If you keep all of your sugar babies as FBs, you'll save yourself all kinds of hassle and trouble. Making normal VYW into MLTRs or OLTRs is hard enough; making sugar baby VYW is double as hard. Just don't do it.

That doesn't mean you can't have a strong bond of friendship and friendly caring with a long-term sugar baby FB. As of this writing, there is one FB I have who is a sugar baby and whom I've been seeing for many years. She's just an FB, and that's all she'll ever be (I already have a girlfriend OLTR so I couldn't make the sugar baby an MLTR or higher even if I wanted to.) Yet, while she's an FB, I still care for her greatly, consider her a close friend, and want good things for her. We have a good relationship.

As I've said in my other writings before, the "F" in FB stands for *friend*, even a close friend. So if you want to make your sugar baby a close friend, do so. But keep her as a friend and don't go further.

What if she's a don't-pay sugar baby? Could she be upgraded to an MLTR or more at some point? The answer is yes, but I would make sure she's had at least *six months* of really good behavior as a sugar baby FB without bitching about money at all before upgrading her to MLTR.

Referral Game Is Extra Effective With Sugar Babies

This is just a reminder about referral game; something that works *very* well with sugar babies. Make it a point to attempt referral game with *every* sugar baby you have sex with at least three or four times (unless she's over the age of about 30; yes, you can go as high as about age 29 for referral game if they're pay-for-it sugar babies). It won't work every time, but you will be shocked at how often, well, and cheaply it does work.

Where Sugar Daddy Game Belongs In Your Life

Sugar daddy game is strictly one of many tools in your toolbox. Like any other tool, it should be used in the scenarios for which it is suited. It's an effective and powerful tool for high income older men who are too busy or too old for normal game. However, it should not be something you use as your only source of sex, all the time, for the rest of your life, nor should it be something you base your life around.

Here are the scenarios where sugar daddy game works best:

- When you are extremely busy with work and don't have a lot of time to date.
- When your travel schedule is extreme and brutal, thus making it hard to maintain normal relationships.
- When you are over age 60 and you haven't been taking care of your looks, making dating much younger women a difficult task.
- When you are in a serious, long-term OLTR or OLTR marriage like me, and you can only have sex with women who are FBs. Sugar daddy game is extremely useful here, since the women won't care if you have a girlfriend or wife. Indeed, many sugar babies *prefer* it. Also, it gives your girlfriend/wife an extra added layer of comfort knowing that you're paying the women for sex instead of the women wanting to have sex with you for free (even if the women *would* have sex with you for free, or for other reasons), and that feelings are less likely to develop.
- If you're unusually picky and have a very specific, narrow, and unusual "type" of woman that you like that is hard to find without paying for it.

My point here is to make sure that sugar daddy game remains a tool you use for the jobs where it's required. Unless you are over 60 (or under 60 but look like you're over 60), or your situation is unusual, I do not recommend sugar daddy game as your only way of getting sex or relationships. Instead, I recommend sugar daddy game as a useful supplement to your overall sex and relationship life.

Chapter 18

SPECIAL RULES FOR FIRST AND SECOND DATES

In this chapter, we're going to talk specifically about what to do and not do when you actually have a VYW (or similar much younger woman) face-to-face in front of you on a first or second real-life date. In *Get To Sex Fast¹*, I go over exactly what to do on first and second dates in great detail, and just about everything I describe in that book applies here. However, there are a few changes you'll need to make when dealing with a much younger woman as opposed to a woman within your own age group. So consider this chapter as a supplement the content in *Get To Sex Fast²*.

A Quick Overview of My Dating Sequence

If you haven't read *Get To Sex Fast³* or my dating and relationships blog for men⁴, here is a brief summary of my dating system that will get you to sex as quickly as possible with the minimum amount of time and money spent. (If you are already familiar with my system, you are welcome to skip this section.)

---

¹ http://www.gettosexfast.com/
² http://www.gettosexfast.com/
³ http://www.gettosexfast.com/
⁴ http://www.blackdragonblog.com/

The basic structure is for you and her to meet up on a casual, non-threatening first date at a cool bar, coffee shop, mall, or whatever, and just talk to her for one hour. During this first date, you will spend the first few minutes getting her comfortable and talking about easy stuff, like her family, friends, job, etc. Then you'll move the subject to her past dating and relationship experiences, and then possibly, if things are going well and you have enough time, talk about sex.

During the entire first date, you are keeping your mouth shut and letting her do 80% of the talking. Most of your talking will be asking her questions to keep her talking. Doing this is actually easier with VYW, since these women will be less interested in you and more interested in themselves, which for our purposes is a good thing, since the more a woman talks during a first date, the more likely she is to have sex with you quickly.

At about one hour you wrap up the date and leave. You do not kiss her or compliment her appearance in any way whatsoever.

The very next day you text her, have a brief text conversation, and pitch the second date, though this "date" will be at your place. You schedule this second date to happen as soon as possible.

On the second date, when she comes to your place, you get her comfortable for the first few minutes, talk on your couch for a while, then sexually escalate, and have sex.

The above formula, once you get good at it, will get you to sex within three or four hours of face time, grand total, and with less than $25 spent in most cities. It works extremely well and has been field tested not only by me but by thousands of men all over the world. It works even better with younger women (once you get the hang of younger woman game) because of their much lower ASD.

Again, if you need more detail on exactly how to do all of this, get a copy of my book, *Get To Sex Fast*.

---

* http://www.gettosexfast.com/

Managing Her Nervousness

Unlike most other women you've met up with on a date, the younger woman you're about to meet up with will possibly be quite nervous during the first few minutes of the first date, particularly if she's a VYW, and even more so if she's a Type Three. This is normal and natural, and it's your job to anticipate and manage this. You must diffuse this nervousness as fast as possible so she can relax. If a woman never relaxes on a first date, you'll never see her again. If she never relaxes on the second date (if any), she'll never have sex with you.

Here are the best ways to reduce or eliminate her nervousness.

1. **Don't be nervous yourself.** Yes, I realize that's easier said than done, especially if you're new at this. You still need to put yourself into a frame of mind where you are as relaxed as possible. *If you're nervous, she'll be nervous. If you aren't nervous (or do a great job at not acting nervous), her nervousness will quickly dissipate within just a few minutes.*

   Make sure your mind is clear. Make sure you've had plenty to eat and have drank plenty of water before the date. Make sure you've had a good eight hours of sleep the night before (that's important!). Make sure you are walking tall and straight, and are dressed in a way that builds your confidence. While sitting with her, make sure your body language is *extremely* relaxed. Smile a lot. Laugh a few times (though not constantly). Speak in a normal tone of voice. *Relax.*

   Remember, you're the older man here. You're the elder, the superior. There's literally no reason to be nervous.

   If you're feeling nervous right before a first or second date, put a big, dumb smile on your face and hum your favorite song to yourself as you walk to the date location. Remember your outcome independence and remind yourself that you don't need her (which is factually true). This is just one girl in an ocean full of girls who would love to meet you and be with a man just like you. If it works with her, great. If not, that's great too, since it's just more practice for when you meet the next one.

2. **As soon as you meet her, act like you're already old friends.** I talk about this in *Get To Sex Fast** but it's doubly important here. Just say "Hey" and start right in talking to her like you've known each other as good buddies for several years. Doing this is amazingly effective even if it sounds strange. I do it on first dates with VYW all the time and it works every time.

3. **Do not judge or criticize any of her young, stupid, or immature behaviors.** As I explained in prior chapters, women under the age of 23 are still teenagers, so when she acts like one, don't call her out on it. Just smile and let it go. If you start acting like her dad and judging or criticizing her immature behaviors, her nervousness will go up, as well as her force fields, and you're not getting laid.

So if she repeatedly uses the word "hella," or talks about how she just got done smoking some weed, or mentions she just got back together with the boyfriend who beat her up last month, just smile and say, "Cool." Accept every dumb, immature thing she says or does.

Once you're in a relationship, past Lock-In, you can judge or tease her on all this stupid stuff if you want, but you can't do this before you've had sex with her twice, and certainly not on a first or second date.

Conversation

In terms of what younger women like to talk about, I've found there are two distinct types of VYW: "shallows" and "singulars."

Shallows are girls who talk about vacuous stuff for hours on end. These are the girls who will spend 20 minutes talking about their hair, that "bitch on Snapchat," or their stupid ex-boyfriend. They enjoy talking

---

* http://www.gettosexfast.com/

about things like music, famous people, parties, makeup, getting drunk, bitchy girls, cute guys, and social media. Deep topics of any kind bore them quickly.

That does not necessarily mean shallows are dumb (though many are). Many shallows are extremely intelligent, with high IQs and even higher social intelligence. It just means they like to discuss a wide array of shallow topics that directly impact their lives as younger women.

Shallows tend to be fun, wisecracking, fast talkers. They switch topics often, laugh a lot, and enjoy being silly. The best thing to do with a shallow is to just *let her talk* (which frankly you should do with all women on a first date or second date). Stay upbeat and match her vocal tonality and speed. Be funny and joke around with her. Do *not* try to get her into any super-deep conversations about any deep topics. Keep the conversation fun and light.

Singulars are very different. Singulars are VYW who are deep, complex, emotional, tunnel vision thinkers. They usually have one key issue that they love to obsess and talk about. Every singular has a different key issue and they will talk about it for hours on end. It could be relationships, fantasy novels, acting, their school or career goals, their kids, travel, or something else. Whatever it is, that's her "thing," and she'll love to talk about it forever and get deeper into it than you ever thought possible.

Singulars tend to be more shy, quiet, and less emotional than shallows. They also tend to be very smart (though some aren't). It's much easier to engage in a conversation with a singular since she'll usually steer you towards her favorite topic. However, you'd better be on your toes because if she senses that you're not as smart or perceptive as her, she's going to disqualify you as "not my type" or a man who "doesn't understand me." That doesn't mean you need to know anything about her topic (though if you do you'll score some major points and increase the odds of success significantly). You just need to demonstrate that you're an intelligent guy with great curiosity about her and her deep thoughts.

The majority of VYW are shallows, as one would probably guess. My estimate is the percentages break down into 70% shallows, 30% singulars.

Talking About Sex and Relationships

One of my core first date techniques is to eventually start talking about sex and relationships. With younger women this is no different. The easiest way to do this is to just ask her about her last boyfriend, assuming she doesn't bring it up on her own, which often she will.

Once again, do not be surprised at the immature or flat-out stupid situations she describes to you about her past relationships or sexual encounters. She's a younger woman, so sexual craziness is a core part of her life (or at least recent past). She may go on and on complaining about something that was clearly her fault or something very minor in a past relationship. Conversely, she may tell you about how inexperienced she is, and that she's (for example) only slept with one or two men in her entire life. Either of these kinds of extremes is possible, so be prepared for them and don't let them surprise you.

No matter what you hear, never get on a high horse and disparage her about anything she tells you unless you're clearly being sarcastic (and even then you need to be very careful; with shallows it's fine, singulars may not like it). As always, just relax, go with the flow, and keep her talking.

Kino

Another technique I talk about is kino; non-sexual touching on a first date. Kino is always a good thing if you can do it, but with much younger women you need to be more careful. If she was *at all* nervous at the start of the date, skip all kino and don't worry about it until the second date. If she's a more confident or sexual woman, then kino is fine. Regardless, when in doubt, just skip kino and save that for the second date for when you actually escalate to sex.

Transportation

One of the biggest differences between VYW and women your age is that a sizeable percentage of VYW are not going to have cars and/or be able to drive. If you live downtown in a large city, then transportation logistics aren't any different with these women since everyone of all ages will be using mass transit. If you don't live downtown in a city core (I certainly don't), you're going to have to figure out transportation logistics for younger women in ways you probably won't need to with normal women.

The most obvious and easiest way is to just pick women up and drop them off. I get a lot of concerned questions about doing this from my readers. The assumption is that picking up a woman and dropping her off for dates comes across as too beta or too much of a try-hard. Normally, that *might* be the case, but with VYW who literally don't have cars and have very low ASD to begin with, this is perfectly fine. I've done it many times, and it does not seem to negatively affect my success rates in any way. Indeed, it will actually help you, since many times VYW won't have any other option of getting to you besides you doing something like this.

What about using taxis, Uber, or Lyft? You are welcome to do this if you have a very high income and don't mind the expense, otherwise forget it, since a very simple round trip on a ride-sharing service like Uber or Lyft can easily cost you $80. This murders the low-cost dating system I normally espouse, but if you're a higher income guy, or if you're doing pay-for-it sugar daddy game anyway, feel free to do this if you wish.

The only danger when providing transportation for younger women for dates is when they're *not* VYW and they're significantly over the age 23. If she's 29 years old and she asks you to come pick her up and drop her off, something is wrong, and you need to dig a little deeper. Also be aware that many Asian, Russian, and Eastern European women living in the West use this "I can't drive" thing as an excuse to "betaize" men. This is obviously not a good idea. I would adopt a general rule that if she's over 25, transportation to and from first and second dates is her responsibility, and to be much more flexible if she's under that age. (Again, this assumes you live in the outer-city or suburban area where mass transit is not an option.) Once you've had sex twice and in an ongoing relationship, if at that point she needs help with transportation every once in a while, that's fine as long as it's reasonable.

Chapter 19

SPECIFIC TECHNIQUES FOR TYPE THREES

As I talked about back in Chapter 3, the majority of the time you're going to be dealing with Type Twos. These are the younger women that legitimately like and want to date older men. You're not going to deal with any Type Ones; they won't even agree to go out on a first date/meet with you, and you shouldn't even try.

That leaves the Type Threes; those younger women who don't *want* to date or have sex with older men but *could* under certain conditions. Sometimes, you will be dealing with them in dating scenarios. A rough estimate, if you date a lot of younger women, is about 15-20% of the women you'll be interacting with in real life will be Type Threes, the rest being Type Twos. This rises to about 25% if you do exclusively sugar daddy game.

Once you get accustomed to the advice in this book, Type Twos are going to be a slam dunk for you. They want to date an older man like you and their ASD is minuscule, so once you become practiced in these techniques, you're going to be surprised at how fast you get to sex with Type Twos once you actually get them to meet you in real life.

Type Threes, on the other hand, are a little more tricky. The process of getting to sex with them is a little more delicate. It's for this reason that I recommend to beginner older men focus on Type Twos first, and quickly weed out the Type Ones *and* Type Threes. Once you get good with the Type Twos, the Type Threes aren't that much more difficult, but tackling a Type Three when you've had limited success with even Type Twos is going to be much harder. So consider Type Threes as an intermediate level of younger woman game.

Overall, Type Threes will be less excited about you than the Type Twos. They will be much more hesitant and nervous. This means you must be less aggressive and allow the process to take a little more time. I have had sex with many Type Threes and they are not necessarily harder to game, just that they require a softer, slower, more patient approach.

Identifying Type Threes

Obviously you need to identify whether or not a woman is a Type Two or Type Three before you adjust your approach accordingly. Here's the rule: *You don't try to identify a Type Three. Instead, you attempt to identify a woman as a Type Two, and if she's not a Type Two but she's still there in person with you on a real-life date, or clearly interested in meeting you, she's automatically a Type Three.* This is because if she's a Type One, she would never have agreed to meet up with you in the first place. So if she's not a Type Two, she's a Type Three. Since Type Twos are easier to identify than Type Threes, it's better to see if she's a Type Two, meaning she's a Type Three otherwise.

There's no precise way to identify a Type Two vs. a Type Three, but there are ways of making good, educated guesses that are likely to be accurate. Here are the possible traits of a Type Two, listed in no particular order. Not all Type Twos will have all of these traits, but if she has many of them, she's very likely a Type Two.

- She's already had sex with one or more older men before you.
- She seems confident and at ease when talking to you (in person, not online).
- She seems to really like you, with good eye contact, interested body language, and perhaps even some compliments.
- Her voice is slightly louder than normal, and she's very talkative.
- She's sarcastic and teases you.
- She expresses disdain for men her own age.
- She flat out says she prefers "older guys" or "guys over 30" or similar. (Note: Most Type Twos are *not* going to verbalize this, so don't expect it. Some will, but most will not.)
- Most (or many) of her male and female friends are significantly older than her.
- She works in a normal "adult" job, like at an office (as opposed to something like a fast food restaurant or being unemployed).
- Her father is older than you are, especially if he's much older (10+ years).
- The number of her past sexual partners is pretty large.

Here are the typical traits of Type Threes:

- She's never had sex with a man more than about four or five years older than her.
- She's a little quieter and reserved when talking to you. She doesn't ask any questions and tends to just answer you without volunteering a lot.
- She demonstrates nervousness before or during the date.
- Over texts, she sends lots of confirming questions and seems a little hesitant or nervous.
- All the men she's dated or had sex with before you were in her age range.
- She's been on first dates with one or a few older guys but never had sex with any of them.

- She acts her age; if she's under 23, she uses a lot of teenage language with words like "OMG," "hella," "slay," "tight," "bomb," "legit," and so on.
- She's unemployed or works at a typical teenage job (fast food restaurants, etc.).
- Her father is around your age or younger.

With those above lists, you should be able to determine if a woman is a Type Two, at least in most cases. If she's not, you need to assume that she's a Type Three.

Less or Zero Kino

With Type Twos, you can kino on the first and/or second date, just like any other woman, and she'll like it. (Though, if you're in any doubt, don't kino at all.) However, with Type Threes, kino will usually make them uncomfortable. It's too much, too fast.

Therefore, if you're at least reasonably confident that a woman on a first or second date is a Type Two, don't kino her *at all*. Wait until you're actually ready to have sex with her. I've had sex with many Type Threes where there was zero kino before the actual clothing came off. This is perfectly normal with these women.

Assume More Time Meet-To-Sex

As I summarized back in Chapter 10, I teach a two-date system. With Type Threes and older men, you may very well be looking at three dates before sex, sometimes even four dates if you're a little new at this. This is normal and often necessary for Type Threes. You're doing something far outside her comfort zone so you need a little more time to get her sexually comfortable. Expect this and don't be surprised by it.

The good news here is that because of VYW's lack of ASD and betaization desires, these extra dates won't reduce the odds of sexual success the way they would with women your age. With most women over the age of 23, every date after date number three with no sex actually lowers the odds of ever getting to sex, since you're pushing "beta" and "provider" buttons within her rather than sexual ones. This is not the case with Type Two VYW (at least usually), so don't worry about this.

However! Do *not* use this as an excuse to keep dating any woman, of any age, past three or four dates without any sex just because you're scared, lazy, or feel guilty. As I talk about in detail in *Get To Sex Fast**, all this does is waste your time, waste your money, and reduce the odds of you ever getting to sex with her. (By the way, this goes double for sugar babies.) Remember, this is about getting to sex *fast*. Getting to sex *slowly* is too often the same as getting *no* sex.

As usual, don't escalate to sex on the first date (unless she's a sugar baby and ready to go). On the second date with a Type Three, you sexually escalate, but be very gentle and don't push it if she resists. Keep sexually escalating on every date, but do so in a very gentle, low-pressure way. If you're doing everything correctly, you will usually have sex on the second date, often the third date, and sometimes the fourth date with Type Threes. I personally think waiting for sex past the fourth date is too long, for any woman, but feel free to make your own decision regarding how long to wait.

Make It Normal

This is an effective technique for being successful with Type Three VYW that I stumbled upon completely by accident when I first started dating much younger women.

If you make it clear to a Type Three that another VYW in her family or social circle have already had sex with an older guy and enjoyed it, she will often be more comfortable with the concept. If such cases exist and she's not already aware of them, it's up to you to educate her. During your conversations with her, ask questions about this. If you discover she

---

* http://www.gettosexfast.com/

has (or had) any female friends, acquaintances, co-workers, or family members who are younger, and have dated or had sex with a much older men, and had a good time with it, you need to reiterate this to her, and really get into that topic. Your frame is that this is normal and fun (which it is!).

The first Type Three I ever had sex with was an 18-year-old Asian girl (though born and raised in the USA). Her close friend was dating me as an MLTR and loving it, and heard nothing but good things about how "older men are better" from her. So although she was a *hardcore* Type Three, getting to sex with her wasn't a big problem. (This is also a textbook example of how well referral game works.) A few years later I was on a second date with a 20-year-old, and through our conversation she revealed that her 19 year old cousin had a fling with a 40-year-old guy. I asked her if her cousin enjoyed it, and she said yes. I asked her if there were any problems, drama, or a bad breakup, and she said no. Then I just shrugged, smiled, and said, "Like you and me." We were having sex within 20 minutes.

Obviously referral game is the easiest way to do this, but if that's not an option, here's what you do:

1. Ask her questions about other women in her family who might have dated, had sex with, or married much older men with positive results, then have her expound upon that experience. Bring out the positives of the experience.
2. Show her other friends or acquaintances she knew of, even if they were distant Facebook friends, who have dated (or are currently dating) an older man and are happy with it.
3. Get her to think back on an experience in her history where she knew a younger woman with an older man. Again, try to get details from her.

This technique is not a cure-all. It will not make her do a sudden 180 and transform her into a Type Two. It's just an effective way to nudge her in the proper direction. I've done this with many women and most times I actually noticed the difference in eye contact and body language when she "gets it," that it really is "okay" and perhaps even enjoyable to be with an older man sexually.

And again, you don't need to nudge very hard, since she's already with you one-on-one on some kind of date in the first place.

Sex and Sexual Escalation Must Be Gentle and Slow

You can initiate sex and have sex with a Type Two just the same way you would with any other woman of any age; there is no real difference. However, with a Type Three, you need to be much gentler and move much more slowly. Here are a few examples of what I mean.

- Don't just start pulling her clothes off while making out with her like a wild man. Instead, make out with her for a while, and do so where you're not ramming your tongue down her throat. Be very gentle and take things slow. Then slowly start to remove her clothing. Take things one step at a time.

- As you're escalating, check in with her verbally every few minutes to make sure she's okay. As you're kissing her and/ or taking off her clothes, you just touch her face and ask, "You okay?" Make sure you're smiling as you ask. Also tell her you're going to "go slow." If you get a little more intense during sex (like I do), tell her that you might get a little intense but that you're not going to hurt her.

- If, at any time, she tells you to stop or that she's not comfortable, STOP. Don't get mad and don't act frustrated. Just nod and say "okay" and stop. Then just talk for a while. You can re-escalate again if you wish, but again, don't push it. If it doesn't happen tonight, don't worry; it will probably happen the next time you see her.

- If you are more intense or crazy during sex, dial it back while having sex with her the first time or two. After you reach Lock-In (sex with her twice on two separate occasions), then you can start letting your hair down and start fucking the way you like. But for the first two times, be a little more gentle and relaxed.

- Don't try any weird stuff. No anal. No odd positions. No sex toys other than very simple vibrators that you use on the outside of her clit (if you're into that stuff). You need to be as vanilla as possible right now.

- Do *not* expect her to cum. She won't. Don't take it personally; she's a Type Three so it's going to take much more time. We'll talk more about sex with younger women in Chapter 23.

- If she verbalizes anything during sex or sexual escalation about what she likes or doesn't like, do what she says. If she says she doesn't like doggy style, or doesn't like fingers inside her, don't do those things even if you love them. Again, you can always slowly introduce those things to her later, after you've had sex at least twice. If she says she prefers a certain position, like being on top or whatever, just do it, again, even if it's not your usual thing.

Long-Term Relationships Are Less Likely

I'm sad to say this, but as an older man, carrying on a long-term relationship with a Type Three VYW is much less likely than with a Type Two. Often, your relationships with Type Threes may only last a few months.

There are always exceptions to every rule of course, but the majority of the time, once she has sex with you for a while, even if she enjoys it, she will eventually return to dating men her own age. The concept is just too far out of her comfort zone. Societal norms are just too important to her.

Regardless, here's some of the good news.

1. Like I said, there are plenty of exceptions. I've encountered a few. You might get lucky. Just don't *plan* on it.

2. All the relationship management techniques in *The Ultimate Open Relationships Manual** directly apply to Type Three VYW just like they apply to any other type of women. Therefore, if you follow the systems I outline in that book, it is easily possible to get Type Threes to keep coming back to you sexually for many years. I'm just saying *consistent* long-term relationships with Type Threes are less likely.

3. Don't forget about all those Type Twos! Long-lasting relationships with Type Twos are not only likely but relatively easy to pull off. Remember, Type Twos should be the mainstay of your younger women diet anyway. I consider Type Threes as a bonus. You should too.

---

* http://www.haveopenrelationships.com/

Chapter 20

YOUNGER WOMEN RELATIONSHIP MANAGEMENT

I have already written an entire book[1] about managing nonmonogamous relationships, and I blog[2] often about relationship techniques, usually from the point of view of open relationships. So I'm not going to attempt to repeat all of that here. Instead, this chapter is strictly regarding having an ongoing relationship with a much younger woman from the standpoint of the older man.

First, we'll cover the positives, then we'll cover the negatives, and lastly, we'll cover how younger women operate in the three different nonmonogamous relationship types. However, before we get to all of that, it's possible you may have a question.

---

[1] http://www.haveopenrelationships.com/
[2] http://www.blackdragonblog.com/

What About Monogamy?

If a monogamous relationship with a younger woman is something you seek, I can't help you, at least not directly. I haven't been in a monogamous relationship for over eleven years (nor wanted to), and I've only had one in my entire life, so I'm not qualified to give men monogamous relationship advice. That being said, you can take the techniques I mention in this chapter (and others) and apply them where they would normally apply in a monogamous relationship. They may work, they may not, I really don't know. Many of my relationship techniques will work with monogamous men, since I occasionally get email from these men saying they've used them and they've helped, but just remember they were not designed for such relationships.

The rest of this chapter, and this book, assumes you're in a nonmonogamous relationship with these younger women, either an FB, MLTR, or OLTR.

The Positives

In no particular order, here are the good things about younger women, particularly VYW, in ongoing relationships.

1. *They're extremely flexible.*

    I don't mean they're physically flexible during sex (although many definitely are!). I mean that in your relationship with her, she will be extremely flexible regarding your lifestyle, who you are, and what you want.

    Work odd hours? She'll work around it. Already have kids? She doesn't care. Don't have a lot of money? Doesn't bother her a bit; she's already accustomed to dating younger men who never have any money. You're emotionally distant, or an asshole, or cheat on her? She'll make it work. (Not that those are good things, or things I recommend, but the point is she'll probably work around them.) You never want to get serious and want to keep things casual forever? Not a problem.

I'm not saying she'll never bring these things up or complain about them. She might, particularly if the relationship is an MLTR. The point is that these things will virtually never be serious problems or deal breakers for her, the way they would for a woman in her thirties or older.

No matter who you are, the problems you might have, or the odd life you might lead, she will likely work with you on it. All she wants is to be with you. She doesn't have this massive checklist of boyfriend/husband "must-haves" that older women constantly operate under. It's very nice.

2. *They're pleasers.*

Younger women tend to be much more focused on pleasing you than older women do. Not all younger women are like this, but the percentage of younger women like this is far beyond the percentage of older women who are.

They want to make you happy. They want to do what you like. They want to make you dinner. They want to clean your kitchen or babysit your sister's kids. They want to make sure that during sex, you are very happy and enjoy yourself.

With women over age 33, this "pleasing" is only a temporary phase before they downshift into betaization mode. Younger women will (usually) always remain pleasers, throughout the length of the relationship (even if they attempt to beta you later).

3. *They're highly compliant (usually).*

Tell your 40-year-old girlfriend, nicely, that you think it would be great if she cleaned your house. Watch the reaction you get. It's not likely to be a positive one. (If you don't believe me, just try it.)

But tell your 20-year-old MLTR the same thing, and her reaction will range from neutral ("Eh… I don't know... maybe next week.") to giddy excitement ("Okay! You don't have any cleaning products here so I'll bring some over from my house!").

Younger women have much less of the I'm-a-strong-independent-woman-no-one-tells-me-what-to-do stuff than older women tend to have.

4. *They have a constant happy, upbeat demeanor.*

One of the first things you notice about younger women as you start dating them, particularly VYW, is how they always seem happy. Even if they've had a bad day or just fought with their girlfriend, mom, or boss, by the time they see you they're smiling, happy, laughing, and joking around as if nothing happened. This is a far cry from the often stressed-out, touchy, complaining demeanor older women are often prone to (particularly women in their thirties; women over 40 tend to be a little happier).

In my opinion, this near-constant happiness is one of the greatest advantages of dating much younger women over women your own age. It really makes a guy's life an enjoyable one. Try it and you'll see what I mean. I'm sure you'll love it as much as I do.

5. *They usually have a higher tolerance to nonmonogamous relationships* (or, if you're that kind of guy, cheating)

This one is interesting. Younger women tend to have more Disney than older women, so they will tend to think that monogamy is more workable than older women. Younger women haven't yet experienced the long string of failed relationships and cheating men that older women have suffered through. However, because of younger women's lower levels of ASD and happy, flexible attitudes, they tend to be easier to manage in nonmonogamous relationships than older women, particularly in FBs and MLTRs. (OLTRs with VYW tend to be extremely problematic, as I explained in Chapter 9.)

6. *They have much lower ASD.*

This means you can do more fun things like have sex with their friends (referral game), have threesomes, and so on. This stuff is much easier with younger women than with older women, as I've already described in prior chapters.

The Negatives

I've already covered some of the negatives of older women you need to be aware of back in Chapter 3. In terms of ongoing relationships with them, here's two more you'll need to be prepared for.

1. *She will love the music you hate.*

   This may not sound like a big deal, but man, if you hate Top 40 music as much as I do, you're going to really have to steel yourself if you want younger women in your life. If she's under the age of about 27, she's going to love Top 40 music (or worse) and will constantly be listening to that crap. In many cases, some women will actually be uncomfortable if they aren't listening to it literally constantly, in the car with you, on their phones while they're with you, and so on.

   You have been warned.

2. *Whining.*

   VYW, still being teenagers, whine. It's not something that I classify as drama, and it's usually not a big deal, but you need to be prepared for it. Often, as soon as you glare at them they'll usually stop, but they'll do it, a lot. Sometimes I will get VYW complaining to me that I have to work (and thus not spend time with them) on, for example, a Tuesday afternoon at 2pm. "Oh my god! You have to work??? That's bullshit, just hang out with me!"

   Maybe they don't have a job. Maybe they have a job but have Tuesday off. It doesn't matter. If she wants to spend time with you and you have to work, even if it's during normal work hours, she will put up with it (as I described in the above section) but there will be whining. The same goes for ten thousand other possible details.

   When she whines, just stay strong, don't get into an argument, but don't put up with it. If you do this, the whining usually dissipates fast.

Do *not* get into a logical conversation with her. If she complains you have to work at 2pm on a Tuesday, you trying to point out that "normal people work on Tuesdays at 2pm" it will simply result in an argument. She's a woman and a young woman at that. She doesn't fucking care you have to work. That's all that matters to her. Just show her that you don't put up with whining, and move on.

VYW in FBs

VYW make fantastic FBs. Their almost complete lack of ASD, their zest for life, their lack of relationship rules, their hidden disdain for monogamy (since they cheat on their boyfriends constantly); all of these things are 100% conducive to FB relationships. My longest and most rewarding FB relationships have been with younger women.

That being said, there are three caveats to this.

First, many younger women tend to get oneitis faster than older women. Just because she's an FB and fully understands it doesn't mean she can't or won't start falling in love with you. This can happen, and *will* happen if you date enough VYW.

This can apply to non-VYW younger women as well. Women in their mid-twenties, in particular, are notorious for lecturing guys about how "This is only sex, okay? We're not dating okay? You're not allowed to start liking me, okay?" only to start getting romantic, girlfriendish feelings for the guy just a few weeks after saying those very words. Be aware.

Second, just like women of other ages, most younger women do not like other people referring to them as a "fuck buddy" or "friend with benefits" even if they themselves fully admit that's what they are, even if they have a boyfriend and you're the guy on the side. They can call *themselves* these things, but *you* can't. Never, ever refer to a woman as a "fuck buddy" or "friend with benefits" even if she's called herself that. (I know that makes no sense. Women don't make sense.) When you're pressed and you have to actually verbalize what she "is", she's your "close friend."

Thirdly, a very high percentage of VYW you'll have in FB relationships will already have boyfriends they're seeing. Either she'll be cheating on him with you (more likely), or she'll be in an open relationship with him (less likely, but becoming much more common, especially with sugar babies). We'll discuss those kinds of relationships in Chapter 26.

VYW in MLTRs

I have had many MLTRs of all ages, from 18-year-old girls all the way to women in their forties. VYW are perfectly fine in MLTRs, even high-end MLTRs. There really is no specific difference to MLTR management with younger women vs. older women beyond what I've already discussed in this book. Interestingly, younger women's sense of timing about when things are "casual," when things are "dating," and when things should "start to get serious" are about the same as older women.

VYW in OLTRs

As I explained in detail back in Chapter 9, I do not recommend you make any woman an OLTR who's under the age of about 25. Since VYW are under the age of 23, that means you shouldn't have any VYW as an OLTR at all. OLTRs usually have long-term expectations, and you can't expect any long-term consistency with a functional teenager. Once a woman hits age 25 (or so), then you can start to expect that she's up for something long-term and consistent.

I'm serious about this. Just about every older man I've ever seen attempt either an OLTR or serious, monogamous relationship with a woman under the age of 23 ends up with a huge cluster fuck in his life, up to and including things like property damage and legal problems. No matter how hot, fun, or smart you think she is, keep her at the MLTR or even high-end MLTR level. Never let her go past that.

What you *could* do, and what I have done, is to start a woman at an MLTR or FB level and then years later upgrade her to high-end MLTR or OLTR, once she gets older. I once dated a woman who was 19 years old as an FB. A few years later I upgraded her to MLTR, and then later a high-end MLTR that was very serious, almost a de facto OLTR. But, she was 24 years old by then, not 19. I would never have made a 19-year-old anywhere close to an OLTR.

The "Having Kids" Issue

Regardless of her numerical age, there are several considerations you need to account for when you get into a serious relationship with a younger woman (high-end MLTR, OLTR, or monogamy with long-term expectations).

The first and largest is the issue of children. *Younger women want kids.* If they're in a serious relationship with you, they'll want them with you. That doesn't mean they'll want them immediately, but it does mean they'll expect them from you eventually. If you already have kids she won't mind or care. She'll still expect you to have more. With her.

If she says "I never want kids," do *not* expect her to stick with that opinion, and the younger she is, the more this is true. In many younger women circles these days, it's considered "tough" or "cool" for younger, left-wing girls to brag about how they "never want any kids." 99% of the women saying this are full of shit. They definitely want kids, just not *yet*. If she lasts long enough in your life under a serious, romantic context, the odds are overwhelming she'll eventually change her mind on this and want you to have her babies.

It also doesn't matter if she already has one child. In my experience (and I believe there is science to back this up), most women want *two* kids. So if she already has one, do *not* assume you're in the clear. It's very likely she wants at least one more, even if she's well over age 30.

Having kids, the decision to have them, or more of them, is obviously far beyond the scope of this book. I have written several articles about this at the Blackdragon Blog[1] and included two chapters about it in *The Unchained Man*[2]. The important thing is to make that decision in a rational, objective way, and then stick with it. Either you never want kids, or already have kids and don't want any more, or have kids but wouldn't mind more, or you definitely want kids. Figure this out. Tell women very clearly what you want and what you don't. Dump any women who complain about your decision or attempt to repeatedly pressure you.

One of the most common dumb things men do is have kids for the primary reason that the cute girl they're dating wants some really bad. *That is literally the worst reason to have children.*

If you don't want kids, don't lie about it. As you already know, I do not endorse lying to women. Therefore, I do not endorse the concept of stringing women along, promising that you'll have babies with her "some day" when you know damn well you won't. Once you're dating and things look like they may move in a serious direction, tell her flat out that you want more babies, or that you don't, or that you could but only under certain conditions. Don't lead women on.

The bottom line is that if you ever get into a relationship more serious than an FB with any younger woman who has less than two children, you are almost 100% guaranteed to get pressure from her to have kids. Prepare for this and expect this.

If You've Had A Vasectomy

All of this talk of kids necessitates a quick segue into the topic of vasectomies. Most older women, particularly the ones who've already had two or more children, *love* guys with vasectomies, and you'll do very well with women over 30 like this when you advertise you've had the procedure done.

---

[1] http://www.blackdragonblog.com/
[2] http://www.alphamalebook.com/

However, with VYW, particularly those with no kids or one kid, it's the exact opposite. If you tell a woman like that you've had a vasectomy, she's gone. Very few younger women are going to stick around with a guy who's had a vasectomy *even* if they only intend for the guy to be an FB. (Exception to the rule: pay-for-it sugar daddy game; these women are getting money so they don't care.)

It's not because they want to get pregnant by you "by accident" (though a small percentage do; be careful with those condoms!). Rather, it's because of their biology, Disney desires, and woman logic. A younger woman will always want the option of having babies with a man she is having sex with, and if you tell her on the first date (or whenever) that you can't have children, she'll be out of there so fast a gust of wind will follow her out of the Starbucks.

I've slept with many VYW where literally the only question they asked about me prior to having sex was whether or not I wanted to have more children. Even if you answer "no," if they know you haven't had a vasectomy, they'll often rationalize it and have sex with you anyway ("I can change his mind!"). But if you tell them you can't have kids, the odds of her sticking around are low.

If you haven't had a vasectomy, you have nothing to worry about. If you haven't had one but plan on getting one, this is something you'll need to consider. If you've had a vasectomy, you're in a tough spot. When she asks about future prospects of kids, you've got three options:

1. Lie and tell her you're able to have more kids. Again, I do not endorse or recommend lying to women for any reason, but it's your life and it's certainly an option.
2. Tell her the truth, and be ready for any consequences.
3. Tell her you're open to getting the procedure reversed and are willing to have kids with the right woman. Again, I would only tell her this if there's some truth to it. Stating this *will* work. It will be enough for her to rationalize being with you. Just remember if the two of you actually end up dating, she'll hold you to your promise. (Rightly so.)

She'll Change

Another significant factor you must be aware of in long-term relationships with younger women, particularly VYW, is that the human brain doesn't finish maturing and forming until around age 25. This means that a woman who is 20 is often a very different person at age 25, or even 24. There are radical, often shocking changes to a woman's personality between the ages of 18 and 25.

This means that the woman you start dating at age 19 is going to be quite different at age 24. She will want different things, like different things, dislike new things, radically change her life plans, and even exhibit large shifts in her overall demeanor and personality.

I have dated many women in very long-term multi-year relationships between the ages of 18 and 25 (and beyond). Sometimes these are consistent relationships, and sometimes these are relationships where the woman comes and goes multiple times over many years. Through these relationships, I've been able to witness first hand the radical personality changes young women go through. Sometimes you'll date a woman at age 21 and then date her again at age 27 and she's almost a completely different person.

This is one of the many reasons you shouldn't get serious with any woman under the age of 23-25, and men who are stupid enough to actually marry women that young are flirting with disaster. That serious girlfriend (OLTR or monogamous doesn't matter) you've got is going to be a completely different person in a few years, and may not even want to be with you by then. Granted, this is risk for dating any woman at any age, since as I described in *The Unchained Man**, women are in a constant state of change. But this is greatly exacerbated by dealing with women who lack fully formed brains; which means women under age 25.

Obviously, I'm not saying you can't have relationships with these women, even semi-serious ones. I'm just saying you need to be aware

---

* http://www.alphamalebook.com/

that the cute girl sitting across from you on your couch is going to be a very different person in a few years, and you need to plan on this and not let it surprise you.

Chapter 21

WHEN AND (WHEN NOT) TO SPEND MONEY ON YOUNGER WOMEN

When dating younger women, there will be an income disparity between you and them that will likely be significant. This means you need to plan ahead regarding the financial aspects of the ongoing relationships you will have with younger women.

Spending money on women is a complicated issue. There are times spending money on women is always bad, and other times where it's a matter of opinion based on your personal preferences, relationship goals, and financial position. It's further complicated by the fact that there are exceptions to the "always bad" rule. There are also different rules and parameters for when you spend money on women during the seduction/ dating phase (before you've had sex with her twice) and during the relationship management phase (after you've had sex with her twice).

Spending Money During the Seduction/Dating Phase

I have always followed the rule of spending the least amount of money on women while getting to sex as fast as possible. As I explain in great detail in *Get To Sex Fast**, most of the first-time sex I get from new women occurs on the second date, and within 3-4 hours grand total of face time (including both dates). About 30% of the time, this process costs me literally zero dollars other than the small cost of gas to and from the date locations. Most of the time when I do spend money, I'm spending less than about $17 grand total between both of my dates (again, not including gas).

Pay-for-it sugar daddy game is an exception to this, but I've only been doing that sporadically over the past two or three years; my standard Blackdragon model stands, and is something I've been doing consistently for over eleven years. Even when doing sugar daddy game, I budget a specific amount of money I'm willing to spend and never go over it.

In terms of getting to sex fast with a new woman, I think spending a little money on gas (or similar transportation) plus buying a woman a drink or two, maybe an appetizer or side salad at the most, in order to have sex with her within a few hours is fine. I don't consider that "spending money on women." So for the purposes of this chapter, "spending money on women" is anything more than that. If you have to take a woman out on two or three full-on dinner dates, that's definitely spending money as I define it here. If you have to rent a hotel room to have sex with her the first time, that is also spending money as I define it. Obviously, if you have to pay her cash under a hooker or sugar daddy arrangement, that's also definitely spending money. You get the idea.

Now that we have a definition, let's discuss when it's okay and not okay.

---

* http://www.gettosexfast.com/

When Spending Money on Women Is Unacceptable

While there are two exceptions to this we'll cover in a minute, spending money on women is unacceptable, in my opinion, if you have no other way of getting laid. If your game, confidence, or physical appearance is so terrible that you literally can't have sex with a new cute woman without throwing cash, gifts, or expensive dinners at her, this is unacceptable. If this is you, either surrender to being a beta male or else come to a complete stop and follow the instructions I laid out in Part One of this book to improve yourself as a man. You're in a feeble life position if the only way you can have new sex is by paying for it.

That being said, there are two exceptions to this rule.

Exception #1

The first exception is if you are so old that improving your appearance really isn't an option. As I explained back in Chapter 1, if you are over the age of 60, and you look quite old, and want to have sex with a hot 23-year-old, then I agree that improving your appearance probably isn't going to cut it no matter how hard you work at it (though I still think you should do it for happiness and lifestyle reasons).

In that kind of case, there's no problem with you throwing a little money around in order to get to sex with a woman like that. Someday, I may be 100 years old and (might) look like shit, and I may have to do this myself at that point. I do admit that with some much older men, improving appearance to the point where you can have sex with cute women 50 years younger than you with zero money spent probably isn't an option.

Exception #2

The second exception to this rule is if you are truly wealthy and money is no object. To be clear, I consider "truly wealthy" as a net worth of *$10 million or more*. If you are literally worth $10 million or close to it, and see no point in learning game or dating techniques, and find it easier to make it rain $100 bills on cute girls while cruising around on your yacht, then fine, I see no problem with this if that lifestyle makes you happy. You've got money to burn, so go ahead.

Just remember I said $10 million or more. If you're worth $2 million or whatever because you have a decent house and a few investments, you are *not* included in this exception, and I still think it's a very terrible condition if you can't get laid without throwing money at women. You need to improve your game/appearance/confidence. I hate to say this, but being worth a few million is not "rich," not with today's inflation rates.

That covers when spending money on women is unacceptable. Now let's switch gears and discuss when spending money on women during the seduction/dating phase becomes less black and white and is more a matter of opinion.

When Spending Money Might Be Acceptable Depending On Your Circumstances

Let's say that you don't have to spend money in order to have sex with new women, beyond the small expenses I described above. This means that you've worked on your game, appearance, and confidence enough where you can get laid reasonably fast, with at least reasonably cute women, without spending more than about $20-$30 or so (ideally zero).

First of all, congratulations. You are an Alpha Male no matter how much money you choose to spend on women at this point, even if we disagree on how much money you choose to spend on women.

So if you can get laid without spending money, does it make sense to start spending money on women to improve your speed to sex or quality of women?

Speaking very generally, the answer is yes, *assuming two things:*

1. You honestly want to do this and are not doing it from a sense of desperation.

2. You make plenty of money above and beyond your monthly bills and investment goals and can easily afford it without screwing anything up in your financial life or going one penny into debt.

If either of the above two things is untrue, you're venturing into a danger zone by spending money on women, and you need to reconsider. But, if the above are both true, I have no problem with it.

How Much To Spend

Assuming all the above is true, the next issue is about how much to spend. What amount is appropriate? How much is too much? How much is too little? There is no objectively right or wrong answer to this question. Assuming you have the ability to get to sex reliably on the cheap, the amount of money you spend is something you must come up with based on the following factors:

1. How much money you make or have.
2. How busy you are.
3. How extroverted or introverted you are.
4. The age of the women you prefer, or more specifically, the age difference between you and them.
5. The part of the world you live in.
6. How frugal you are.
7. Your sexual and relationship goals.

All seven of these factors are going to drive the appropriate amount of money up or down based on your personal situation and personality.

I'll give you the example of how I've determined this for myself. Again, this is only an example to show you my thought process as I go through the above seven factors; I am not describing what is "right," since all of us are different.

I am a very busy, high-income, 46-year-old man, who hates spending money because of a frugal Myers-Briggs INTJ personality type and a financially poor upbringing that, for better or worse, still rolls around in my subconscious. I am also an introvert (though a very high functioning, socially calibrated one) who hates going to parties, events, and clubs (with or without women). I'd rather go see a movie or be cozy at home and have sex. I live in the United States, in the Pacific Northwest. I am extremely busy, working literally seven days a week, since I'm a motivated guy with big goals. These days, I am in an OLTR marriage with a woman in her late thirties, and because of this I prefer to have FBs on the side who are reasonably young, ages 21-27 or so. I have extremely strong game and confidence, and can easily have sex with hot new women under age 33 very quickly, pretty much whenever I want. My goal with women has always been to have long-term FBs and MLTRs with every woman I have sex with. I hate one night stands and short-term relationships and never do them if I can avoid them. Today, since I have an OLTR wife who lives with me, all new women I meet must be FBs, but again, I want all of these women to be long-term relationships, not brief flings.

That's me. You may be radically different, so remember that. Based on my situation, here is my evaluation of how much money is appropriate for me to spend...

I can have sex with new women for virtually free, but it does take me three, sometimes four hours of face time, in addition to some (but not much) time sending out copy and paste openers on dating sites. I'm a time management nerd and time is very important to me, so the faster the sex, the better.

If I wanted to drop this 3.5-hour average to 5 minutes, I could just pay a hooker. That would be a perfectly valid thing to do at my income level and with my time management goals. However, with my hatred of spending money, and my goal of having long-lasting FBs with women, hookers aren't really an option for me.

Other higher income guys who love one night stands and think five-minute meet-to-sex times are awesome will have no problem paying hookers. Totally fine; that works for them. See how this works? But let's continue.

My next option would be to drop my 3.5 hour meet-to-sex times to perhaps 1-2 hours or less by using pay-for-it sugar daddy game. At my income level I could afford this with no problem, and it would certainly increase my speed to sex, which is a big plus for me. Thus, over the past few years, I have chosen this option several times, mixed in with my normal online dating and don't-pay sugar daddy game. Perfectly fine, at least for me. However, if I made less money, or had no idea how to get laid without paying for it, I would not choose this option, and instead focus on my dating/seduction skills to get to the point where I am today, where I *can* have sex for free or very close to it if I choose to take the time.

So, look at the above seven factors as I did, and figure out how much money you're willing to spend during the seduction/dating phase. If it's $30, that's great. If it's $200, that's fine, again, as long as you've carefully evaluated the above factors.

Spending Money on Women in Ongoing Relationships

That covers dating, what about once you're in a relationship with her? How much money do you spend then?

First, let's cover the two extremes of money spending relationship models most common in society, neither of which work if you want harmonious, happy, long-term, low-drama relationships with women (younger or otherwise).

The most common extreme is the one most of us are familiar with. This is the (usually) monogamous beta male who showers his gal with cash, loans, gifts, financial support, romantic dates, food, drinks, trips, clothes, jewelry, and in more extreme cases, more expensive things like cars, fake boobs, expensive handbags, and the like.

Hopefully, I don't need to outline here why this is a terrible idea. Treating a woman this way invites drama, betaization, demands, and all kinds of other things you don't want. Treating a woman this way also tends to speed up the end of the relationship, since women tend to get bored with a boyfriend (or husband) to the degree to which he kisses her ass. If you keep spending money on your monogamous girlfriend, don't be surprised when she suddenly goes serial mono on you (which means she'll dump you).

The opposite extreme is far less common but does happen from time to time. This is when a stronger man is in a relationship with a very submissive woman, and over time *she* starts paying for *him* in just about every way. I've seen a few relationships over the years where the woman goes and works and the guy sits at home, smokes weed, and watches TV all day. This kind of relationship is extremely unlikely if you're an older man dating a much younger woman, so that isn't even an option unless something very weird is going on.

You need to spend money on women only to the degree where it doesn't create future problems in the relationship, regardless of if you can easily afford it or not. If you follow the guidelines in this chapter, this will never be a problem for you.

Spending Money on FBs

You should never spend money on FBs, period (unless they are pay-for-it sugar babies, and even then there must be a set per-visit amount that never increases, and nothing beyond that). Once you spend the minimum you need to spend on the first few dates and start having sex with her on a regular basis, you should never spend money on an FB at all, ever. If she doesn't like it, she's more than welcome to leave. (She won't if you're following all the usual correct techniques I lay out in *The Ultimate Open Relationships Manual*.*)

There are a few minor exceptions to this. Normal gas/bus/subway transportation costs are okay. If you need to go to her place or transport her to yours, that's fine as long as you aren't sending limousines to pick her up. Once you've evaluated how much money you want to spend (as we discussed in the above section), and it falls within your spending parameters, you are welcome to use things like taxis or Uber. (Just

---

* http://www.haveopenrelationships.com/

remember she always has the option of having one of her friends or needy guy orbiters to drive her over to you; I've done this a lot with younger women.)

The world also isn't going to end if, for example, while she's with you on the way to your place to have sex, you stop off at a Taco Bell drive-thru and spend $2 to get her a burrito. I've done this kind of thing once or twice with some FBs, and as long as it doesn't happen very often and the rest of your relationship technique and frame is rock-solid, there's no big problem with this.

What you *don't* want to do are things like take an FB out to dinner. No, no, no! This is wildly incongruent, will send all the wrong messages to her, and is guaranteed, yes *guaranteed* to cause trouble with her down the road.

An objection to this I hear semi-regularly is that some men *like* to spend money on people. Some men assume that since they occasionally enjoy buying dinner for their guy buddies, it's fine if they do it for their FBs.

These men aren't acknowledging that you're not having sex with your guy buddies and your guy buddies aren't women. If you buy dinner for one of your buds, it's not going to change the dynamic of your friendship at all. He's not going to start consciously or subconsciously changing the nature of your relationship, or start asking himself all kinds of emotional internal questions about "where he stands" in your relationship with him.

A female FB will do all of these things. You're not comparing apples to apples. I've bought a dinner or two for one of my guy buddies before, but I have never bought dinner for an FB, and I never will. I don't want the drama and betaization that I know will arise down the road.

If you really want to take one of your FBs out to dinner, and you like her more than a friend, then just upgrade her to MLTR. That way, things like an occasional dinner are allowed.

Spending Money on MLTRs

An MLTR is someone you're actually dating; someone for whom you have romantic feelings and intentions. Therefore, spending money on an MLTR *within reason* is perfectly acceptable.

The key here is that while an MLTR is someone you really do like, an MLTR is not your girlfriend. Therefore if you go the standard beta-male-with-a girlfriend route on the spending money stuff, she's going to assume "girlfriend status" whether you intended it or not, then say hello to all kinds of drama, demands, and/or betaization.

With MLTRs, I will have many "dates" that are actually cozy meetups at my house (cost to me: zero). While I don't like socially awkward women, I do tend to lean more towards women who aren't extreme extroverts who constantly have to "go out" all the time specifically for this reason; more extroverted and/or outgoing women tend to cost more money.

Don't get me wrong. I have indeed had MLTRs, even serious ones, with women who were high-extroverts. I'm just saying that I try to make as many "dates" at my place as I can.

When I do go out with an MLTR, I will usually pay. Notice the word is "usually" and not "always." A general rule of thumb to follow is to make sure your MLTR pays for at least some of the event costs at least 40% of the time. She must understand that you are not her beta boyfriend and that she must have some skin in the game if she wants you to stay in her life.

The issue here is that in many cases, VYW have little or no money. In that case, you can indeed pay 100% of the time for outings in an MLTR, but even then, I stipulate that she needs to, at least sometimes, *help* with the expenses, even if it's just $20 here or there. That's an extreme example; I once had a long-term MLTR in her early twenties who paid for almost all of our dates when we went out because I didn't want to pay for them. She was employed full-time and lived with family so she had no bills, so she could easily afford it. It was great!

Spending Money on an OLTR

Spending money in an OLTR is a highly complex topic and is beyond the scope of most of this book, particularly because, as I said earlier, a VYW shouldn't be your OLTR to begin with. If you're dating younger women who are older than 25 and wish to make one your OLTR, then follow all the other guidelines I outline in this chapter. I also strongly recommend you read *The Ultimate Open Relationships Manual** if this is the case, since OLTRs are a little complicated and easy to screw up.

For High Income or High Net Worth Men – Spending Money When You Can Afford It

As an older man, it's entirely possible that you have a much higher income than average ($100,000 per year or more) and/or have a high-end net worth ($1-2 million or more). When you're in this condition, the rules for spending money on women do indeed change a little.

However, it's extremely important to remember that just because you *can* do something *doesn't mean it's a good idea.* If you can afford to drop thousands of dollars per month on a woman you're having a relationship with, that it doesn't mean this won't cause major problems for you in the relationship down the road, as well as with your long-term future finances.

With that in mind, there are five factors at play you must consider when making decisions about the issue of throwing money at women because "you can" or because "you like it."

1. Your personal net monthly income after paying all taxes, expenses, and debts.
2. Your personal net worth and liquidity (and remember that these are not the same thing!).

---

* http://www.haveopenrelationships.com/

3. Her possible reaction to you spending money on her like a girlfriend, and the bullshit, drama, and demands that will ensue if this is the case.

4. The type of relationship you have with her: FB, low-end MLTR, high-end MLTR, or OLTR.

5. Your level of drama tolerance.

Only after dispassionately evaluating these five things will you be in a place where you can make a rational determination of how much money to spend within a long-term, consistent happiness framework. I will cover each.

Your Net Monthly Income

By "net income" here I'm talking about the money you have left over after taxes, required lifestyle expenses (going out to a fancy restaurant is not a required lifestyle expense, but your mortgage or rent payment is), and any payments on debts.

Clearly, if you have thousands of dollars left over every month after these three things, then you're certainly able to afford to throw all the money at women you like (within the next four factors we have not yet covered, that is).

However, the issue of debt is an important one that a hell of a lot of high-income men don't factor in. If you've read the wonderful book, *The Millionaire Next Door*, you know that the majority of so-called "rich" people in the US are both illiquid and absolutely drowning in debt. A study that was recently published showed that 38% of Americans who make over $100,000 a year would have trouble coming up with just $1000 in case of an emergency.

That doctor or corporate vice president who lives in the large, nice house, drives a Mercedes, whose wife drives an Escalade, whose kids go to private schools, and who vacations in Europe every year is likely to be cash poor. Statistically speaking, he's smothered in a gigantic home mortgage, car loans, college loans, credit card debt, personal loans, child support and alimony from a prior marriage, and all kinds of other debt, on top of massive lifestyle expenses. He also likely has zero or near zero liquid savings to draw upon. Not to mention he's paying 60-70% in grand total taxes whenever he gets paid, since because of our corporatist society and ridiculous two-party political system, we Americans get raped when it comes to taxes. Europeans, Canadians, and Australians don't fare much better with their quasi-socialist economic systems.

So when I say you have plenty of net income, I'm talking about being cash rich, not outwardly rich. Many higher-income men *feel* like they have a lot of money, when in fact they do not. If you have a high income but you have massive debt or high lifestyle expenses, you should not be throwing money at women at all, and instead should be focused on paying down your debt with a vengeance (as I had to do many years ago). Once you're completely debt free, then throw a big party (I did), but until then, your personal financial picture is more important than any woman should be.

Your Personal Net Worth and Liquidity

I consider truly "rich" as a net worth of around $10 million or more. If your net worth is $10 million or more, and it's in solid investments (instead of something like a tech startup that can radically shift in value at any time), then you're good to go and can spend all the money you want, any way you like, and you're welcome to move on to the next section. But if you aren't worth at least $10 million, you need to take a harder look at your financial situation before you think about throwing money around with wild abandon with women.

There's also the issue of liquidity. If you've got two men, each with a net worth of $2 million, there's a huge difference between the guy that has it all in rental real estate versus the guy who has it all in a portfolio of diversified ETF's. The second guy is far more liquid than the first. This is something to consider. (I'm not saying rental real estate is a bad investment or inferior to ETF's. I'm only talking about liquidity here.)

Her Reaction to Being Treated Like A Girlfriend

I have spoken about this issue at great length at the Blackdragon Blog[1] and in *The Ultimate Open Relationships Manual*[2]. To summarize, the more money you spend on a woman, regardless of what kind of relationship it is, regardless of your frame, and regardless of what your intentions are, the more boyfriend behaviors she will start to expect from you. Boyfriend behaviors include things like talking every day, going out on dates more often, sexual monogamy/exclusivity, meeting each other's family, more money spent on her, and all kinds of other Disney trappings. She will start to expect at least some of this stuff, then *demand* this stuff, and when she doesn't get it, you'll get drama.

If you don't like drama and or a bunch of relationship rules, you need to avoid spending money on women whenever possible, regardless of your income. Realize that just because you A) can afford to take women out to expensive steak dinners and B) you *like* taking women out to expensive steak dinners, doesn't mean she isn't going to start in with the betaization and drama when you do so. She will. Just give it time.

The Type of Relationship

I already discussed above the appropriate amounts of money to spend depending on if a woman is an FB or MLTR. The amount of money you spend on a woman must precisely match the type of relationship you have with her. Taking an MLTR out to dinner every once in a while is fine, but taking an FB out to dinner is an insane idea that's going to cause all kinds of confusion, drama, and hurt feelings down the road (which will be all your fault). Taking a woman out to an expensive, super romantic night on the town would be a terrible idea for a low-end MLTR, a perfectly fine idea for an OLTR, and only good for a high-end MLTR if your Alpha frame was very strong and 100% perfect.

---

[1] http://www.blackdragonblog.com/
[2] http://www.haveopenrelationships.com/

If it's a pay-for-it sugar daddy relationship, then spending a set amount on her per visit is perfectly fine, but just make sure that:

1. It's purely an FB relationship only. No MLTRs for sugar babies (unless you're doing something very usual).
2. There is a set amount you pay her per visit, and that amount never rises, and you don't give her any more money beyond that, for any reason (unless, again, you're doing something unusual like actually having her do work for you).
3. There is a specific expectation for how much time and/or sex she's going to spend with you based on these amounts. If she doesn't follow through, you take corrective action, or just dump her and find someone else.

Your Level of Drama Tolerance

I talk about the four levels of drama tolerance in great detail in the *Ultimate Open Relationships Manual**, but to summarize, there are men who like drama, men who don't mind drama, men who hate drama but put up with it, and men who hate drama and never put up with it.

I'm in the last category (hate drama, never tolerate any of it), but I realize there are lots of men in the first and second categories. If that describes you, you are free to discard many or even all of the guidelines I've set forth in this chapter regarding spending money on women. You'll get some drama, but you may not care, or at least may not care as much as I would.

If you're more like me and hate drama, you need to be very careful about spending money on younger women, even if you can easily afford it.

---

* http://www.haveopenrelationships.com/

Going On Trips

A lot of older men enjoy taking younger women on trips with them. I don't do this often with women unless they're an OLTR or high-end MLTR, but I know many men love to take women on trips even if they're just FBs or low-end MLTRs.

My general rule for going on trips is that this is only allowed with high-end MLTRs and OLTRs, and even then, she should be expected to kick in for at least some of the cost, even if you're paying for most of it. For example, you pay for the plane tickets and food, and she covers the hotel. When we're dealing with older men and much younger women, we have to make a few adjustments to this.

If she's an FB, don't take her on any trips, period. This is very incongruent and is almost guaranteed to cause problems in the relationship later, for all the reasons I've talked about in this and prior chapters.

If she's a pay-for-it sugar baby, then taking her on trips and paying for everything is acceptable, but only if you've been seeing her consistently and regularly for at least two or three months and there hasn't been any problems whatsoever. Also, the nature of the relationship and what is expected of her on this trip needs to be very clear. She's just a friend, we're going to XYZ location to have some fun and sex every night, and that's it. If there is any trouble on the trip, you'll need to dump her as soon as you get back, and she needs to know this before you go. Going on trips with pay-for-it sugar babies is only for very strong, confident men who can set hard parameters and abide by them. If that doesn't describe you yet, hold off on trips with sugar babies until you have some more experience with younger woman.

If she's a standard MLTR and very young, as in age 25 or younger, then it's a judgment call on your part as to whether or not to go on a trip with her. If you do, she should pay for at least some of the costs, whatever she can afford.

If she's a standard MLTR and she is age 26 or higher, I would not take her on any trips. Her ASD and betaization tendencies are just too high. She'll assume it's a "boyfriend behavior," and trouble will likely ensue.

If she's a high-end MLTR of any age, then trips are fine. Again, she should help pay for some of the costs.

If she's an OLTR of any age, then obviously trips are fine, even if you pay for it all (though you need to always keep your outcome independent, Alpha frame).

The length of trips is also important. Going away on a two or three-day weekend getaway is fine. Going on a four-day trip is fine, but a little riskier. Going on any trip that is longer than four days is usually asking for drama, unless there is significant time during the trip where you and her will be separated for many hours a day. This is very important and you need to remember this. On just about any trip longer than four days where you're spending pretty much the entire time with her, regardless of her age, you're virtually guaranteed to get some drama. This is because of the extended period of time you have with her, coupled with the fact that a woman tends to "save up" their drama for a man when she can unleash it on him during a long trip like this, where she thinks he's "stuck" with her.

If you want to keep your life as drama-free as possible, keep your trips with women very brief, as in two to four days maximum, and reserve any future long trips for your current or future OLTR.

Loaning Money

Never, ever, *ever* loan money to VYW unless you essentially view it as a gift where you will never see the money again. Loaning money to a teenager (and remember, if she's under age 23, she's a teenager) with any expectation of ever getting it back is one of the stupidest things men do. If you want to *give* money to a younger woman you're regularly having sex with, to help her out or something, you may do so as long as you're following all the guidelines in this chapter as to when and when it's not appropriate. But *loaning* money to women this young is just flat out stupid. You're not going to get it back.

Regarding giving or loaning money to a younger woman when she has an "emergency," remember that younger women have "emergencies" all the damn time. If you give or loan her money when she has an "emergency," you are 100% guaranteeing that she's going to ask you for money again for the *next* "emergency" very soon. This is why I don't recommend giving (*or* loaning) money to women just because they ask (set amount pay-for-sex sugar daddy arrangements notwithstanding). It opens a dark door in your relationship that will never be closed.

Chapter 22

CONNECTING EMOTIONALLY WITH YOUNGER WOMEN

Here's a question often asked by older men whenever the topic of dating much younger women comes up:

> *If I'm in my forties (or older), and I'm on a date with a 19-year-old or 21-year-old, how do you connect with a woman that young? I understand the physical attraction, but what if you can't connect, despite a mutual attraction, because she's so young. Or dumb. Or just too different. How do you even maintain normal banter? How do you not get bored? How do you not get turned off? How do you connect?*

This reminds me of the very first time I had a first date with a much younger woman, about a decade ago. I was still somewhat new at all this, and it was the first time I finally got the balls to start messaging much younger women online. Up until then, I was dating women primarily in their forties, thirties, and very late twenties. I figured that if I messaged women in their late (legal) teens or early twenties, they would just call me a creeper and vanish. Indeed, my response rate suddenly plummeted, but to my surprise, a few Type Two VYW responded to me, and quite enthusiastically.

Not yet having my online dating system fully developed, I fumbled through it as best I could, and finally got one of these girls to agree to a first date at a local Starbucks. Her pics were not super-hot, but cute enough. I considered it an experiment to see if A) I was attracted enough to actually want to have sex with a woman that young, and B) if a woman that young was actually interested in having sex with *me*. I was about 36 at the time; she was 20, 16 years younger than me and essentially still a teenager.

When we met up at the Starbucks, I was shocked to see that she was way better looking in real life than her pics indicated (a common occurrence back in the days when I used to hit online dating really hard). Though she wasn't blonde or short, which are my two favorite traits, the rest of her was fantastic. Perfect, beautiful face. Young, perfect, tan skin. Long, light brown hair. Trim, fit body. Big perky boobs. The works.

So being physically attracted to her was easy. More so than I thought, as you'll see in a little bit.

Then she opened her mouth and started talking.

Oh shit.

For the first few minutes, everything was fine. We talked about her mom and her best friend. I was getting pretty good at first dates by then and knew that the more she talked and the less I talked, the higher my odds of fast sex would be. So I just kept her talking about whatever she wanted to talk about.

Soon, the topic of her mom and friends morphed into a detailed conversation (mostly on her part) about… wait for it… her hair. Coloring it. Maintaining it. Shampoo and conditioner. She went on and on about this crap, literally for at least 20 minutes. I couldn't stand it, but I knew I had to keep her talking, so I just kept her going, which was easy. It was stupid, but I still couldn't deny the physical attraction. She was amazingly hot and I got a little turned on even as she was talking about her conditioner.

Eventually, we wrapped up the first date, keeping it to one hour as per my dating model, and went our separate ways. I remember walking out of that Starbucks, shaking my head. I was a grown man, a business owner, and father of two. What the hell was I doing? Her stupid conversation about her hair reinforced my false Societal Programming about dating someone "too young."

Then something very interesting happened. I drove home to my apartment (I was still living in an apartment back then since I was still going through my divorce), parked, walked into my home, and immediately a huge wave of monstrous, caveman-like horniness overtook me.

I've always been a high sex drive guy, but this was different. I had never experienced anything like it before. It was a massive, sudden surge of sexual desire. It hit me like a truck. I suddenly felt so horny I literally stood in my living room for a few moments, my eyes squinted, trying to figure out what was happening inside my body, and why. I was so randy I was ready to fuck my couch. I didn't understand what the hell was going on.

Today, I know exactly what was happening. We men, of all ages, are biologically hard-wired to be sexually attracted to very young women at prime child-bearing ages, meaning mid to late teens and early twenties. This reality is offensive in left-wing cultures that were formerly puritanical, such as the USA and Canada, but biological facts are biological facts. As I've pointed out many times before in my other writings, a particular culture's discomfort with something doesn't mean it doesn't exist.

They've even done studies, several of which I discuss in *The Unchained Man**, where they took old married men, measured their testosterone levels, then had these guys have a nice conversation with a flirty, hot teenage girl for just 20 minutes, and then measured their testosterone again. This resulted in an average increase of 14% in testosterone blood content levels. In just 20 minutes.

---

* http://www.alphamalebook.com/

Trust me, if your testosterone shot up 14% in just 20 minutes, you'd feel it. This is what happened to me so many years ago. Not only was I talking to a hot young woman, but I was talking to one on an actual *date* with the intention of (maybe) having sex with me. That was many years ago and today I'm accustomed to this feeling, but back then, as a recovering beta male, getting punched in the face with this level of instant horniness was as intense as it was unexpected.

Little Ms. Shampoo and I never had sex. I screwed up the second date pitch and waited too long. I would have to wait a few more months before having sex with my first much younger woman, but I'll never forget the lessons I learned that day.

This brings me to my first and primary point. When you're an older guy (over age 35 or so) and you're on a date with a woman who is under the age of 23, you're not there to connect. You're not there to find commonality. You're not there to have a deep, meaningful conversation. You're going to have to look for that kind of thing with women who are a little older. When on a date with a VYW, you're there to enjoy the deep, visceral feelings of sexual desire and masculinity that much younger women can give you. That's it. If you look for anything deeper or anything beyond that, you're likely going to be disappointed.

That doesn't mean you can't find some kind of emotional connection with a much younger woman. I certainly have. Just consider that an exception to the rule and not something you should normally expect. Remember, if you're on a first or second date with a 22-year-old or younger, you're sitting across from a teenager. You must adjust your expectations accordingly (or stick with women over the age of 23).

In other words, don't try to "connect" or have a "meaningful conversation" at all. Just sit back, relax, and feel the wonderful horniness and sexual attraction nature designed you to feel (assuming you're attracted to her of course). Don't have any other goals beyond that (and eventual sex).

If that sounds like torture to you, or if you can't stand listening to a hot younger woman talk about her hair or Snapchat or "that cunt on Facebook" who flirted with her last boyfriend, then don't date women under age 23. Draw a line at 23 or 25 and only date women older than that. There's nothing wrong with that at all.

I actually stopped going below age 23 for FBs (more or less) several years ago, mostly because A) I've been there done that (a lot) and B) my schedule is so jam-packed busy these days I can only afford to interact with reliable people. A little while later I returned to under-23 women, somewhat, only for new women I added to my roster, strictly because I'm now in a live-in OLTR marriage and it's easier to deal with women under 23 because of their lower levels of ASD. Yet, I still have to tolerate a lot of disorganization from these women when I go that low in age. That being said, my OLTR wife is 38, and my primary FB is 25.

If you still want to date women under age 23 (or so) but are still concerned about the conversation aspect, just do what I do; let her talk about whatever the hell she wants. If you can't stand that, try to find something you both can relate to, at least a little.

"Relate to" can mean something as simple as entertaining stories she tells. I had nothing in common with my first 18-year-old, but she was able to tell the funniest, strangest stories from her life that I was at least mildly entertained, and this was someone who ended up being in my life for many years. As an introvert, I didn't need to do much talking, and she was an extreme extrovert who could go on and on about stupid stuff for hours. It worked, and I never needed to get "deep" or "meaningful" or find "commonality."

Lastly, don't forget that if you are sexually attracted enough to a woman, you won't need to find as much depth or commonality as you think. I'll prove it. In your mind, picture the hottest, most perfect ten you can possibly imagine. A woman who is physically flawless and 100% your type in every possible way. Make her about age 21. Now imagine her sitting across from you on a first date. She's a little dumb and you have nothing in common, but she's not irritating, she clearly likes you, she's clearly a happy person and is smiling, laughing, and having a great time with you.

Now answer honestly: do you really care that you have nothing in common and aren't connecting mentally? Be honest. You probably would consider that a bonus, but not an absolute requirement.

Dating much younger women requires this more relaxed mindset. It's not a good thing or bad thing, just something you must be aware of and prepare for, if, as an older guy, you intend on dating women this young.

Chapter 23

SEXUAL DYNAMICS OF YOUNGER WOMEN

Though there are indeed some differences, sex with younger women is not that different from sex with older women. There are all kinds of stories people tell about how women in their mid-thirties are at their sexual peak, hornier, and better in bed than younger women. Some of these things have some truth to them, and some do not.

Regardless, I've slept with a large number of women and of a very wide range of ages, from 18-year-olds to women in their mid-fifties, and I can tell you for a fact that most of the biggest differences are based on the *person*, not the *person's age*. With both younger and older women, some women are fantastic in bed, some are bad in bed. Some are loud, some are quiet. Some are very active, some lay there like a dead fish. Some are naturally enthusiastic, others are reluctant (or seem that way), and yet others are clearly putting on an act for you. Older or younger, it doesn't make much difference.

Are older women actually better in bed though? It's true that older women are more comfortable and understanding of their own bodies during sex than younger women, but whether or not that directly translates to better sex or a better sexual experience for you, really depends.

All I can go from is my own experience, as well as the experience of the men I've communicated with about this topic over many years. I've slept with a lot of older women and younger women, and I have to say that *in general* and *on average* (and there are many exceptions), younger women *tend* to be more enjoyable in bed. I know that sounds like the opposite of what you've been told, but it's true, at least in my (extensive) experience. During sex, younger women *tend to be* (and again, there are many exceptions to this) more enthusiastic, willing to try new things, willing to follow instructions, and are way less picky. There's a light and eagerness in younger women's eyes during sex that frankly, most older women don't have. Many women in their thirties have had much of that "light" burned out of them by stressful kids, numerous failed relationships, financial pressures, and all kinds of other baggage.

One of the more obvious celebrity examples of this is Britney Spears. Hit up YouTube, and watch a few interviews of her when she was 19. Then watch a few of her today, in her mid-thirties. You will see two completely different women on every level. The first woman is bubbly, happy, enthusiastic, bright-eyed, and excited. The second woman is a near-robotic zombie with dead eyes. Both beautiful, but two very different people.

Some may argue that some younger women are faking this enthusiasm during sex, and under certain scenarios this can be true, but that reinforces my point; it shows they care more about your experience than an older woman who refuses to show any enthusiasm, fake or otherwise.

It's true that older women tend to orgasm easier during sex since they know their own bodies better, and that many younger women either can't cum at all or take a very long time to do so. It's also true that there are some older women who will absolutely blow your mind and body during sex, and that a hell of a lot of younger women are absolutely horrible during sex. Yet overall, younger women tend to be better on the overall.

Frankly, this surprised me, since before my conversion to Alpha Male 2.0 status many years ago, I bought into the societal narrative that said, "older women are better in bed."

When it comes to women's bodies, again I may surprise you. Societal Programming, particularly in the manosphere, preaches that younger women have perfect bodies, and as soon as they cross over age 30, their sexual market value instantly plummets and their bodies instantly get disgusting.

As much as I like younger women, I have *not* found this to be the case. Indeed, I have encountered a hell of a lot of the exact opposite; younger women with stretch marks and other weirdness from babies, weight gain, smoking weed, drinking alcohol, tats, and piercings. On the flip side, I've had sex with numerous women over 30, often well over 30, with perfect, amazing, tight, trim, teenager-like bodies.

When women hit 40, then yes, I start to see a consistent set of problems with the naked female body. But prior to 40, I've encountered too many women in their thirties with amazing bodies and too many women well under 30 with average or problematic bodies.

Also, women in their legal teens or early twenties just don't give a shit about health, fitness, eating right, exercising, taking care of their skin, and staying thin, whereas women over 30 tend to be obsessed with this stuff. I have definitely seen this reflected in the numerous naked bodies I've been up close and personal with in terms of women in both age groups.

Am I saying that women in their thirties have better bodies than women under 30? No, I can't go that far. I've been with too many perfect-bodied younger women. However, I can say that in terms of women under 40, I consider the quality of the *average* naked body from the *average* American woman in her twenties and the *average* American woman in her thirties about a tie. It's about the same, on average, across the board, with about an equal spread of hot bodies and flawed bodies in both age groups. Over 40, most women do indeed lose that tie, so women under 40 definitely are better looking naked than those over 40. (Though this is rapidly changing as the entire human race continues to get younger-looking.)

I'm sure you could find some statistics that conflict with what I just said, i.e. perhaps statistically speaking there are more overweight women in their thirties than in their twenties. That might be true, but are you going to have sex with a bunch of fat women in their thirties? Of course not. So overweight women aren't even relevant here (unless that's what you're into).

Therefore, in terms of the women in their thirties you'd actually have sex with, I don't see a huge disparity in body quality between modern Western women in their thirties and modern Western women in their twenties. (Outside the West is an entirely different story, of course. For example, women in many South American and Asian countries tend to age shockingly well.)

Female Sexual Motivations

Speaking generally, older women, particularly those over age 30, like sex primarily because it feels good and it makes them feel sexy. Younger women, VYW in particular, like sex primarily because of the attention it gets them. I'm not saying 19-year-olds don't think sex feels good. They certainly do (most of them anyway). I'm saying that for younger women, sexual *attention* is just as important, if not more important, than the act of sex itself.

I've dated women in their forties who wanted me to just come over to their houses and fuck them. You will rarely get requests like this from VYW. She might call you up to hang out, and she may want to have sex, but that's not all she wants; often she'll want to go "do something" too. Whereas after sex, the 42-year-old woman probably wants to just have sex again.

This is the reason why a cute 21-year-old girl loves to dance on tables down at the local bar but a still-attractive and fit 40-year-old woman has no desire do to that at all, even if she thought she could get away with it without judgment. You might think that's because the older woman is more "mature" or has already "gone through that stage," and some of that might be true. However, the overriding reason is that pure sexual attention is less important to the 40-year-old, while sex still is. The 21-year-old girl thrives on sexual attention, loving it just as much as (or even more than) actual sex.

There are few ways as effective to command a man's total and complete positive attention as having sex with him, and younger women learn this very quickly. That's the overwhelming reason why they want to have sex, in addition to the fact she's got raging hormones (more on this in a minute) and sex feels really good.

How does all of this relate to you?

In many ways, her desire for sexual attention is a good thing for us. It means she has far less ASD than her 40-year-old female counterparts. If you play your cards right, she will have sex with you much faster and with much fewer rules and strings attached than the 40-year-old will (whereas the 40-year-old woman can and usually will deny you sex even if you play all your cards right in a dating environment).

It also means if the woman in your life is really young, as in a VYW, she's going to be far more tolerant of you sleeping with other women, including women she knows personally. (That's what referral game is all about.)

The bad news is that your new 19-year-old or 23-year-old MLTR is likely not going to be as pure a sexual creature as your last girlfriend who was 39. Your new younger girl is probably not going to want to have sex three times a day. I'm not saying she *won't* do that, I'm saying she won't be begging for it. Your older woman would love to have sex three in a row late into the evening, but your new 19-year-old is ready to go "do something fun!" after having sex just once. She may think having sex all night is "boring" when she'd rather go to the club with you instead. (And I will repeat, there are exceptions to all of these generalizations. Doesn't matter; the generalizations generally tend to be true.)

Going back to the plus side of all this, your new 19-year-old is going to have far, *far* less rules about your relationship than your 39-year-old ex ever did. Your 19-year-old is going to let you do just about whatever the hell you want. Your 39-year-old ex had a list of expectations and "proper boyfriend behaviors" for you that was a mile long. Violations of any of these resulted in a long "discussion" about things like "mutual respect" and "how hard she works." (If you've ever dated a woman over age 33 you know exactly what I'm talking about.)

Teenage Biology

As I have written about extensively in my other books and blogs, we human beings possess, more or less, the same brains and bodies of ancient cavemen from tens of thousands of years ago. We like to think we're all high tech with our smartphones and driverless cars, but the reality is we are operating the same bodily machine as Grog the caveman from 100,000 years ago sitting in a cave with a spear and a stinky loincloth. Nature has been very slow in catching up with our technological advancements and culture.

Back then, when food was scarce and tribes of humans were small, nature designed you to grow fast, reproduce fast, and die fast. Nature made sure you matured from childhood to adolescence by age 11 or so. Then it wanted you to have lots of babies as quickly as possible. So, it designed your body with all kinds of hormones to improve your looks, make you stronger, metabolize food efficiently, and make you really horny for sex. This is why teenagers are so damn horny. This is why parents fantasize about locking up their teenage daughters and why you used to masturbate seven times a day back when you were 13.

After a few years of this, nature didn't want you hanging around as an old person, draining the tribe's sparse food supply. It ensured you died at age 25 or sooner. This is why people start actually aging at age 25. It's also why the brain isn't fully formed until around age 25. Up until then, people look great. After that, the slow process of death begins. The reason people over age 25 eventually run into things like sagging skin, balding, wrinkles, gray hair, cancer, heart attacks and Alzheimer's Disease is that nature never designed any of us to live past age 25. It's quite interesting when you think about it.

If you're a man over 35 dating a woman who is under age 25, certainly if she's under age 20, you need to remember her body is in a very different stage than yours. No, I'm not talking about puberty; most women have that handled by age 11 or 12 at the latest. I'm taking about this adolescent caveman-stage where her hormones are powerfully flowing through her body in an effort to get her to reproduce, among other things.

This will help put the next part of this into prospective...

Levels of Sexual Experience and The "Slut Phase"

Sexually speaking, VYW almost always fall into one of two extremes. Either she will be very sexually inexperienced, as in she's a virgin or near-virgin who has only has had sex with perhaps one or two men, or she has been some kind of super-player, and had sex with a *huge* number of men already, even if she's only 18 or 20. Rarely have I met or dated VYW who did *not* fall within one of these two extremes, and there's a very specific reason for this.

In the modern era, most women hit a temporary "slut phase" sometime between the age of 16 and 22. At some point between those ages she snaps, and suddenly has sex with a huge number of guys within a very short period of time, even if she was a very "good proper little girl" beforehand. We're talking 10 to 20 men (or more!) within timeframes as small as six to nine months. This happens because of various factors including cultural pressures, parental deficiencies, immaturity, the desire for attention, possible ADD, and the extremely powerful biological factors we just talked about.

Then when the smoke clears, she snaps out of it, looks back and says "OMG! I was a slut! I don't want to be a slut!" Then she calms down a little, keeping it to just one or two guys at a time.

This slut phase is normal, natural, and predictable. Most women I know went through something like this. Most older women will (reluctantly) admit that they too went through this slut phase back when they were that age. (If you don't believe me, just ask them.) Of course there are exceptions to every rule and there will always be a few women who never do this, but the vast majority in the modern era, and in the Western world, do. I don't care how innocent, sweet, smart, or responsible she seems, or how good her grades are, or how good her parents were. She's either done this or will be doing this very soon.

When you meet up with a VYW who is very sexually inexperienced, that means she hasn't hit her "phase" yet. There is nothing inherently good or bad about this. These women are just as easy to get to sex with as the post-slut-phase girls, so proceed as normal. Just realize that if you get into an ongoing relationship with her, the day will come when she's going to explode and go get slammed by a bunch of guys. You need to be prepared for this. Often, I see younger guys get into serious relationships, or even marriages, with pre-slut-phase younger women, only to be shocked and horrified when these girls break up with or divorce these poor schmucks and go sleep with a huge pile of men, or worse, cheat on them.

Just as often, perhaps more often, the younger woman you meet up with will already have had her slut phase. That means despite her age or appearance, she will be very sexually experienced and she'll know exactly what she's doing in bed. However, she will put up a *little* ASD with you initially because she doesn't want to "be a slut like she was last year." The memory of her slut phase will still be fresh in her mind and she will be conscious of not repeating it. However, she won't be any more resistant than a typical VYW; her ASD will still be low as compared to older women.

Sometimes, the timing for you will be just right and you'll meet up with a VYW while she's right in the middle of her slut phase. Happy day for you! Get ready for a very fast, very easy lay. However! Don't expect her to be around long. Soon, she'll be off you and on to the next guy. Be double sure to wear that condom!

The best thing to do with VYW right in the middle of her temporary slut phase is to fuck them fast and for as long as you can, (which probably won't be very long), and make sure you get their phone number, email address, and get them on your social media ASAP. Then, when she vanishes out of your life, hit her up in four to six months later and re-acquire her. By then her slut phase will be over and she'll be more normal to deal with. I have done this with more than one VYW and it works well.

Sexual Teachability

Cougars (older women who like to date much younger men) have talked about how they like younger men because they're more "teachable" in bed than older men. Well, guess what? The same is true for younger women. Once you're in a relationship with a VYW who really likes you, you can indeed take her from an inexperienced near-virgin to an absolute sex goddess who is amazing at all the things you like. I have done this with several women, including with women who had not yet hit their slut phase.

Do not hesitate to do this! As an older man, she's going to expect you to be dominant and take the lead in sexual areas anyway. Being her sex teacher is yet another fantastic way to assert your dominance and raise her attraction for you to extremely high levels. Of course, if she's only a short-term thing or a pure FB only, this is less important. But if it's with someone you plan on dating for a while, you should do this.

Here are the sexual areas younger women tend to have the most trouble with, and where they are the most teachable, listed in order.

1. Being less self-conscious and more comfortable with their own body.
2. Learning how their own body works and what they like (because all women are different and like different things).
3. Learning how to easily and reliably get to orgasm (clitorally and vaginally).
4. Learning how the male body and mind works and does not work.

This is not a book on sex or sexual techniques. I cover that topic in great detail in *The Ultimate Open Relationships Manual**. The point here is if you lovingly address those four areas with her (in about that order)

---

* http://www.haveopenrelationships.com/

THE ULTIMATE YOUNGER WOMAN MANUAL

you're going to quickly have one amazing woman in your life. Not to mention the fact that even if you break up later, she will remember you, very fondly, for the rest of her life. I mean that. You're not here to just get laid. You're also here to bring happiness to the women in your life. Getting comfortable sexually is a very difficult thing for women of all ages to do. Assisting a younger woman in becoming a happy, comfortable, sexual being is one of the many ways you can do good for others.

Also, just because a woman in her twenties has gone through her slut phase and has slept with a bazillion men does not necessarily mean she is now comfortable with her body or knows how to orgasm. All my life I've been surprised at women who have been with large numbers of men but who still have body image issues, problems with being self-conscious, sexual hang-ups, and/or trouble getting to orgasms. This is because 95% of the men out there are either terrible in bed or don't give a shit about making a woman feel good. Don't be one of those guys.

How To Handle Sexually Uncomfortable Women

If you date enough younger women, particularly VYW, you will eventually encounter one or more women who are attracted to you and want to have sex with you but are very sexually nervous and/or uncomfortable. Examples of these women include:

- Some Type Threes
- Virgins
- Near-virgins, i.e. women who have only had sex with perhaps one or two men before you
- Women who have never had sex with a much older man before, only very young guys her age
- Women who suffer from social anxiety
- Women who have very low self-esteem or have body image issues
- Women who have been raped, sexually assaulted, or physically assaulted in their past

Again, I am *not* referring to women who aren't attracted to you and legitimately don't want to have sex with you. I'm referring to women who want to be physically intimate with you but are nervous about it because of one or more of the reasons above.

When in a sexual encounter with such a woman, you need to move very, *very* slowly, gently, methodically and go step-by-step. Here's how I usually handle it, and I've literally never encountered a problem using this system.

Sexually escalate as normal, as I describe in detail in *Get To Sex Fast**. Talk for a while, get her comfortable, then start touching her arms, shoulders, hair. Then kiss her on the mouth, but do so very lightly and gently. Do not go full tongue or anything like that (at least not yet). Kiss for a little while, then escalate as normal, slowly removing her clothes.

Of course if she says no, stop immediately. However, with this kind of woman, you usually you won't get a verbal no; instead you'll just feel her body tense up, or at least not relax. Or she'll sexually escalate with you but will talk a lot at the same time (ask lots of questions, make lots of requests, crack jokes, and so on). If she asks questions, answer them. If she makes a request, like to turn the lights off or have sex in a different location in your home, or whatever, then agree to all of them. Say, "Good idea," and then just do it.

As you continue, if she still seems tense (physically or verbally) or keeps talking, stop what you're doing and ask her if she's okay. When she says yes (and she will say yes), say, "Are you sure? We don't have to do this right now if you're not comfortable. It really is okay." If she says she's uncomfortable, stop escalating right there, put your clothes back on, and try to have sex with her on the next date after this.

If she assures you that she's okay, then proceed. Usually, she'll say something like, "No, no, I want to do this. I'm just a little awkward." Then proceed, but proceed slowly, taking time on each step.

If you want to do anything other than normal, vaginal sex in the missionary position, tell her or ask her what you're going to do before

---

* http://www.gettosexfast.com/

you do it. It doesn't matter what it is; doggy style, fingering, going down on her, whatever. Ask or tell her you're going to do it before you do it, so she has a chance to tell you that she doesn't want that. Sexually awkward or inexperienced women will often have a list of things they don't like that other normal women really like, such as fingering, receiving oral sex, and so on. If she tells you she doesn't like something or doesn't want to do something, don't do it. You'll have plenty of time to experiment with her later once she's more comfortable with you, but at this first time, don't do anything out of the ordinary.

That means that if you really like certain out-of-the-ordinary things, like anal sex or odd sexual positions, you need to relax about that stuff the first one, two, or three times you have sex with a sexually uncomfortable woman. Just relax, and don't worry about that stuff right now. Again, you'll be able to teach her all kinds of fun stuff… later.

If you're loud during sex (I am), warn her about this and try to keep as quiet as you can. Tell her, "I make some crazy noises; don't worry, I won't hurt you, and it's normal for me. It means I feel good." I've actually scared some women during sex with some of the crazy, dominant noises I make. Just be aware of this if you're dealing with a sexually nervous woman.

Don't pound her hard during sex if that's your usual style (it is certainly mine). If you're an intense guy during sex, dial it down a few notches this first (and perhaps second or third) time. Once she's accustomed to the way you have sex, she will *love* your intensity (trust me on that), but right now, you need to take it easy.

During sex and right after sex, verbally assure her that she makes you feel really good. Sexually awkward women are really concerned that you won't/don't like them during sex, or that they don't make you feel good. Telling women this helps them relax. Look them in the eye when you tell them this, and say it with feeling.

Right after sex, ask if she's okay (again, she'll always say yes) and if she needs anything. Women like this are usually very self-conscious about their bodies (even if they're perfect tens to you) so make sure you cover them with a blanket or towel as soon as you're done having sex so they can relax.

Chapter 24

YOUNGER WOMAN DRAMA MANAGEMENT

If you're familiar with my other work, you already know that one of my core concepts, not only regarding women but of all life, is that I have a zero tolerance for drama. Life is too short, and I have bigger and better things to spend my time than arguing with a woman (or a man, for that matter).

A zero drama tolerance policy may seem antithetical to a man who dates younger women, especially VYW. After all, aren't younger women big balls of childish drama? I'll answer that question in a minute. First, I must clearly define the word "drama" because I use a very specific definition. Per my glossary of terms*, my definition of drama is this:

> *Drama – Any harsh negative actions directed from a woman to man where the man is the target of said negativity. Screaming,*

---

* http://www.blackdragonblog.com/glossary/

nagging, complaining, arguing, demands, crying, threats, ultimatums, the "silent treatment," refusing sex because of non-medical reasons, all of these things are drama, and there are many others. Drama is not "anything negative." Specifically, it must be harsh (sweetly lying would not be considered drama) and focused at the man (angrily complaining about her boss at work would not be considered drama). Drama is a female trait. (Men have guy-drama.)

If she screams at you, that's drama. If she gives you the silent treatment, that's drama. If she spends 20 minutes complaining about her bitchy best friend, that's not drama. Nor is it drama when she lies to you. These might be bad things, but they don't fall under the definition of "drama" as I define the term.

While we're at it, let's also be clear about what guy-drama is. Again from my glossary:

Guy-Drama – A particular form of drama directed from a man to a woman. Unlike drama, which is feminine and takes many forms, guy-drama takes the form of a lecture issued in order to correct behavior. "Setting her straight," "straightening her out," "laying down the law," commands to "respect" him, or issuing "rules" are all forms of guy-drama. Guy-drama is extremely ineffective at managing a relationship and only creates more drama or at best simply delays (instead of preventing) future drama.

Now that we're on the same page with definitions, let's get back to our question. Do younger women have more drama than older women? The answer is yes. And no.

Drama – Yes

Indeed, younger women, and VYW in particular, can be full of silly, ridiculous, childish drama. All you have to do is watch some 18-year-old girls talk to each other or watch the social media banter of women under the age of 23 to see the sheer amount of up-and-down, useless, dramatic bullshit that permeates the lives of younger women (or more accurately, younger people).

VYW who don't attend college live in a world of casual fun, lots of free time, and a decent amount of freedom. While they live very poorly in terms of their finances, in most cases, they have their day-to-day expenses covered by parents, relatives, friends, boyfriends, or baby daddies. They will often be surprised that you actually have to spend time during the day working instead of spending it with them. Many of them will also be confused when you're not available to them at a moment's notice like most of their younger friends (who also have no lives) are. This can generate complaining and drama.

VYW who attend school or who work full time are actually much better in terms of drama. They understand that normal human beings have responsibilities and they accept that you have them as well. On the other hand, many of these women can be pretty stressed out with the workload of school and jobs, and this can create moments of drama as well.

Lastly, often *men* are the source of drama in older man / younger women relationships. Many older men attempt to order younger women around in ways that they wouldn't with women their own ages. If a younger woman has a more submissive personality, then this will probably be fine. But most younger women do not have personalities like this, and this authoritarian behavior can and will create friction in the relationship. I've seen it happen with older man / younger women relationships a lot.

Younger women today have grown up in a participation trophy, high speed internet, microaggression, Instagram, attention-whoring culture that caters to their every desire in lightning speed and coddles them in ways older guys like you and I never had when we were that age. This can, and often does, create frustration for them when they don't get what they want.

Lastly, VYW are essentially teenagers, who have less maturity and certainly less emotional control than more mature adults with fully formed brains.

To be clear, I'm not saying that older women don't have drama as well. They absolutely do! Modern-day women in their thirties are going through the most stressful decade of their entire lives and live in an almost constant state of stress. Women in their forties are better, but not much better. This obviously creates drama where none would occur with a younger woman.

I'm also not saying that all VYW have more drama. Rather, certain common types of VYW have heightened states of drama that you'll have to manage.

Drama – No

There's a big *but* to all of this. Yes, VYW can often be volcanoes of immature drama, *but*, in the face of a confident older man, their drama can be permanently redirected away from you, and in ways that are impossible to redirect with an older woman.

If you stand firm without being a jerk (we'll discuss how in a minute), your 22-year-old FB or MLTR will quickly learn to redirect her drama away from you and instead aim it towards her girlfriends, family, and friend-zone guy friends.

No, she won't *stop* being dramatic. That's like expecting a dog to never bark. She'll simply throw her drama at other people in her life besides you.

This is a key difference between younger women and women over age 33. If you even start implying that your 39-year-old MLTR, girlfriend, or wife should throw her drama somewhere else instead of at you, she will actually feel insulted and offended. To her, she has a "right" to throw drama at you. That's part of your role in her life: a target of her drama when she's in a bad mood. I'm not joking; this is literally how most women view perceived-permanent male fixtures in their lives, particularly husbands and live-in boyfriends. Moreover, the older a woman is, the more this is true. (There are many psychological and societal reasons for this that go beyond the scope of this book.)

The point is your 22-year-old MLTR isn't adamant about this "right" to throw drama at "her man" like a 38-year-old would be. The 22-year-old is more than happy to redirect her drama away from you and towards other people as long as she can vent on *someone*. The actual target of her drama isn't that important, the expression of the drama is.

In just about every MLTR relationship I've had with a younger woman (this only applies to MLTRs since you should never receive actual drama from a properly managed FB), within a few weeks, I had her "trained" to get mad at other people instead of me. A semi-regular occurrence is that she would get upset, instantly catch herself getting upset before she actually said something, turn around, leave the room, call one of her friends or family and scream at *them*. Then I would smile and get back to work. It's very nice.

Here's how you do it…

How To Redirect Her Drama

When I was a kid, I played in a large sandbox in my backyard that my dad built. I spent hours creating tiny rivers inside it. I would carve out a trench, give it a little angle, then turn on the garden hose that was laying on the high end. Then I'd watch the little river I'd created.

As the river was flowing, I would dig another trench, attached to the first trench, and watch as the water was diverted from the main river to my new secondary river. This was a lot of fun when I was little and I used to do this kind of thing for hours in the summer time.

A woman's drama, particularly that of a younger woman, works the same way. It's an unyielding river that never ends. Through all of my relationship structures, techniques, and frame, I can dramatically reduce the size of this river, often substantially, but I can never dry it up completely. What remains I simply divert away from me, around me, and "aim" it towards other areas in her life. Since I hate drama and love happiness, I've become very skilled at this.

Here are four ways you can divert the drama of the younger women in your sex/romance life away from you and towards other targets. I have personally field tested all of these techniques over many years with numerous women of various ages and personality types, and I can tell you for a fact they all work for most women under the age of 33. They can also work for women over the age of 33, but they're less effective and can often take more time and effort to embed into her behavioral pattern.

1. *Encourage her to call her friends or family and yell at them when she's feeling angry at you.*

   If a woman is pissed off at you, she often needs to yell at somebody. Why does that "somebody" have to be you? Really think about that; why does it have to be you? It actually doesn't. Like a boiling teapot, she needs to vent her anger so she can calm down and get back to normal, but a teapot doesn't care who is standing next to it. If she's mad at you, but rather than yelling at you, screams at one of her girlfriends about what an asshole you are, it actually accomplishes the same thing. She gets her anger out of her system and eventually returns to her normal, happy self, though without giving *you* any drama.

   Let her go scream her head off at one of her girlfriends, who themselves are women and thus will enjoy the drama. Let her go yell for ten minutes at one of the friend zone guys who want to have sex with her. If these men want to be her emotional tampon, let them, while you get back to work on your goals or go have sex with one of your other women.

   Encourage her to do this. Tell her that you don't do drama, but she is more than welcome to call up anyone she wants on her phone when she's mad (specifically mad at you, since if she's just mad about something else I don't categorize that as drama) and scream at them for as long as she likes about what a horrible person you are. Then back up your words with actions by letting her do this without complaint, or by soft nexting her whenever she insists on giving you drama instead (as I'll explain below).

As I mentioned above, most women are under the impression that the man they're dating automatically becomes the repository for all negative venting she needs to express. This is worse with women over age 33 and with women you live with, but younger women have some of this too. From the very beginning of the relationship (or at least the first time she actually gives you drama), she needs to clearly understand that when she's upset at you, regardless of the reason (yes, even if it was really your fault) she can not raise her voice at you, insult you, or threaten you, and if she needs to do these things, you are the *last* person to receive this bile, not the *first* person.

The first person should be her friend, friend zone guy, sister, whomever. The man who makes her happy, takes care of her, and gives her frequent orgasms should be the last person. That's you.

2. *Completely ignore her if/when she says bad things about you to other people.*

    Reading the above, you may realize that doing this might be harder than you think. Letting her scream about you to other people will be harder for men with certain personality types. If you're a more emotional guy, you're going to want to talk with her and argue with her rather than tell her to leave and go call someone else. If you're a more controlling guy, have stronger outcome dependence, or have stronger Alpha Male 1.0 tendencies (as I talk about in *The Unchained Man*[1]), it's going to be very hard for you to let her go badmouth you to someone else, particularly while you're within earshot.

    If you want a happy woman life with younger women, you need to man up and get over this. As I talk about in *The Unchained Man*[2], developing a strong sense of outcome independence makes everything in your life easier, particularly

---

[1] http://www.alphamalebook.com/
[2] http://www.alphamalebook.com/

your relationship life. So what if some 20-year-old girl says you're an asshole to one of her 20-year-old girlfriends you've never met and probably never will? Does this really bother you? Should it bother you? Nope. Particularly when she'll calm down in about 10 minutes or less and she'll probably be having sex with you again.

I admit I had trouble with this in the beginning. Years ago, when I was first experimenting with nonmonogamous relationships, occasionally I'd have women complain about me in a very public way on social media. As you might imagine, I got a little upset. At one point I even found myself getting a little Alpha Male 1.0 and telling women to "not say bad things about me in public on social media."

Then I caught myself and realized how outcome dependent I was being. I made a pact with myself that I would never, ever tell a woman not to complain about me or even badmouth me to other people. I would be outcome independent and not give a shit. If they ever asked me about it, I would say, "I will never badmouth you to anyone else, but if you want to badmouth me to other people, I think that's a shitty thing to do, but hey, you're more than welcome to do it. Cool with me."

It worked. Soon, I didn't care what women said about me to anyone, even their own mothers, and was even a little embarrassed at how childish I was being earlier.

If one of my women ever badmouthed me on social media, I just smiled and clicked "Unfriend." When they begged me to re-friend them, I said no. I've done this many times over the years, and it's worked great. (Keeping your more drama-prone women off your social media to begin with is also a good idea.)

You need to get to the point where if someone tells you "Hey, your girlfriend told Suzi that you're an insensitive asshole!" you just smile and say "Cool" and then eat a potato chip. Diverting her drama is not going to work if you freak out every time she bitches about you to one of her friends. Hey, she's a woman, and a teenager if she's a VYW. Bitching about men/boyfriends/ husbands is what these people do. Get used to it, ignore it, and move on. Who gives a shit? You have more important things in your life to focus on.

Just Remember I said badmouthing you *to other people*. If she badmouths you to *you*, that's drama, and unacceptable, and it's probably time for a soft next. (I'll describe how in a minute.)

3. *Strongly encourage her to spend lots of time with other women.*

    I have experienced overwhelming evidence that strongly suggests the following: *the amount of drama a woman gives you is inversely proportional to the amount of time she spends with female friends.*

    If a woman has "no friends," or is one of these women who "hates women" and only has a bunch of guy friends, then, in my experience, she is far more likely to throw drama at you. Moreover, the drama is more likely to be angry and intense.

    However, if she spends a lot of time with female friends, this seems to allow her to vent her drama on her girlfriends, like that teapot. By the time she gets around to spending time with you, she's all "vented," and is less likely to give you drama.

    I have dated women who were hardcore, emotional, drama- bitches who treated me like absolute gold because they had lots of girlfriends they were always spending time with and talking to. They had lots of drama with everyone else, but never with me. On the flip side, I've dated women who were sweet, pure, submissive sweethearts who actually gave me drama more often than the drama-bitches because of their lack of female friends or an engaging social life.

    I always encourage the women in my life to spend time with more women. If any women in my life clearly have no friends, no social life, or just have male friends, I know I'm probably in for some more drama unless there are other factors that make up for this. And even then, I will still encourage her to go spend more time with more women if the relationship is more serious (if it's just an FB relationship then I don't care).

The more time she spends with female friends, the better. Men who get pissed off when their women spend "too much time" with their girlfriends are making a huge mistake. In my experience, women who spend a huge amount of time with other female friends are, generally speaking at least, the lowest-drama women out there (in terms of how much drama they give *you*, that is; their girlfriends get a shitload of it).

4. *Master the technique of the soft next, and get comfortable doing it. VYW may require it more often.*

By far, the single, most powerful weapon in your relationship management arsenal is the **soft next**. The act of soft nexting a woman once or twice will *instantly* reduce her drama and teach her to divert it away from you faster than just about anything else you can do.

I explain exactly how to do a soft next in step-by-step detail in *The Ultimate Open Relationships Manual**, a book I highly recommend you get if ongoing relationships with younger women is something you desire. It's something you do when she's clearly giving you drama and won't stop. I will briefly summarize the process here:

1. Don't get mad, don't get defensive, and don't argue.
2. Immediately terminate the conversation, but do so nicely.
3. Physically leave her.
4. Don't answer her texts, messages, or phone calls, at all, for any reason for 1-7 days (usually 1-2 days is all you need).
5. Text her again and return to her and resume the relationship like nothing happened.

When you soft next a woman for the first time, you will be shocked at how well it works. It takes a screaming, raving bitch and turns her into the sweetest, kindest girl you've ever seen. Try it and you'll see. (Get the

---

* http://www.haveopenrelationships.com/

The Ultimate Open Relationships Manual* if you need more detail on how it's done.)

What <u>Not</u> To Do When Receiving Drama

The above is what to do when she gives you drama. It's also important to lay out what not to do. The first step in redirecting her drama is to *not* do what your instincts tell you to do. When a woman (of any age) starts giving you drama, your biological male instinct will be to react in one of three ways:

1. *React back.* You'll want to instantly defend yourself and throw shit right back at her. "What the fuck are you talking about?" or "I never did that! She's lying!" or "Well if you don't like *that*, then stop doing *this*!" or "Why are you screaming at me? I didn't do anything!" This reaction is more common with more emotional men and more immature men.

2. *Acquiesce / Surrender / Apologize.* In psychological circles this is called conflict avoidance, saying things like, "Okay, okay, fine!" This is especially common with men with strong oneitis or beta males in long-term relationships or marriages.

3. *Respond with guy-drama.* I already defined guy-drama above. This is saying things like "Alright, look! That's it! From now on, you are no longer allowed to hang out with her! I don't want you ever talking to that bitch. Delete her off your Facebook page and call Verizon and block her phone number right now. I'm going to stand right here and wait until you do it." This is common with stronger men and Alpha Males, particularly older men.

Here's the problem. ***All three of those responses are bad.*** All three are extremely ineffective at the primary goal of not having drama in your relationship in the first place. The first response creates more

---

* http://www.haveopenrelationships.com/

drama. The next two simply *delay* drama until a future date (in addition to creating the environment for future drama to fester). None of them *remove* the drama.

Father-Like Qualities

The correct response to drama from a younger woman is to respond like a kind, loving, but stern father.

Not a jealous boyfriend. Not a drama queen. Not a pussy. Not her son. Not a drill sergeant. Not her boss. Not an abusive or insecure father. No, instead you respond like a strong, confident father figure who loves her but *also* doesn't have time for her crap.

Your words and actions need to make it clear to her that while you love her (I use the word "love" loosely in these examples, since you probably don't actually love her, depending on the type of relationship) you will not spend time with her while she acts out like a child. Other men might. Her girlfriends might. Her sister might. But you will not.

Therefore, you're not going to respond to her drama, surrender to her drama, or issue your own kind of drama. You're just going to calmly smile, tell her to calm down, and if she doesn't, you're going to calmly remove her from your home and go do something else, i.e. a soft next.

The difference in soft nexting and drama management with you as the older man and her as the younger woman is you need to be a little less of the Alpha Male badass and a little more of the strong, stern, but loving father. Many younger women, particularly the Type Twos, have been lacking a strong father figure in their lives (or in some cases, *too strong* a father figure, which is also unhealthy; very common with Asian girls). In many ways, you're the security and balancing force in her life she craves. Moreover, she's not going to give her strong but loving father figure drama. Not if he's both strong *and* loving, and you need both components to make this work.

A few years back I was dating two VYW simultaneously who were both friends. One day, after some furious whispers between them, they came to me and started asking me very nicely if we could have a party at my house and invite their friends. Immediately they started making all kinds of promises and assurances.

One of them suddenly stopped, looked at the other, and said "You know… this is funny… this is just like we're asking our dad."

That's when I first knew I had nailed the confident, non-needy, loving, strong, drama-free frame of a quality father figure. By the way, both of these girls were drama queens to everyone else in their lives (and remain so to this day), but neither of them ever gave me drama.

Let Them Vent

The technique of letting a woman "vent" applies to women of all ages, and it's key to keeping drama low and redirecting a younger woman's drama.

When a woman comes home and bitches about her horrible day to her lover, I call that "venting." Venting isn't drama. It's a very important part of the feminine psychological process. Women process the world by talking. Only by talking things out do they get to the point where they can relax. This is, of course, the opposite of what most of us men like to do. After a rough day, we'd rather just crawl into our cave and watch football. We don't want to talk to anyone. Talking about stuff often just stresses us out even more.

Women are the opposite. They need to talk it all out. While drama should not be tolerated, not even a little, you should allow her to vent all she likes (especially if she's at the MLTR level or higher), or at least for a while (if she's an FB). If she wants to complain to you for 20 minutes about her dumbass boss or ex-best friend or her bitch sister-in-law, let her. Just smile, nod, and let her talk. This concept was first introduced in the 1980's by John Gray, writer of *Men Are From Mars, Women Are From Venus*. While he was dead wrong about a lot of things, he was absolutely right about this one.

If you don't let your woman vent when she needs too, she's not going to feel like you are a safe place for her, and she needs to feel this in order to stay with you for the long-term. Remember, it's not directed at you, so it's not drama as I define it, so venting is okay. Also, as I said above, if she's just an FB, you don't need to listen to her venting for very long if you don't want to (but a few minutes is acceptable).

Of course, if in the process of venting she starts complaining about you, *that's* drama and it's time to nip that in the bud immediately. Just follow the sequence of 1) a warning, 2) changing the subject if she persists, 3) soft next if she still persists.

Women, including younger women, are extremely fast learners. She'll figure out the difference between drama and venting and modify her behavior accordingly. I've done this countless times over the years with many women. It works.

Chapter 25

POSSIBLE PROBLEM AREAS AND HOW TO SOLVE THEM

Younger women are wonderful. I really mean that, despite some of the negatives I've pointed out about younger women in some of the prior chapters. My life has been enhanced in every way since learning how to attract and date VYW, as well as younger women who are not VYW, and I recommend it for every older man who has decent energy levels and a healthy sex drive.

However, as with all things, there are pro's and con's; it's not all sweetness and roses. Having a sexual and/or romantic relationship with a girl 20 years (or more) younger than you does introduce some challenge areas that would be less likely to occur with a woman closer to your age.

I have eleven years of experience having sex with, dating, and being in relationships with much younger women, and in large numbers. In this chapter I'll give you a heads up on all the pitfalls I've observed and learned, as well as the problems other older men have reported to me over the years, so that you can be prepared for them and ensure they're alleviated if and when they do happen to you.

Challenge Area 1: Underage Women Sometimes Lie About Their Age

I already discussed the issue of age of consent laws back in Chapter 1. I'm just stating here for the record that underage women can and do lie about their age. If you don't verify their age, proceed to have sex with them, and they complain about it to one of their parents, if you live in the USA or Canada the government will gleefully throw you in jail and brand you as a sex offender for the rest of your life, even if you can prove in court she lied to you.

So don't do that. If you live in more sexually relaxed places like Europe, Asia, or South America, this is not a big deal, but if you live in uptight places like the USA or Canada, know the age of consent laws in your local area as well as your attorney does. Always verify a younger woman's age before you touch her, either by checking ID or by using a private investigator or web service. Do not touch women whose age you cannot verify, no matter how hot, willing, or mature they seem. If you absolutely can not verify her age, move on. There are plenty of other fish in the younger woman sea.

Challenge Area 2: Family Issues

Even younger women who are 100% sexually legal still may have parents they live with who are not going to approve of their perfect little angel dating an older man.

The good news is that as the world becomes more progressive, this is much less of a problem than you might expect. I've actually been extremely surprised at the number of parents who really don't have a problem with their 18 or 19-year-old daughters going out with a guy 15-25 years older. The majority of the parents of VYW I've been with who were aware of my existence in their daughters' lives have been surprisingly supportive, or at least neutral to the concept.

However, this doesn't mean *all* parents will be supportive. Some are going to be downright creeped out or worse, very upset. This is especially true if her parents are younger than you. The good news is younger women aren't stupid, and most girls, particularly Type Twos, usually keep the older man a secret from their parents. The problem is, with younger women being who they are, secrets tend to get out.

You must be prepared for any fallout that might occur in your life, or hers, if the issue of disapproving parents (or other guardian-like family members) arises.

Here are a few ways you can help prevent or alleviate this problem.

1. Always treat the younger women in your life with the utmost care and respect. You should do this with all women in your life anyway, but it's going to serve doubly as well if you do it with VYW. The more you treat her like crap, the more you lie to her, the more you take her for granted, and/or the more you get involved in her drama, the more likely she'll go complain about it to her friends and possibly her family, and the more likely there will be trouble for you.

   I am not saying you need to act like a pussy or beta male. Hell no. You can still be a strong, dominant Alpha Male with the younger woman in your life and still treat her with kindness, care, and respect.

2. Do not lie to women. Again, this should be a maxim for all romantic relationships, and I follow this as a personal rule religiously. Telling the younger woman in your life hard truths or just keeping your big mouth shut are both better than lying. Most drama in non-married relationships stems from dishonesty of some kind. Moreover, VYW are already accustomed to men constantly lying to them, so your confident honesty will be a nice retreat for her.

3. Do your best to only date VYW who do not live at home with their parents. Just doing this alone removes all kinds of possible relationship and logistical problems from your interactions with her. VYW are indeed ten times easier to deal with if they do not still live at home.

Not only are there logistical benefits to dating her when she doesn't have her parents at her place, but VYW who do not live at home are far more likely to act like mature adults than those who still live at home with mommy and daddy. I've dated many VYW who lived on their own, or with roommates, who owned their own cars and/or had their own full or part-time jobs. I usually have smoother relationships with more responsible younger women like this.

The next best situation, though still not ideal, is if they live with just one parent. 50% less parents in the picture means 50% reduced odds of problems. Moreover, the single parent will often be working hard at a job to support the family and thus not be home very often; another plus for you (and her).

If you indeed end up with a VYW who is still living at home with one or both of her parents, you need to be extra respectful and honest with her if you want to avoid parental entanglements.

Challenge Area 3: Excessive Alcohol Usage

Regardless of the law, it's a hard fact that women age 16 to 23 drink more alcohol and get drunk far more often and intensely than women in any other age group. I have dated large numbers of women in all age groups and can attest to this personally.

Women under age 24 drink and/or do drugs more often to ridiculous levels and (this is the important part) *it does not matter how smart or mature they are in the other areas of their life*. Many extremely intelligent and capable VYW will still get drunk to the point of puking all over the carpet on a semi-regular basis or sit around and get high on their couch all weekend. Do not be fooled by the cute 20-year-old who acts "mature for her age." She could easily still be a little party animal just like all the rest.

Of course, when VYW are physically with you, you can control this to a degree, and you should. (Not to mention the legalities involved in being an older man in the presence of drunk, underage minors.) However, when she's not with you, that's where she'll often get into trouble. Sometimes, big trouble. I first realized this many years ago when I watched one of the first 18-year-old FBs I had down three-fourths of an entire bottle of 151 rum within about ten minutes. Wow. I can't even put a shot of 151 near my face without getting disgusted with the pungent aroma, but here she was, guzzling it like it was beer. (She spent the rest of the night puking in the toilet of course.)

In my time with younger women, I've had these situations:

- One 18-year-old FB of mine got drunk downtown with friends (I was not there) and was wearing a pair of sweat pants that were too large for her (she was borrowing from someone else). They were constantly falling down and she was constantly pulling them up. She got a little too drunk and didn't pull them up fast enough when the cops drove by. She was arrested for public drunkenness and indecent exposure and had to spend the night in jail.

- One 20-year-old FB got drunk and stoned, had sex with one of her younger guy friends at a party, and got pregnant. It was her third child from as many men. She snagged the guy as a boyfriend so they could "make it work," until a paternity test revealed he was not the father. She was so drunk she didn't even remember who the real father was. Today, her daughter is about seven years old, and will literally never know who her father is.

- One 19-year-old MLTR of mine (one of those very smart, mature, capable ones) was so drunk one evening at my house that she kept me awake until 4am while I held a bowl under her face to catch her puke. Fun. I had an important business appointment the next morning and needless to say I was not happy.

- A 25-year-old MLTR of mine once saw something another woman put on my Facebook page she didn't like. In a fit of jealousy, she stopped seeing me, then quickly went out on a first date with a guy from an online dating site she had never met, got shitfaced drunk with him, and had sex with him on the first date. Unprotected sex, of course, because when you're drunk you don't care. So far so good, until a few days later her genitals started bleeding. He had given her genital herpes and she is now HSV-1 positive for the rest of her life.

- Years ago, before I had most of this younger woman stuff mastered, I stupidly held a party at my house, and most people there were guys and gals under age 24. Two guys got drunk, got into a fight with each other, smashed some of my glasses, got blood all over my carpet, and scared the crap out of everyone else. At about 2am, I had to physically remove them from my house (thankfully I'm a big guy), drive them 30 minutes away, and kicked them out on the sidewalk. One of them refused to get out of my car because it was raining, so I had to literally threaten him with violence to get out, which he eventually did. Man, I was pissed. (Though I did get a threesome with two 18-year-olds out of the deal, and they cleaned the mess for me while I was gone, so the evening wasn't a total loss.)

I don't want to give you the impression that these are common occurrences in my life. They aren't. These are just a few instances over an eleven year-period of me dating a lot of women. Regardless, if VYW are in your life, especially multiple ones (like I have), you need to be prepared for these scenarios.

Challenge Area 4: Lack of Birth Control or STD Protection

Birth control and STD prevention is a big topic, and I cover it in great detail in *The Ultimate Open Relationships Manual**. Suffice it to say that unless you know the younger woman very well, *and* she's demonstrated a history of responsible sexual behavior, *and* you've seen a recent STD test from her, you always need to wear a condom when you have sex with her.

---

* http://www.haveopenrelationships.com/

This is even more important with VYW than with women your age. VYW, even the very intelligent and mature ones, usually don't give a shit about preventing pregnancies or STD's. I shouldn't have to tell you about the epidemic of young single mothers out there for you to understand that VYW just don't care if they get "accidentally" pregnant. Many even secretly desire it. If you want to cum inside them for weeks on end without wearing a condom, many won't bat an eyelash.

But *you* should! Not only will you end up having to pay child support to some dingy 20-year-old for the next 18 years, you may end up with chlamydia or herpes or some other fun disease.

When having sex with any woman, but especially a VYW, condom up. I don't care if she said she was "just tested and is clean" (unless she can show you actual test results) or that the "doctor said she can't get pregnant." Bullshit.

Look, I understand that when a super-hot younger woman is laying naked before you and she clearly doesn't care if you wear a condom, the temptation is very high. Really, I get that. It doesn't matter. You need to wear a condom.

If you absolutely hate condoms, remind yourself that if she becomes a longer-term, regular sexual partner, and builds a level of trust with you, then at that point you can take the condom off. I regularly have sex without a condom and have for over a decade, *but only with those women who have demonstrated a level of sexual responsibly I can depend on.*

Challenge Area 5: Super High Energy Levels

I actually consider this a good thing, at least sometimes, but you might not. As I've talked about in prior chapters, VYW have young teenage bodies bursting with powerful metabolisms, flowing hormones, and almost boundless energy... possibly more energy than you want or are ready for. Here are some examples of what I'm talking about:

- You might want to have a quiet evening at home, but she wants to go to the clubs and dance until 3am.

- While you're at work she's texting you, bitching that she wants to go to the mall with you or smoke weed with you, *right now*. (And no, she doesn't care it's 2pm on a Tuesday and you're at work.)
- You're cleaning your garage on a Saturday and she's bouncing off the walls, wanting to go camping or jet skiing.
- It's 10:30pm and you're both cozy in bed. She's "starving" and wants to go out and eat right now, even though you both just ate full meals two hours ago and she ate more than you did.
- It's 1am and you're ready to fall asleep, but she's wide awake, jumping on the bed, and wants to stay up and watch The Simpsons with you. Again.

You get the idea. Humorous as they sound, these kinds of situations are not unusual.

I happen to be a healthy, high-energy guy, so this kind of thing is not a big deal for me (usually!). I'm also at the point where I'm accustomed to it. However, I know plenty of older guys interested in younger women who have moderate or even low energy levels. You need to be prepared for the occasional energy level disconnect with your younger companion. If you're only interested in infrequent FBs or very short-term relationships, this is less of an issue for you, but it's something you need to be prepared for if you want anything beyond that.

Challenge Area 6: Lower Sex Drives

You'll especially notice this difference with VYW if you are accustomed to dating women over age 35.

Speaking generally, women between the ages of 35 and 45 often have wildly insatiable sex drives once they get comfortable having sex with a particular man. Often, you can have sex two or three times in an evening and they're still ready and willing for more. Younger women, especially VYW, not so much. Yes, they like sex, but they will usually not crave sex like older women do. You can often have sex with women over age 35 multiple times, but once you have sex with a VYW, it's more likely she'll be ready to "go do something fun" rather than have sex again.

When I date older women, I will sometimes get phone calls and texts from them begging me to come over to their place to fuck them. I almost never get these kinds of requests from the VYW I date. (Though there are always happy exceptions to this!)

As I talked about in Chapter 23, over time, you can teach a younger woman to relax and enjoy sex (including orgasming regularly). I've done this many times. At that point, she *might* be as horny as an older woman, but this takes time, and will only happen in a longer-term, regular relationship.

Challenge Area 7: Extreme Promiscuity During the "Slut Phase"

This may sound like the complete opposite of challenge area six, but it's true. In Chapter 3 I talked about a VYW's "slut" phase. If you happened to be dating her during this phase, you need to be prepared for some very promiscuous behavior. Don't be shocked or offended when you see it.

You might have to worry about the 27-year-old woman in your life fucking another man when you're not looking, but you may have to worry about the 18-ear-old in your life fucking *two or three* other men when you're not looking.

You'll probably never have to worry about the hot 28-year-old gal in your life dancing on a table in front of a bunch of men when you're not around. Not true if she's a VYW.

You'll probably never have to worry about the 38-year-old woman in your life dressing in overtly sexual clothing when it may not be appropriate to do so. Not true if she's a VYW.

You'll probably never have to worry about the 31-year-old in your life constantly flirting inappropriately with other men when you're not around. Not true if she's a VYW.

This is why extreme outcome independence on your part is key. If any of the above behaviors make you angry, you're going to have to force yourself to relax and accept that the world of VYW is a little more sexually free than what you're accustomed to or think is appropriate.

This is one of those "take the good with the bad" situations. The good news is that younger women have much less ASD than older women, which is a very, *very* good thing for you and me. The flip side of this is they will often flaunt their sexuality far more than older women. Accept this and make this okay in your world… or you're going to be upset quite often.

Challenge Area 8: Addictions To Phone and Social Media

Women of all ages like to mess around on social media, but younger women treat it like oxygen. Her phone is the most important thing in her life. Facebook, Snapchat, Instagram, and so on is the blood that runs through her veins. She needs these things constantly, at all times, 24/7.

While talking to her at the restaurant while having dinner, much of the time her little face will be planted in her phone while she texts someone and talks to you at the same time. It's a classic generational difference. You might consider this behavior rude, but people in her generation do not. It's considered perfectly normal in her social world, and if you tell her she's being rude, you'll just confuse and annoy her. It's simply part of the new communication paradigm of her era (and frankly, of yours too).

That phone of hers rules her life. It doesn't matter if you're having a quiet emotional moment or in the middle of watching a movie at the cinema… if that phone makes any sounds or vibrations, she must stop whatever she's doing and respond to the text, email, Facebook message, or phone call. Even if she loves you, her phone will (seemingly) be more important. Be prepared.

Again, outcome independence must be practiced. Let her be a phone addict. That's her problem. If she starts looking at it while you're talking to her, just stop talking and go do something else. Don't get upset and don't order her around (unless you don't mind drama).

The only time I ever forbid a VYW to look at her phone is during sex. Yes, a few younger women are so addicted to their phones that they will actually want to check it during sex. Obviously that's not going to fly. But other than that, let her do what she wants with the phone. Trust me, if it's a war between you and her phone, her phone will win… eventually.

Challenge Area 9: Jealous Younger Guys

This is a big one that can really cause you some headaches if you're not careful.

If she keeps you a secret to her social circle, then you have nothing to worry about. However, if she starts telling her social circle about you (either verbally or on social media), some of her circle are going to include younger men her age, and *all* of these guys are going to universally hate you with a white-hot passion. You'll be some "creepy old guy" fucking "their girl." Older, more confident, more wealthy men as competition strike to the core of sexual threat and masculine competitiveness, so at least some of these guys are going to be really, really pissed off.

She's going to constantly hear complaints and insults regarding you (when you're not around, of course). Take her out to a bar, and even random strangers, guys closer to her age than you are, are going to badmouth you to her when you turn your back to get a drink.

Bottom line, you are not going to be welcome in her male social circle. The other young men in her life will at best fear you, at worst hate you. Be prepared for this. I've even had one or two instances of young, jealous friend zone guys of young FBs or MLTRs I was dating try to harass me. (Online of course, never in person.)

If you're a more emotional, touchy, or dramatic guy, this is going to be a problem. It's no big deal for me however, because of my no-drama policy, I simply refrain from spending any time with any younger guys in her social circle. I suggest you do the same unless you enjoy drama and conflict.

The younger *women* in her social circle… now that's a completely different story! You want to talk to them! We already talked about referral game back in Chapter 15.

Challenge Area 10: "On Blast" With Relationship Details

"On blast," if you have not heard the term, it is a common term among the millennial generation that means to reveal personal information to a large group of people. Over time, that term has morphed to mean "revealing anything personal to people who don't need to know."

Women under the age of about 26 have a different concept of privacy than you might, especially if you're over age 40. In an internet world of 24/7 video-capable smartphones, YouTube, Facebook, Instagram, and Twitter, the term "privacy" has changed dramatically to say the least.

Let's say you have a little argument with the younger woman in your life. You might be surprised to find the next morning she's posted about it in great detail on her Facebook page so that all of her 523 friends and family members can read about it.

Again, this is a generational difference you need to accept, at least to some degree. Contrary to what we older guys from a bygone era might think, she's not doing this because she's being a bitch, or because she's trying to get back at you, or anything like that. She's doing it because that's what her generation does. If something upsets them, they plaster it all over social media regardless of how personal or private you think it should be.

For a while, when I was new to the world of dating much younger women, I tried to fight this with all the VYW I dated. Over time, I realized this was a losing battle. This is just how "kids these days" work. It's the way it is, and you're not going to stop it.

I'm at the point now where as long as the crap that is posted about me isn't too explicit or specific, I just let it go. Unless you want to be constantly battling a key generational difference that you'll never win, I suggest you learn to do the same. Again, outcome independence.

I'm also not saying every younger woman does this, but many do. It also only applies to MLTRs, rarely to FBs (though there are exceptions to this).

Challenge Area 11: Sugar Daddy Scammers

This challenge area only applies to sugar daddy game. The rise of sugar daddy websites has, sadly, also given rise to a subset of younger women on these sites who flat-out scam men out of money. These scams have become more common in recent years and will continue to grow.

Here are some of the common scams women run on men on sugar daddy sites that I have seen attempted or have been reported to me by other men:

- Demand that you send them money electronically (PayPal, Venmo, Cash App, etc.) *before* they ever meet up with you on the first date. They will threaten to not see you unless you do this. The excuse they give is that "guys keep trying to scam them." You pay them, then they ghost you (or demand a non-sexual date).
- Meet with you but keep one of their friends nearby in a car outside, demand you pay them cash before you have sex, then ask you to take a shower or some other activity away from them. As soon as you're gone they run out of your house, hop in their friends' car, and leave with your cash.
- Demand several non-sexual dates, usually "dinner," where you pay them cash on every meet. When you try to have sex with them, they dangle sex in front of you as a carrot but push for more non-sexual (and paid) dates. After several of these, when you finally put your foot down, they ghost you, block you on the site and their phone, and never see you again.

THE ULTIMATE YOUNGER WOMAN MANUAL

- Have sex with you several times (and get paid for it), then, once you're comfortable with them, ask you for a larger amount of money as a loan (or gift) in order to take care of some catastrophe, real or fake ("I need to pay my rent by Friday!"). You pay them, and then they ghost you, never responding to your texts again.

- Agree to go on some big, fun trip with you (for a price) and have sex. You pay them, fly them out to your fancy trip, and once there, they don't have sex with you, usually making an excuse about how they're on their period or have cramps.

Obviously, if you follow the advice I've given you in this and my other books, none of the above scams will ever be a problem for you. *Never* give a sugar baby *any* money before you've actually put your penis inside her, and immediately dump her if she demands otherwise. *Never* give a sugar baby you're already having sex with extra money unless you are 100% okay with never seeing that cash ever again, no matter what she promises. Follow those two rules and you'll never have a problem. Let those women scam all the other needy betas on the sugar daddy sites; you're better than that.

Challenge Area 12: Excessive Drug Use

Just like excessive alcohol, women between the ages of 16 and 23 also do more drugs, and harder drugs, more often than older people. Smoking weed is one thing that most people (including myself) don't have a problem with, but when you date a lot of VYW, you're going to run into women who regularly do the hard stuff like meth, heroin, and/or opioids. This is in addition to the more common recreational drugs like acid, Ecstasy, and prescription stimulants like Adderall.

You need to set some standards about how much of this you will tolerate. I can't give you guidance on precisely where to draw the line, because every man is going to have a different opinion about this. I'm just saying you need to draw a line somewhere and stick with it. Otherwise you're going to be pretty surprised when a younger woman shows up to a date totally whacked out of her mind, or if she pulls out a meth pipe or heroin needle right after having sex with you (yes, this shit happens).

I can tell you what my standards are, just if you're curious, but remember your standards can be anything you want based on your age, family situation, country you live in, personality, and lifestyle.

In my case, I'm an American libertarian and father of two, so I think all drugs should be legal, and I have a pretty permissive attitude about drugs, even though I've never done drugs myself, and never will, because I personally think they're stupid. With that in mind, for most of the last decade or so, my personal standard was that all of my FBs and MLTRs could smoke all the weed they wanted when with me, but cigarettes needed to be smoked outside of my house and car. This is because weed smoke seems to dissipate better than cigarette smoke and not get into furniture, at least in my experience. They could also do harder drugs when they were with me, but not when I was at my home, because I didn't want that stuff around my children.

I did this for several years without any major problems. One day, one of my distant VYW FBs, after sex in a hotel room, pulled out some needles and shot up heroin right in front of me. I found the experience so disgusting that I then set a rule that women could do all the hard drugs they wanted to, but not when I was around. That's worked well for me since then.

So think about it, set your own standards for drug use (not just for VYW, but all women you date), then make it clear to the women you date and stick with it, so there isn't any confusion or arguments. And again, if you live a very clean, conservative lifestyle, don't freak out when you hear a VYW talking about doing hard drugs. It *will* happen if you date enough of them.

Chapter 26

"TAKEN" YOUNGER WOMEN

On my blogs and in many of my books, I talk extensively about how sexual monogamy really doesn't work, how human beings were never designed for it, and how no one, men or women, really want it despite intense Societal Programming teaching us that it's the only appropriate way to be sexual with someone.

Sexual monogamy is hard for anyone of any age, but for sexually active women under the age of 23, it's effectively impossible. They literally don't know how to do it, even when they try. (And yes, there are always rare exceptions to every rule.)

This means that the plurality, and in many cases, the majority of the women you will date under the age of 23 in any context will have young men in their lives they identify as "boyfriends," whom they are cheating on by being sexual with you. In terms of women under the age of 23, you should roughly estimate that 25% of all MLTRs, 40% of all FBs, and 70% of all FB sugar babies you will have will have boyfriends. Many of these women, especially the sugar babies, will attempt to hide these men from you.

This is yet another reason why, regardless of my personal opinion regarding monogamy, you shouldn't even attempt a monogamous relationship or even an OLTR with a woman under the age of 23. If you're monogamous, she will cheat on you. If you have an OLTR, she will eventually break the rules. Just don't bother, and if you really want a relationship like that, stick with women age 23 and over, 25 or over being better (as we discussed back in Chapter 9).

The fact that so many of VYW you will date will have boyfriends means two things. First, it means you need to really work on your outcome independence if you haven't yet already. If you're going to be jealous that your cute 20-year-old FB who is great in bed is regularly posting lovey kissy pics of her and her boyfriend on social media, then you have a lot more work to do on your outcome independence (or you shouldn't date VYW at all, and just stick with women over age 23).

Second, it means you're going to have to manage some level of discretion with these girls. If you're too indiscreet about your sexual relationship with her, she's going to suffer blowback from her boyfriend, girlfriends, social circle, and perhaps even her family. You also risk blowback personally from these sources. All of this increases the odds of problems, damages your relationship with her, raises the odds that she'll leave you, and reduces the odds of her ever returning.

However, if you're discreet and non-judgmental about the fact she's also regularly having sex with a "boyfriend," she will stay with you a very long time, and even if she leaves, the odds are overwhelming that she'll return to you over and over again for many, many years; far longer than she stays with any boyfriend. I discuss this in great detail in *The Ultimate Open Relationships Manual**.

---

* http://www.haveopenrelationships.com/

Being Outcome Independent About Her Boyfriend

If the fact she has a young, needy, beta male boyfriend, even if he's really good looking, bothers you, you are viewing this all ass backwards and distorting the facts. You need to learn and emotionally internalize that as an older man, you have a much higher sexual market value than some young, dumb 22-year-old guy who spends most of his time smoking weed, working for minimum wage at the local pizza joint, and playing video games. Why in the hell are you jealous of *that* guy?

So what if he's sometimes having sex with your 22-year-old FB, MLTR, or sugar baby? Trust me, this guy is absolutely no threat to you whatsoever. Let me count the reasons why:

1. He's needy as fuck, and you aren't. This guy is constantly blowing up her phone with texts, phone calls, and social media messages. You aren't doing any of that. You're just texting her when you need to schedule another meet with her, and not much else. Your behavior is far more attractive to her than he ever could be.

2. He's absolutely terrible in bed. He enters her, thrusts four times, cums, and then rolls over. I'm not exaggerating. A hell of a lot younger men fuck just like that. If you don't believe me, ask a few younger women about the sex they've received from younger men and they'll tell you. I have had many VYW who were shocked that I actually lasted 15-20 minutes the first time they had sex with me. They had never had sex with any man that long, because all of the men they'd had sex with were needy young guys who couldn't hold their loads for more than a minute or two.

3. He has no idea how to make her orgasm and doesn't care. He pumps her, cums, and he's done. You actually take the time to make her feel good, and cum if she can. If she's never cum, you take the time to show her how, even if it takes many sexual sessions. Mr. Needy Younger Guy never does this.

4. He's lots of drama, all the time. He and her argue about stupid crap constantly. He's a big pain in her ass. You never give her drama, ever. 100% of the time you spend with her is happy and fun, rather than about 40% of happy time she experiences with him.

5. Lastly and most importantly, *he's not going to be around for very long, so don't worry about it.* In less than six months (at the most!) she's going to dump this guy and move on to her next serial "monogamous" victim. But she'll keep seeing you. Even if she dumps you, it's only temporary; she'll be back (provided you do everything correctly).

You need to reach the mental state where you don't give a shit at all about the fact she has a boyfriend in addition to you. This is a normal and natural condition of many or most VYW you will date. Moreover, as I've said in my other books, FBs who have boyfriends are actually the best FBs to have. They are less work and less drama, since all the pressure of having a "real relationship" is on him rather than you. I love it when my FBs (sugar babies or normal FBs) have boyfriends, and I prefer it. I've gotten to the point where I actually get a little concerned if they don't. (Though this is okay too of course.)

Managing Discretion

In terms of staying out of trouble by regularly having sex with a woman who has a "boyfriend" (and I use that term loosely when discussing VYW, thus the quotes), here are a few things you should do.

1. Always operate under the assumption that any new VYW you start to see has a boyfriend that she's hiding from you. This goes double for sugar daddy game. Keep operating under this assumption until you determine with 100% certainty that there isn't one. Remember, the odds are as high as 70% that she has a boyfriend (or some guy she's calling a "boyfriend") *even if she says she doesn't.*

2. Once you're having sex with her, don't friend request her on any of her social media without verbally asking her to do so first. If she has a boyfriend, she'll be terrified to add you onto her friends list. Respect this! If I can't add her on social media for whatever reason, I will locate her on Facebook and/or Instagram and bookmark her profile page in my browser instead of friend requesting her. This way I can keep an eye on her if/when she dumps me for proper resurrection later, and as a way to get a hold of her if/when she loses her phone or changes her phone number, which happens constantly with VYW.

3. If you are a friend/follower of hers on social media, **never** post anything on her page, including a comment or a like. Remain her friend/follower, but never post anything on her page for any reason. Private messaging over the social media platform is usually acceptable though, since it's private.

4. If you engage in messaging over social media, never say anything that will get her in trouble. Saying stuff like "your pussy felt so good last week," might sound fun, but if/when her "boyfriend" gets access to her social media page because she left her phone or computer on and never logged out (again, a very common occurrence with our wonderfully disorganized younger ladies), he'll read that and there will be hell to pay, either with you, her, or both. Keep comments on the social media page friendly enough to where if her boyfriend sees them, she has plausible deniability and can say you're "just a friend," and there are no clear statements he can point to that indicate otherwise.

5. Everything I just said above should also apply to any normal phone/texting conversations, though I realize that might be harder if you have a more sexual or emotional personality. I personally almost never say anything overtly sexual to my younger women over texts. It's just too risky on multiple levels. Save that stuff for the women you date who are your age. They'll enjoy it more anyway.

6. This one is something you have to experience a few times yourself before you actually believe it. Amazingly, many VYW who have boyfriends will actually use their boyfriend's phone to text you and set up dates. I've had this happen with many women over the years. Yes, it's dumb in the extreme, but remember, we're talking about functional teenagers here. Just remember this. They will usually delete their texts when they do this, but that won't help you when you contact them again at the same number. If you send her a message out of the blue saying, "Hey cutie. Wanna meet up on Friday?" and suddenly get a response that says, "Who the fuck is this?" be aware that you're probably talking to her boyfriend. Therefore, whenever you send the first text in a text conversation, make sure it's 100% platonic and friendly-sounding. "Hey. Are you free Friday?" is a better text to send than the above. Often, if I'm texting a brand new phone number they gave me recently, and I'm sending a text out of the blue, I will usually start with a text like, "Is this still Suzi?" before I actually start having a real conversation.

7. It should go without saying that you should have zero contact with her boyfriend. Any social contact with her boyfriend, either in person, over the phone, or over social media, is a very bad idea for all parties concerned.

If you ever get into a scenario where you have to deal with a jealous boyfriend (or husband!) who is contacting you, do not engage him in any way whatsoever. Just ignore him and don't respond to his messages or phone calls. Once, a VYW FB of mine used her boyfriend's phone to set up a meet with me and she didn't delete all the texts. This guy texted me pretending he was her, trying to get info on the nature of our relationship (which he already knew). Fortunately for me, he was a pretty bad actor, and I determined very quickly the person texting me from this number wasn't her and likely was some guy she was dating.

I just stopped responding to his texts. This young, needy beta male started bombarding me with texts, begging me to tell him what happened and what the hell was going on. When that didn't get him anywhere, he started calling me. I just let it go to voicemail. He called me about four times and left two voicemails, begging me to call him back ("Hey man, I just have two questions man, that's all. Just two questions. Please just be a man and call me back!"). I deleted his voicemails and blocked his number. Problem solved. She dumped him about a month later and continued to see me for many years (even to this very day).

Let that be a lesson to you. Remember that these young women are going to dump the guy soon no matter what, so these problems will always solve themselves as long as you stay out of it. Don't respond to any drama from any men if your VYW are stupid enough to leave blatant evidence about what they're doing. You're not the one cheating on anyone, and this guy isn't *your* boyfriend, so it's her problem, not yours. You have better things to do. At least I hope you do.

AFTERWORD

Dating younger women and having them in my life ranks up there with one of the most pleasurable and downright happy experiences of my life, despite the manageable downsides. If you get to experience even one-tenth of what I've experienced with younger women (and it's my hope you experience more than that!) you will understand exactly what I'm talking about.

If younger women are something you want to experience, then take the knowledge from this book and put it into practice as soon as you can. Please don't read this book, nod your head in approval, and then go back to your business-as-usual life and forget about it. Do this stuff! You will be rewarded, I promise. Moreover, this stuff isn't nearly as difficult as you think it is. Much like men when they try nonmonogamous relationships for the first time, you will be shocked at how easy dating much younger women is.

I love to hear about success stories. If you're an older guy who has made even one much younger woman work in your life, email me at theonlyblackdragon@gmail.com and tell me about it.

Unlike women, as we men age, we become more attractive, more in our prime. It's time we started taking advantage of this.

Good journey to you, and good luck!

~Blackdragon

CPSIA information can be obtained
at www.ICGtesting.com
Printed in the USA
BVHW03s0131120718
521405BV00025B/47/P